I Just Got My New Mac!

What's Next?

Stan Smith

CONTENTS

Helpful Hints

1. **Write down your login names and passwords.** Most people create them, then forget about them. Don't be one of those people! Every time you set up a new account for anything, anywhere take a few moments to write down your login and password. There's even a handy page at the beginning of this book for you to do just that. I have some clients who keep a little notebook with all of this information. It has saved many of them when they've had subsequent issues with their systems.

2. **Keep an inexpensive keyboard and mouse (both with cords) on hand, just in case.** Wireless peripheral items are great, however any number of things can render them temporarily (or permanently) useless. The batteries may die, the communication link may fail, you just spilled coffee on them.... Do yourself a favor and keep an inexpensive keyboard and mouse with cords in the desk drawer or closet. Chances are your wireless items will fail at the exact moment when you need to finish that big project.

3. **Buy an external hard drive and start backing up with Time Machine.** You don't need to get anything big or fancy for the hard drive, just whatever is on sale that week. Plug in the USB cord, and follow the instructions in this book to use Time Machine. Running a simple backup is much better than losing your files and photos completely, or pay someone a lot of money to retrieve them.

4. **If you have a laptop, use the battery.** At least once a week, unplug the machine and just use it until the battery life drops below 10%. Then plug it in again to recharge. Giving the battery a little workout like this greatly extends its life.

What is an Apple ID?
Why do I need one?
What if I have more than one?

An Apple ID is a unique login that allows you to access Apple's online products and services. If you want to set up an iCloud account, buy a new app, or update your operating system, you'll need to use your Apple ID.

When you first purchased your Mac you probably set up an Apple ID or had one set up for you. Usually it's your email address. If you can't remember it, or have forgotten your password, go to the Apple ID Account page at appleid.apple.com then click "Forgot Apple ID or Password?" at the bottom.

All of your purchases from the App Store are tied to your Apple ID. This is important because if you need to replace your Mac or if you buy another device, you will still have access to your purchases and can download them again.

Many people are not aware that they have multiple Apple IDs. Remember that any item that you download form the App Store, or any iCloud account, will be associated with one Apple ID. Having multiple IDs can cause confusion because you will not have access to all of your purchases or iCloud data through one single account.

RECORD KEEPING

Your Mac's Serial Number: _____

Your Mac's Make and Size: _____
                                    (for example: "MacBook Air, 11 inch")

Your Mac's Hard Drive Space: _____ Your Mac's RAM: _____

Date You Purchased Your Mac: _____

Your Mac's Administrator Login: _____ Your Mac's Password: _____
(needed for updating or upgrading software)

Your Apple ID: _____ Your Apple ID Password: _____
                  (usually an email address)

Email Accounts (for example: gmail, AOL, Yahoo, etc.)

Login: _____ Password: _____

Login: _____ Password: _____

Login: _____ Password: _____

Software Accounts (for example: Adobe, Microsoft Office, etc.)

Account: _____ Login: _____ Password: _____

Account: _____ Login: _____ Password: _____

Account: _____ Login: _____ Password: _____

Other Accounts

Account: _____ Login: _____ Password: _____

Account: _____ Login: _____ Password: _____

Account: _____ Login: _____ Password: _____

About This Book

Often, Apple has provided many different methods for doing the same exact thing. We have explained one or two ways for each topic, but you may discover others that work better for you as you use your Mac. Remember, it's *your* Mac so use it the way that works best for you! Also, Apple likes to change things frequently, so the information in this book may not exactly match what you see on your Mac.

To comment or ask questions about this book, please email:

info@macsmithsupport.com

1 – THE BASIC SETUP

What's Next in this chapter...

- Menu Bar (Left and Right Sides)
- Dock
- Windows
- Apple Menu

When you first power up your Mac, you'll see a screen that has four distinct zones:

- Menu Bar – Left
- Menu Bar – Right
- Dock
- Desktop

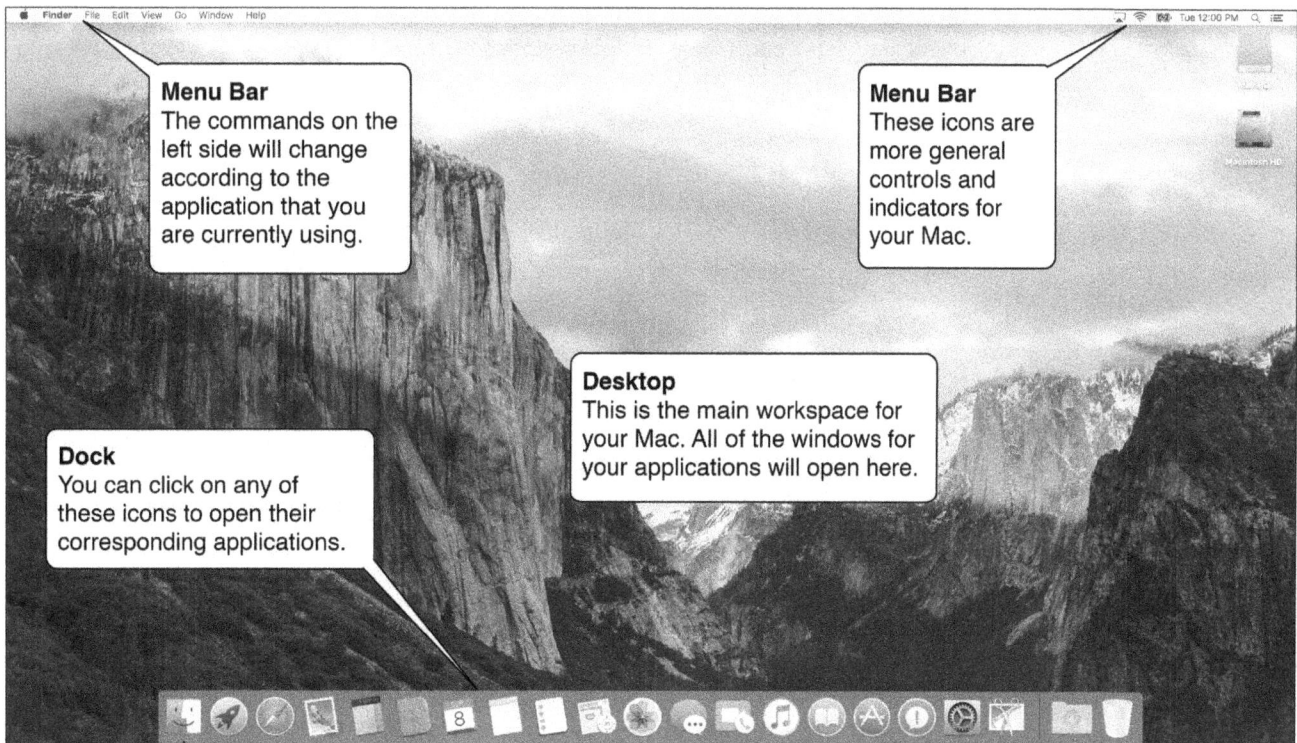

Menu Bar
The commands on the left side will change according to the application that you are currently using.

Menu Bar
These icons are more general controls and indicators for your Mac.

Desktop
This is the main workspace for your Mac. All of the windows for your applications will open here.

Dock
You can click on any of these icons to open their corresponding applications.

Menu Bar – Left Side   (Top Left of Screen)

The band at the top of the screen is called the Menu Bar. On the left side of the Menu Bar, your current application is shown. You'll see it in bold type beside the little Apple logo in the upper left corner.

An application is a program that performs a particular function on your computer. For example, Safari is an application used for browsing the Internet. Mail is an application used to access your email. Your Menu Bar will change to show which application is currently active.

Each application has its own set of commands. When you're working within an application, the specific commands for it will appear in the Menu Bar.

Here's the Menu Bar with Mail in use: 🍎 **Mail** File Edit View Mailbox Message Format Window Help

And here it is with Safari in use: 🍎 **Safari** File Edit View History Bookmarks Develop Window Help

Menu Bar – Right Side
(Top Right of screen)

The white area at the top of the screen on the right is also part of the Menu Bar. This Menu Bar section contains various items that let you monitor your machine, such as a clock, the battery life indicator, the Wi-Fi status icon, etc. Just as with the other side of the Menu Bar, these items can change depending on what you have open or available.

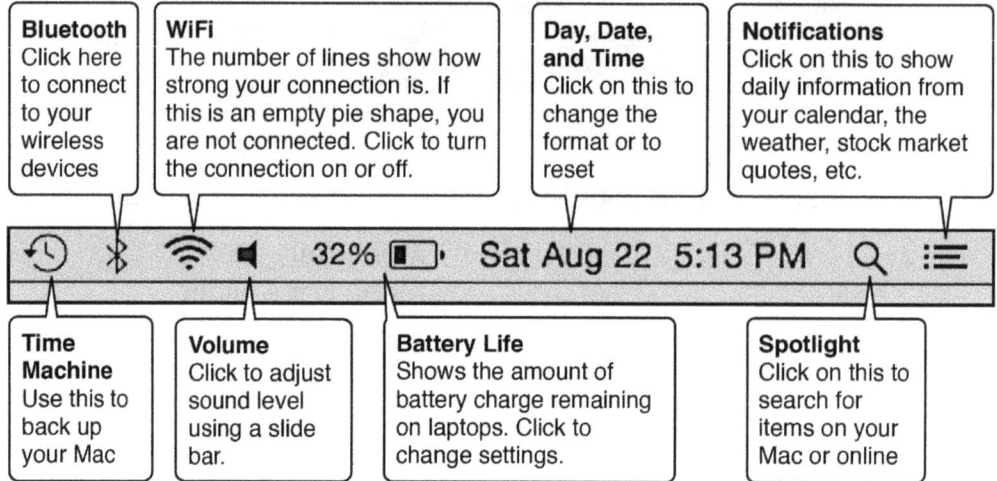

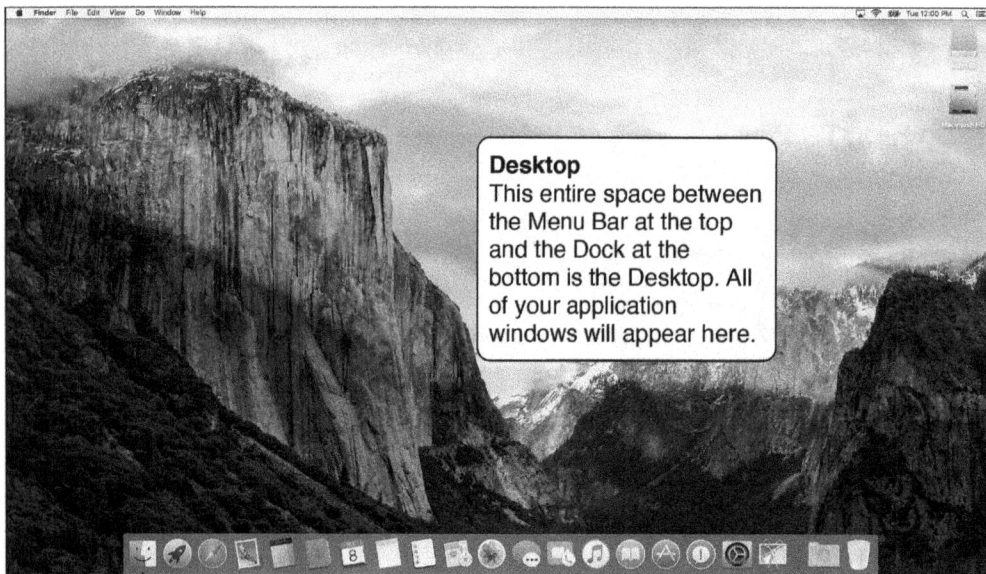

Bluetooth
Click here to connect to your wireless devices

WiFi
The number of lines show how strong your connection is. If this is an empty pie shape, you are not connected. Click to turn the connection on or off.

Day, Date, and Time
Click on this to change the format or to reset

Notifications
Click on this to show daily information from your calendar, the weather, stock market quotes, etc.

🕑 ✳ 📶 🔊   32% 🔋   Sat Aug 22 5:13 PM   🔍 ☰

Time Machine
Use this to back up your Mac

Volume
Click to adjust sound level using a slide bar.

Battery Life
Shows the amount of battery charge remaining on laptops. Click to change settings.

Spotlight
Click on this to search for items on your Mac or online

Desktop
This entire space between the Menu Bar at the top and the Dock at the bottom is the Desktop. All of your application windows will appear here.

Desktop
(The big space between the Menu Bar and the Dock)

The Desktop is the space where all of your various application windows will appear. You can have lots of different applications open (and lots of overlapping windows) on the Desktop.

Dock
(Bottom of screen)

At the bottom of the screen you'll see lots of icons lined up beside each other. This is called the Dock. All of these icons give you quick access to various applications. To open an application, you just click on its icon in the Dock.

Open Application
The tiny black dot beneath this icon for the Finder application shows that it is currently open.

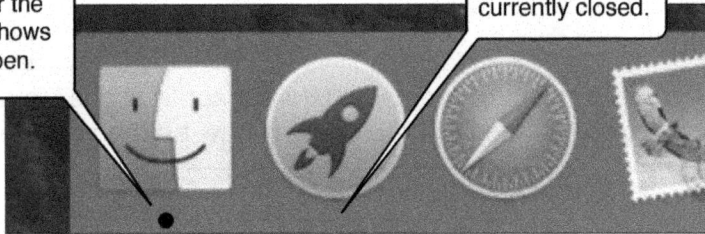

Closed Application
This application has no black dot. It is currently closed.

If you see a dot beneath an icon on the Dock, that means that the application is currently open. Closed applications have no dot beneath them.

One important aspect of the Dock is that it always shows icons for the applications that are open (they'll have a black dot under them), but it does not necessarily show icons for applications that are closed. The only closed application icons that you will see are either the ones Apple put there for you, or the ones that you've put into the dock yourself. (We'll learn how to do that in the next chapter.)

For example, the chess application is open on the desktop here. Notice that the chess icon is in the Dock with a dot under it.

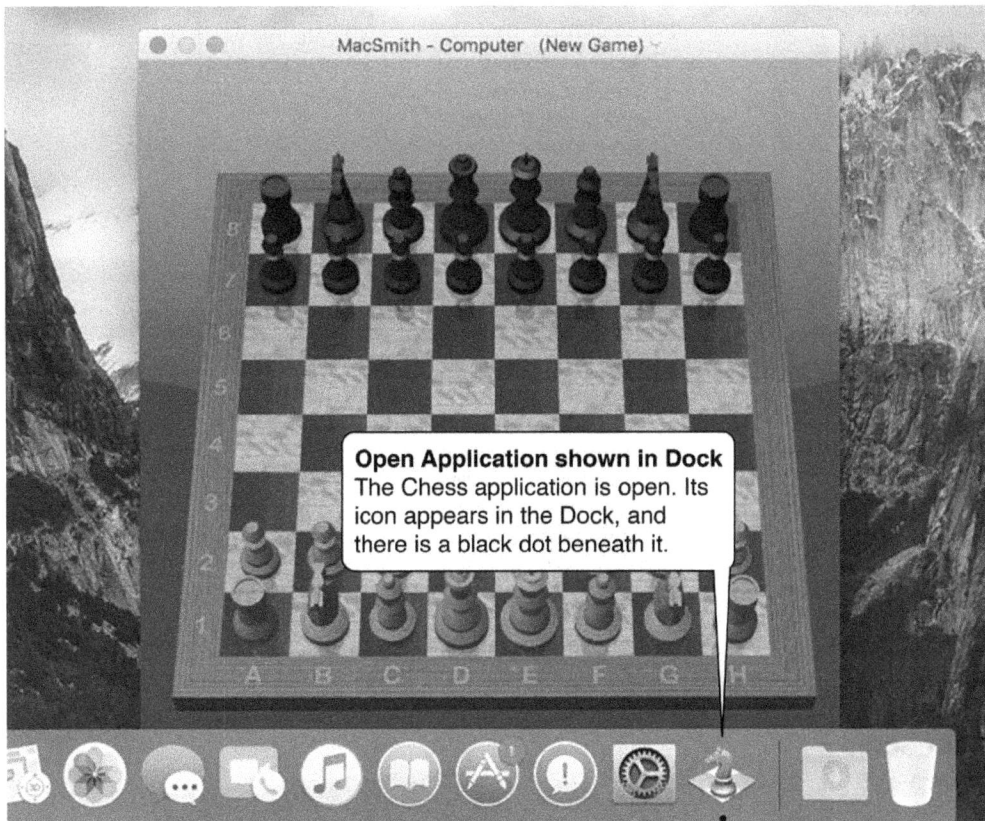

Open Application shown in Dock
The Chess application is open. Its icon appears in the Dock, and there is a black dot beneath it.

Icon Disappears
The Chess application has been closed, so its icon has disappeared from the Dock.

Now we'll quit out of chess. The icon no longer appears on the Dock.

If you don't see an icon for an application in the dock, don't panic! That doesn't mean that the application is gone from your computer. It just means that you don't have quick access to it from the dock.

3

Windows

Any file, folder, program, or application that you open and use on your Mac will appear in a window. You can have many windows open at the same time. However, only one window will be active at any time.

Activating a Window

You can have many windows open on your desktop for many different applications. To activate a window just click on it once. It will move to the front on the Desktop and will now be the active window.

When you make a window the active one by clicking on it, the Menu Bar on the upper left will change to show the application that this window uses, and the commands that are available.

For example, the active window on the right is a Finder window. The word FINDER appears in the Menu Bar on the upper left corner, and the commands that are available to you are shown in the Menu Bar. We can tell that this is the active window on the desktop by the bright red, yellow and green buttons in the upper left corner of the window. Since it says FINDER in the top left corner of the Menu Bar, this would be a Finder window.

In the example on the right the active window is now the Safari window. The word SAFARI appears in the Menu Bar on the upper left corner, and the commands that are available to you for Safari are shown beside it in the Menu Bar. We can also tell that this is the active window by the red, yellow, and green buttons that appear on it.

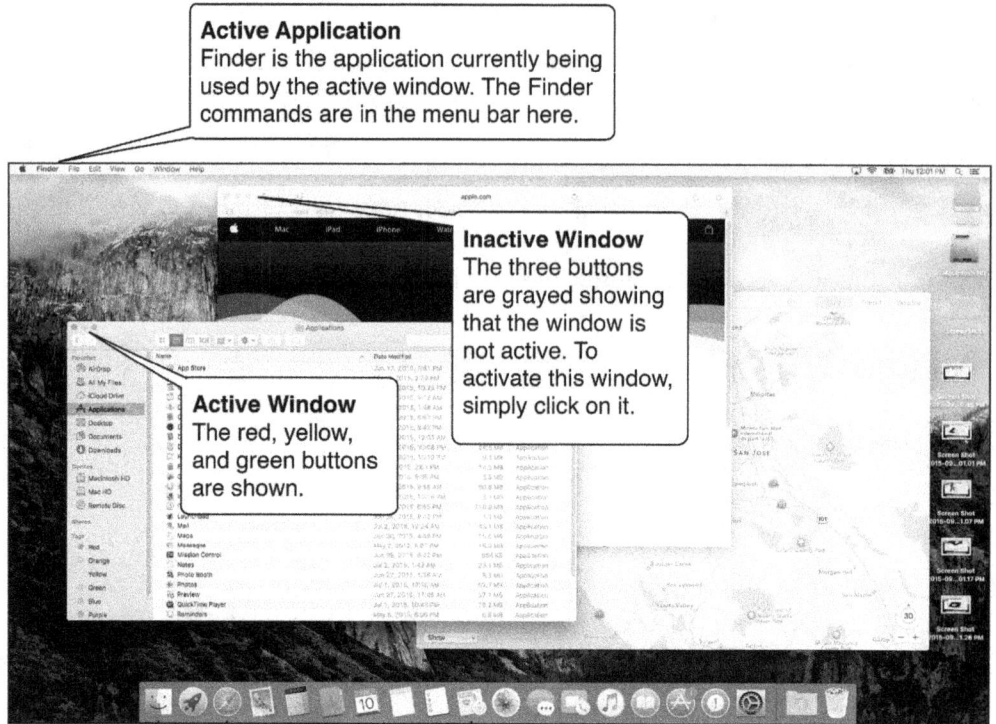

Active Application
Finder is the application currently being used by the active window. The Finder commands are in the menu bar here.

Inactive Window
The three buttons are grayed showing that the window is not active. To activate this window, simply click on it.

Active Window
The red, yellow, and green buttons are shown.

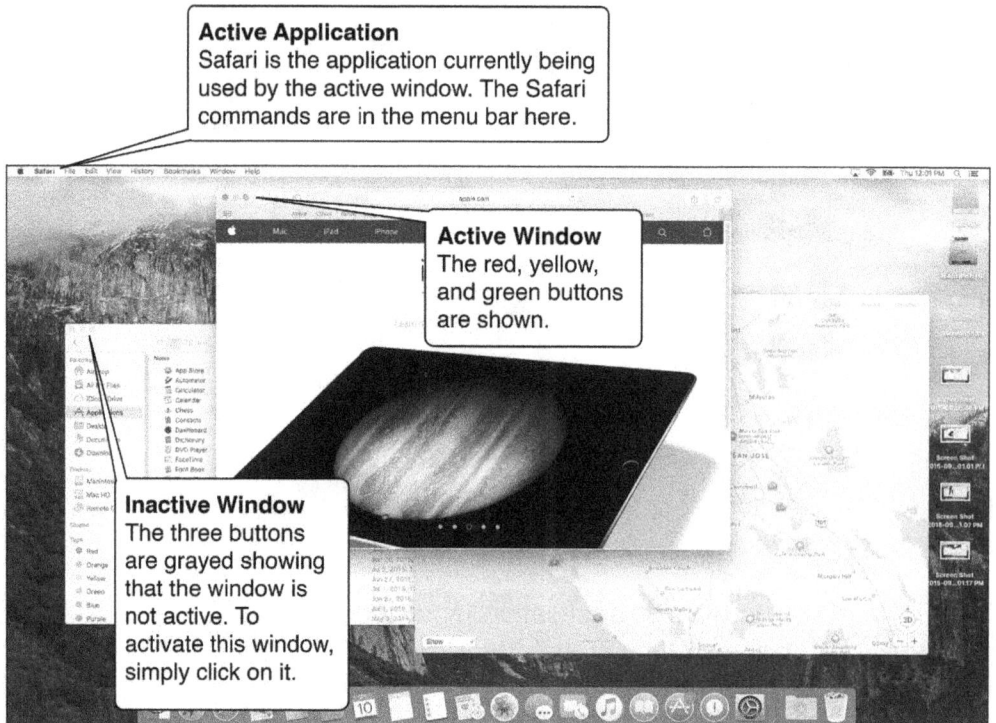

Active Application
Safari is the application currently being used by the active window. The Safari commands are in the menu bar here.

Active Window
The red, yellow, and green buttons are shown.

Inactive Window
The three buttons are grayed showing that the window is not active. To activate this window, simply click on it.

Minimize, Expand, or Close a Window

You can have many windows appearing on your desktop at any one time, but the only active window will be the one with the red, yellow, and green buttons. These buttons not only indicate which window is active, they control the window as well.

The red button closes the window. Don't confuse this with closing or quitting out of an application! We'll cover that below.

The yellow button minimizes the window to a small icon in the dock. This is helpful if you have many many windows open but find that they are cluttering the desktop.

Red
Closes the window. It will go away completely. (Note, this is not the same as quitting out of a program.)

Green
Expands the window to fill the entire desktop. These three colored buttons will disappear. To see them again, place the cursor all the way in the upper left corner of the screen until the buttons reappear.

Yellow
Minimizes the window. It will shrink down to a tiny icon to the right of the dock. If you click on it there, it will enlarge again so that you can use it.

The green button expands the window so that it covers the entire screen. You'll note that when you use this option, even the three colored buttons will disappear. To see them again, hover your mouse in the upper left corner of the screen as far as it will go. The buttons will then reappear.

Opening a New Window

Note that you can have a program or application open, but without any active windows appearing on the desktop. Remember to always look in the upper left corner of the screen to see which program is active. If you are in the correct program but don't see an active window (one with the red, yellow, and green buttons), you can create a new one by clicking on FILE then the NEW command (see the example on the right for Finder). We'll talk about this more a bit later in this book.

Finder	**File**	Edit	View	Go	Window	Help

New Finder Window	⌘N
New Folder	⇧⌘N
New Folder with Selection	⌃⌘N
New Smart Folder	⌥⌘N
New Burn Folder	
New Tab	⌘T
Open	⌘O
Open With	▶
Print	⌘P
Close Window	⌘W

Resizing a Window

You may have many windows on your desktop and find that you need to change their sizes. Resizing windows manually will help to clean up your desktop. Place your cursor on the lower right corner of the window and hold down the mouse or trackpad button. Keep holding it down and move the cursor. See the window change sizes as you move the cursor? Let go of the mouse or trackpad button when you're at the size you want.

Active Application
Calendar is the active application, as shown in the menu bar here.

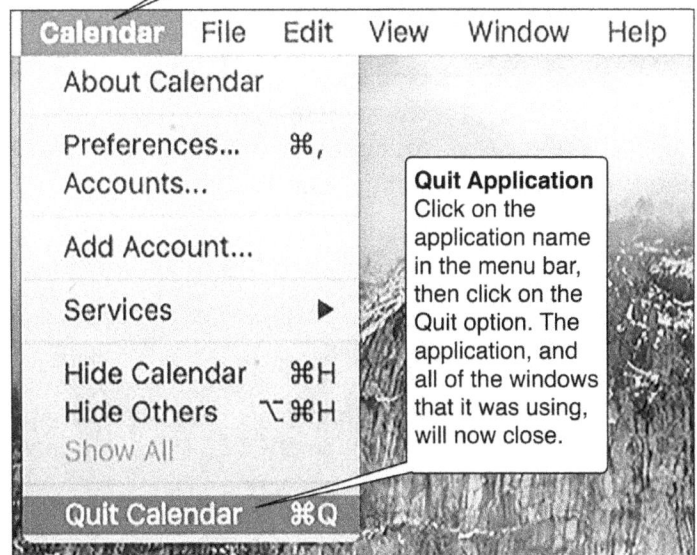

Calendar	File	Edit	View	Window	Help

About Calendar	
Preferences...	⌘,
Accounts...	
Add Account...	
Services	▶
Hide Calendar	⌘H
Hide Others	⌥⌘H
Show All	
Quit Calendar	⌘Q

Quit Application
Click on the application name in the menu bar, then click on the Quit option. The application, and all of the windows that it was using, will now close.

Quitting Out of an Application

To quit out of an application, make sure that it's the active one (its name is in the upper left corner), click on the name, then click on the QUIT command at the bottom of the drop-down menu.

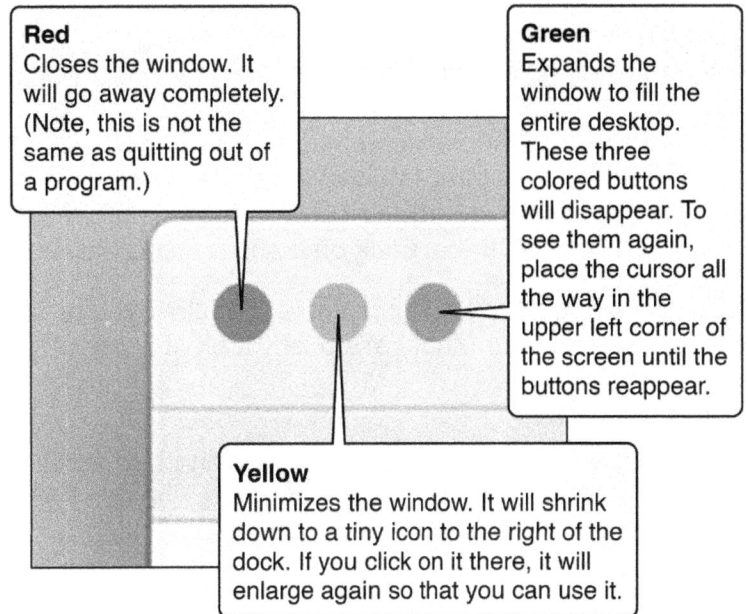

Apple Menu
(left corner of the screen in the Menu Bar)

Every Mac has an Apple Menu that is always accessible. It's the little Apple icon at the upper left corner of the screen. No matter what program you're in, regardless of what the menu bar looks like, the Apple icon will always be there. Click on it and a menu will drop down.

These items can be very important, especially if you're talking with someone about servicing your Mac. Let's briefly look at some of the options.

Apple Icon
Click to access the drop-down menu

Finder File Edit View
About This Mac
System Preferences...
App Store... 1 update
Recent Items ▶
Force Quit Finder ⌥⇧⌘⏏
Sleep
Restart...
Shut Down...
Log Out MacSmith... ⇧⌘Q

About this Mac

Click on this option in the drop-down menu and you'll see a window pop up that will tell you all of the technical information about your Mac. Here you can find out how much memory your system has, the size of the hard drive, the serial number of your machine, and lots of other technical stuff. You may never need to know any of this, but good to know where to find it if you do.

Operating System
This shows the operating system and the version of that system that your Mac is using. Here it's OS X 10.11

| Overview | Displays | Storage | Support | Service |

Processor
This is the hardware that functions as the brain of the computer performing all of the computations.

OS X El Capitan
Version 10.11

MacBook Air (11-inch, Mid 2013)
Processor 1.7 GHz Intel Core i7
Memory 8 GB 1600 MHz DDR3
Startup Disk Mac HD
Graphics Intel HD Graphics 5000 1536 MB
Serial Number C2QLL03QQQQQ

Memory
This type of memory is the RAM or Random Access Memory. Think of it as short-term memory. Usually, the more RAM you have, the faster your machine will run.

[System Report...] [Software Update...]

Serial Number
Every Mac has a unique serial number. If you ever need to contact Apple, they will probably ask for this. It's a good idea to write it down somewhere (on the Record Keeping page at the front of this book!)

Apple Inc. All Rights Reserved. License Agreement

The OVERVIEW window shown above provides the basic information on your specific Mac. This includes the serial number of your specific machine, the operating system that you're using, your Mac's processor, and the amount of memory your system has.

What's a Hard Drive and What's RAM?

Every computer today has a Hard Drive. That's the memory module that stores all of your files, applications, pictures... pretty much everything on your Mac. Every computer also has RAM (Random Access Memory). RAM is a different kind of memory. It temporarily stores pieces of information so that computers can load files, retrieve images, play video, or get information from the keyboard. Think of RAM as short-term memory while the Hard Drive is long-term memory. If your Mac has lots of RAM, it can multi-task all the more and everything will run faster (usually). If your Mac has a bigger hard drive, you can store lots more files, folders, pictures...all of your stuff!

Click on the STORAGE button to find out about your hard drive. This shows you how much hard drive memory you've used to date, and also how it's currently being used.

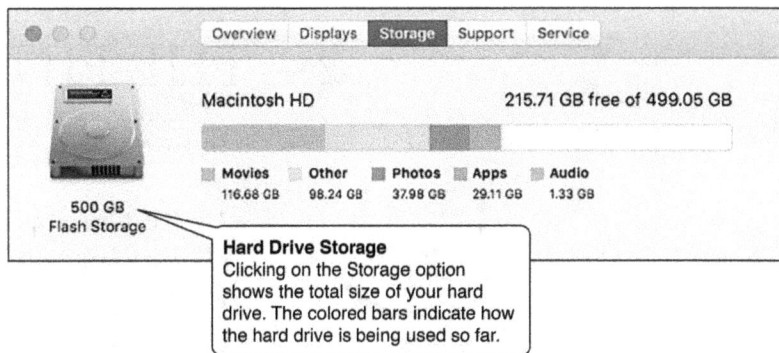

Hard Drive Storage
Clicking on the Storage option shows the total size of your hard drive. The colored bars indicate how the hard drive is being used so far.

System Preferences

This option from the Apple Menu brings up a large window filled with icons. It's the control system of your Mac. We have a whole section on these coming up in a later chapter.

App Store

Apple requires that you access all updates for the Mac's operating system, Apple programs and apps through the App Store. You'll need to know your Apple ID and password to access anything in the store. We'll cover more on the App Store in a later chapter.

Select the application that you want to Force Quit.

Click on the Force Quit button. This window will disappear, and the application will quit.

Force Quit Applications

If an app doesn't respond for a while, select its name and click Force Quit.

- Calendar
- Mail
- **Microsoft Word**
- Pages
- Photoshop
- Preview
- Safari

You can open this window by pressing Command-Option-Escape.

Force Quit

Force Quit

This option comes in handy if you have a program that isn't responding (i.e., if it seems "stuck"). Click on this option in the Apple menu, then find the program in the list that you need to get out of (often it will say "not responding" beside it). Highlight it, then click the Force Quit button, and you're free!

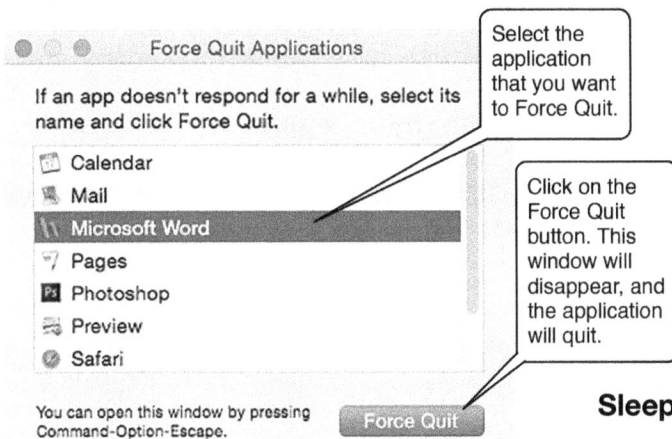

Sleep

In order to save energy your Mac has the ability to go to sleep. In this mode it is still technically powered on, but the screen will be blank and everything but vital operating functions will be inactive. To put your Mac in Sleep mode, select SLEEP from the Apple Menu. To wake it up again, just press any key on your keyboard.

Restart and Shutdown

Restarting the machine is a good way to let your Mac reset itself, especially after you've been running it without shutting it down for some time (as in, a few days). It doesn't do quite as much as a full shutdown, however. The Shutdown option actually stops everything and requires that you physically start your machine again by pressing the power button.

2 – THE FINDER

What's Next in this chapter...

- Finder Window Setup
- Finder Viewing Options
- Staying Organized with Finder
- Using Finder to Find Things

Finder is an application that allows you to see all of the files, folders, utilities, and other applications that are on your computer. It also gives you access to other drives and devices that may be connected to your computer. It's the most important application on your Mac, and you'll be using it often! You'll use the Finder to create and save files and folders. You'll also use the Finder as the starting point for installing and opening new applications.

You can always access the Finder quickly and easily by clicking on the smiling face (pictured above) in the Dock. You can also access it by clicking anywhere in the open desktop space (but not on another window).

Finder Window Setup

We'll start working in the Finder by looking at a Finder window. Click on the Finder icon (the smiling face) in your dock. Notice how two things happen immediately. First, the word "Finder" appears in the menu bar at the top left of the screen along with the basic finder commands.

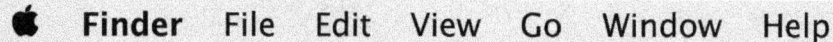

🍎　**Finder**　File　Edit　View　Go　Window　Help

Second, a Finder window appears on the desktop. The Finder window contains two different sections, the Sidebar and the Toolbar, that help you to navigate around and find your various files and programs.

Toolbar

At the top of the Finder window you'll see a Toolbar that contains various icons. This allows you to change the views in Finder so that you can access things more easily.

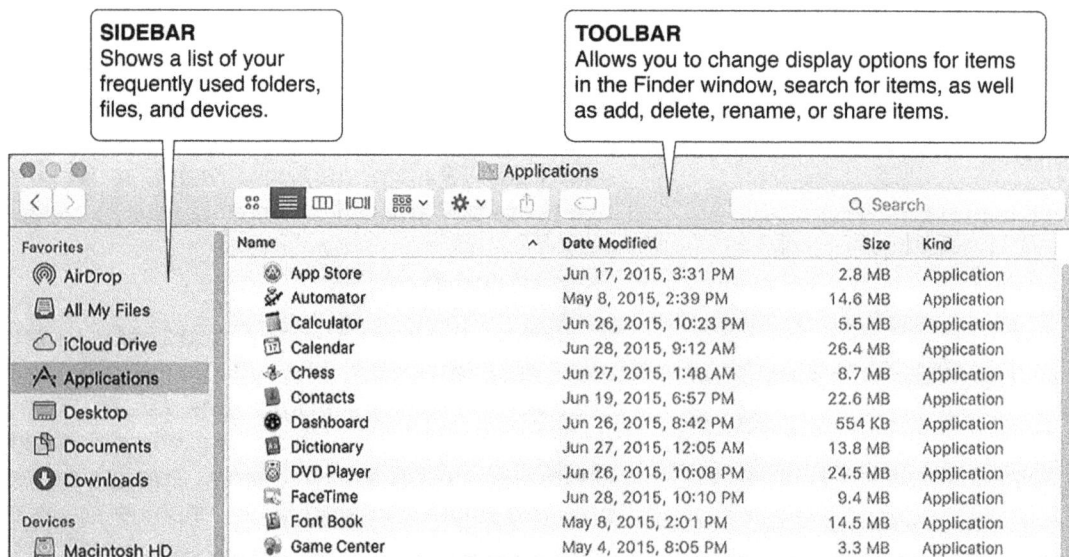

SIDEBAR
Shows a list of your frequently used folders, files, and devices.

TOOLBAR
Allows you to change display options for items in the Finder window, search for items, as well as add, delete, rename, or share items.

Name	Date Modified	Size	Kind
App Store	Jun 17, 2015, 3:31 PM	2.8 MB	Application
Automator	May 8, 2015, 2:39 PM	14.6 MB	Application
Calculator	Jun 26, 2015, 10:23 PM	5.5 MB	Application
Calendar	Jun 28, 2015, 9:12 AM	26.4 MB	Application
Chess	Jun 27, 2015, 1:48 AM	8.7 MB	Application
Contacts	Jun 19, 2015, 6:57 PM	22.6 MB	Application
Dashboard	Jun 26, 2015, 8:42 PM	554 KB	Application
Dictionary	Jun 27, 2015, 12:05 AM	13.8 MB	Application
DVD Player	Jun 26, 2015, 10:08 PM	24.5 MB	Application
FaceTime	Jun 28, 2015, 10:10 PM	9.4 MB	Application
Font Book	May 8, 2015, 2:01 PM	14.5 MB	Application
Game Center	May 4, 2015, 8:05 PM	3.3 MB	Application

Favorites: AirDrop, All My Files, iCloud Drive, Applications, Desktop, Documents, Downloads

Devices: Macintosh HD

Sidebar

The Finder window has a list on the left side that shows your frequently used files, folders, drives, devices, etc. The Desktop folder is a typical item in the sidebar. It shows the same files and folders that are saved on your Mac's Desktop. Another typical item in the Sidebar is the Applications folder. It contains all of your Mac's applications ("apps").

Finder Viewing Options

Let's go over some possible viewing options within the Finder. We'll look at the Applications folder, something that is found on every Mac.

1. Click on the FINDER icon in the Dock (the dark & light blue smiling face).
2. If a Finder window does not appear, click on the FILE command, then select NEW FINDER WINDOW.
3. Click on APPLICATIONS in the SIDEBAR.

You will now see the Applications folder. Note that whenever you click on a folder in the Sidebar, the name of the folder appears at the top of the display window.

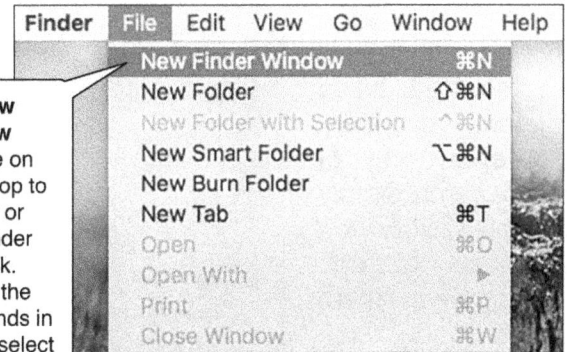

Finder   File   Edit   View   Go   Window   Help

New Finder Window	⌘N
New Folder	⇧⌘N
New Folder with Selection	^⌘N
New Smart Folder	⌥⌘N
New Burn Folder	
New Tab	⌘T
Open	⌘O
Open With	▶
Print	⌘P
Close Window	⌘W

Creating a New Finder Window
Click anywhere on the open desktop to activate Finder or click on the Finder icon in the Dock. When you see the Finder commands in the Menu Bar, select File, then New Finder Window from the drop-down menu.

Applications Folder
Select this folder to view your applications.

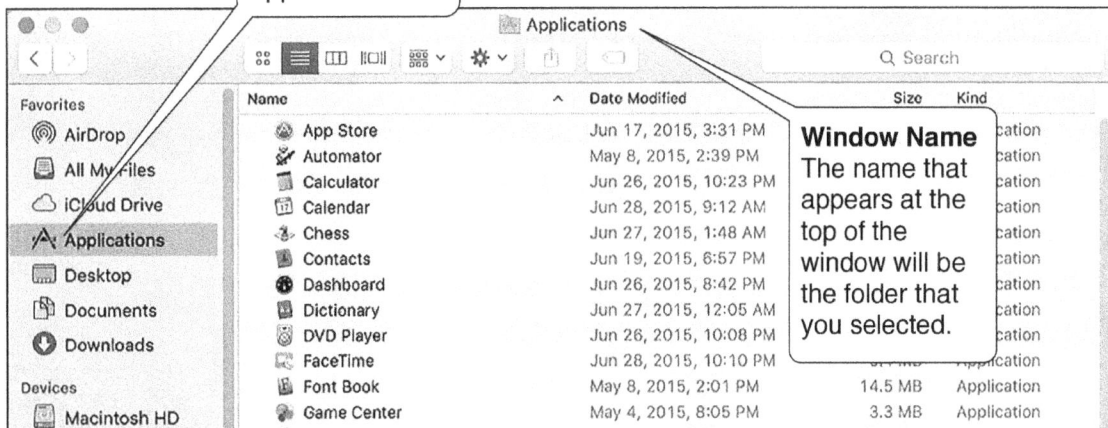

📁 Applications

Favorites	Name	^ Date Modified	Size	Kind
🔴 AirDrop	🅰️ App Store	Jun 17, 2015, 3:31 PM		cation
💾 All My Files	🤖 Automator	May 8, 2015, 2:39 PM		cation
☁️ iCloud Drive	🧮 Calculator	Jun 26, 2015, 10:23 PM		cation
🅰️ Applications	📅 Calendar	Jun 28, 2015, 9:12 AM		cation
🖥️ Desktop	♟️ Chess	Jun 27, 2015, 1:48 AM		cation
📄 Documents	📇 Contacts	Jun 19, 2015, 6:57 PM		cation
⬇️ Downloads	🌐 Dashboard	Jun 26, 2015, 8:42 PM		cation
	📖 Dictionary	Jun 27, 2015, 12:05 AM		cation
	💿 DVD Player	Jun 26, 2015, 10:08 PM		cation
Devices	📹 FaceTime	Jun 28, 2015, 10:10 PM		cation
💾 Macintosh HD	📚 Font Book	May 8, 2015, 2:01 PM	14.5 MB	Application
	🎮 Game Center	May 4, 2015, 8:05 PM	3.3 MB	Application

Window Name
The name that appears at the top of the window will be the folder that you selected.

What is a File? What is a Folder?

Think about an old-fashioned file cabinet. All of those papers were organized into folders. Folders could hold other folders. Your Mac organizes things in the same way. Each electronic File is like one of those papers (or sets of papers). Files can also be entire documents, images, or even programs. Each Folder can contain these files, other folders, or it could even be empty, waiting to be filled with something later. And just like the old-fashioned filing cabinet, your filing system will be as organized, or as messy, as you make it!

You have the option to view your files in one of four ways: Icon view, List view, column view and cover flow. Each one has benefits and drawbacks.

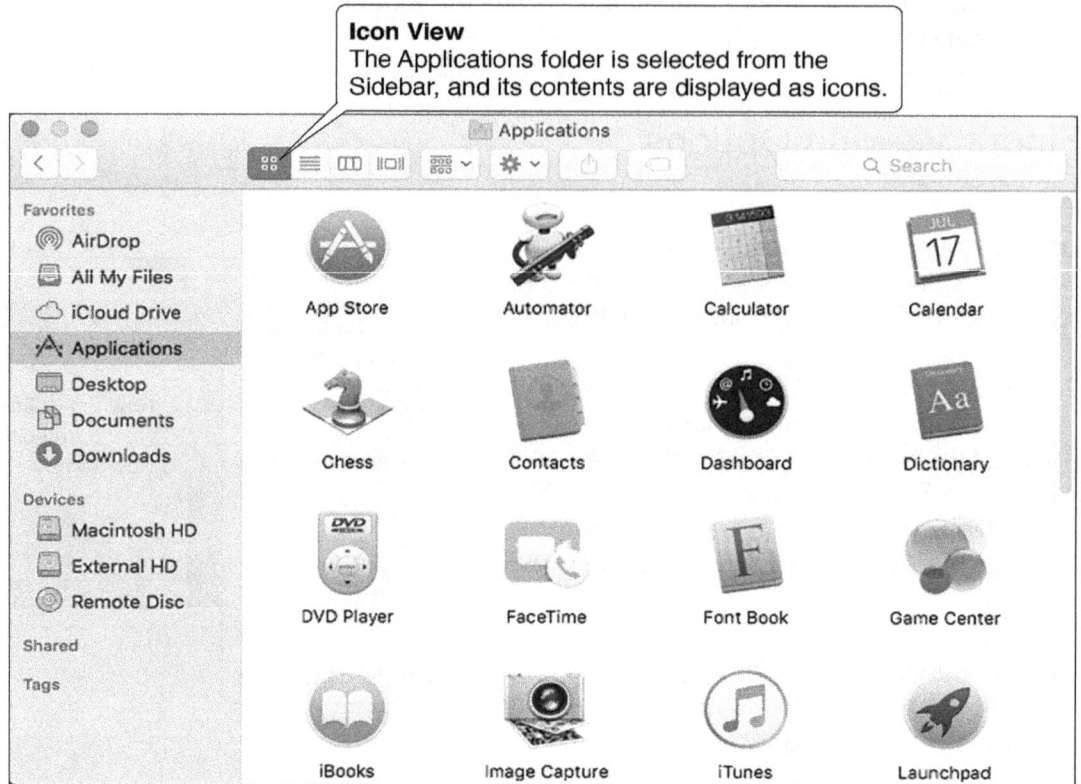

Icon View
The Applications folder is selected from the Sidebar, and its contents are displayed as icons.

Icon View

In Icon View, each file or folder is represented by a picture, or icon. To open any of these items, simply double click on the icon. You can also move them by dragging them around.

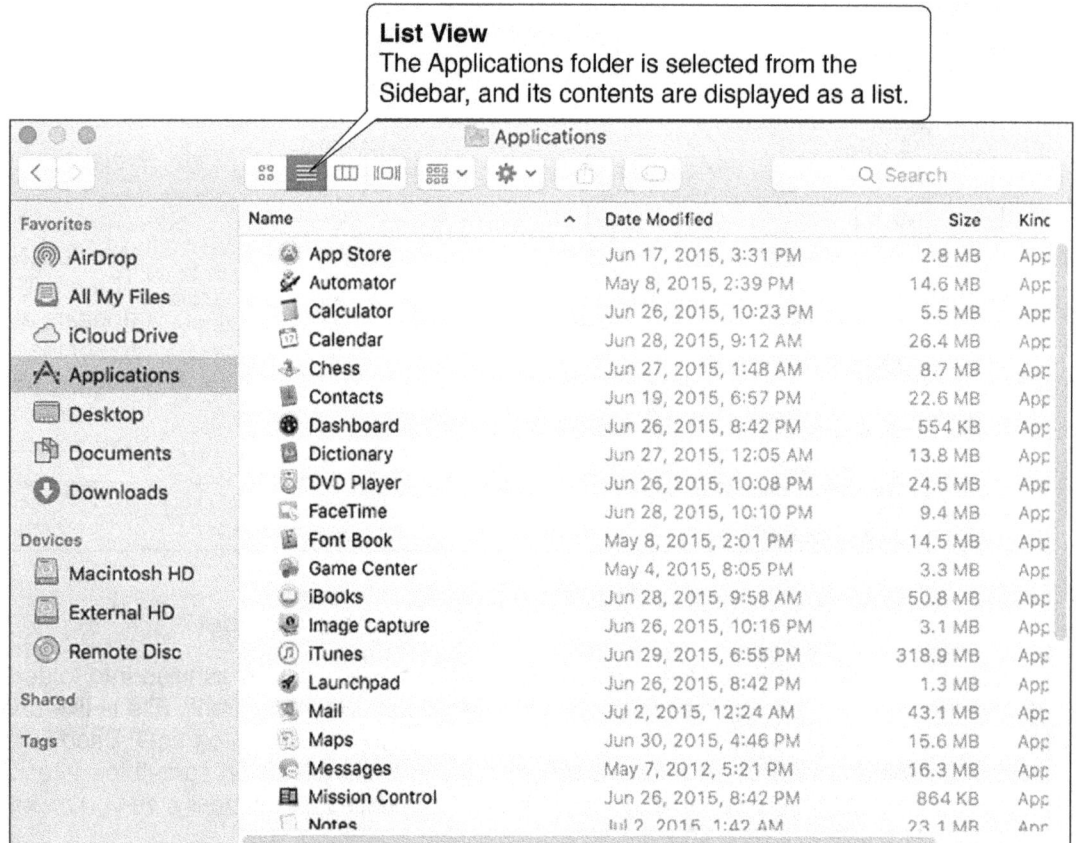

List View
The Applications folder is selected from the Sidebar, and its contents are displayed as a list.

List View

In the List View on the right, each file or folder appears in a list with additional information such as the date it was last modified and the file size.

Name		Date Modified	Size	Kind
App Store		Jun 17, 2015, 3:31 PM	2.8 MB	App
Automator		May 8, 2015, 2:39 PM	14.6 MB	App
Calculator		Jun 26, 2015, 10:23 PM	5.5 MB	App
Calendar		Jun 28, 2015, 9:12 AM	26.4 MB	App
Chess		Jun 27, 2015, 1:48 AM	8.7 MB	App
Contacts		Jun 19, 2015, 6:57 PM	22.6 MB	App
Dashboard		Jun 26, 2015, 8:42 PM	554 KB	App
Dictionary		Jun 27, 2015, 12:05 AM	13.8 MB	App
DVD Player		Jun 26, 2015, 10:08 PM	24.5 MB	App
FaceTime		Jun 28, 2015, 10:10 PM	9.4 MB	App
Font Book		May 8, 2015, 2:01 PM	14.5 MB	App
Game Center		May 4, 2015, 8:05 PM	3.3 MB	App
iBooks		Jun 28, 2015, 9:58 AM	50.8 MB	App
Image Capture		Jun 26, 2015, 10:16 PM	3.1 MB	App
iTunes		Jun 29, 2015, 6:55 PM	318.9 MB	App
Launchpad		Jun 26, 2015, 8:42 PM	1.3 MB	App
Mail		Jul 2, 2015, 12:24 AM	43.1 MB	App
Maps		Jun 30, 2015, 4:46 PM	15.6 MB	App
Messages		May 7, 2012, 5:21 PM	16.3 MB	App
Mission Control		Jun 26, 2015, 8:42 PM	864 KB	App
Notes		Jul 2, 2015, 1:42 AM	23.1 MB	App

Column View

In Column View a separate column is displayed for each nested folder. On the left, Applications is selected from the sidebar, and its contents are listed in the first column. In this list is the Utilities folder. Selecting this folder shows a list of its contents in the second column. We could keep going with more columns of lists if there were additional folders. When a file is finally selected, its icon and information will appear in the space on the right side of the window (for example, here we see AirPort Utility). The successive columns will appear from left to right until a final file is selected.

Cover Flow View

The Cover Flow view gives a preview of each file or folder in a rotating carousel. You can drag the scroll button (the small gray button on the horizontal line beneath the images) to the left or right to preview items, or simply select items from the file list and the preview window will locate your selection in the carousel. Photo and text files will show the actual image or first page of text allowing you to search visually for a particular item.

Column View
The Applications folder is selected from the Sidebar, and its contents are displayed as a series of columns. Notice that the second column shows the items that are in the Utilities folder selected from the first column.

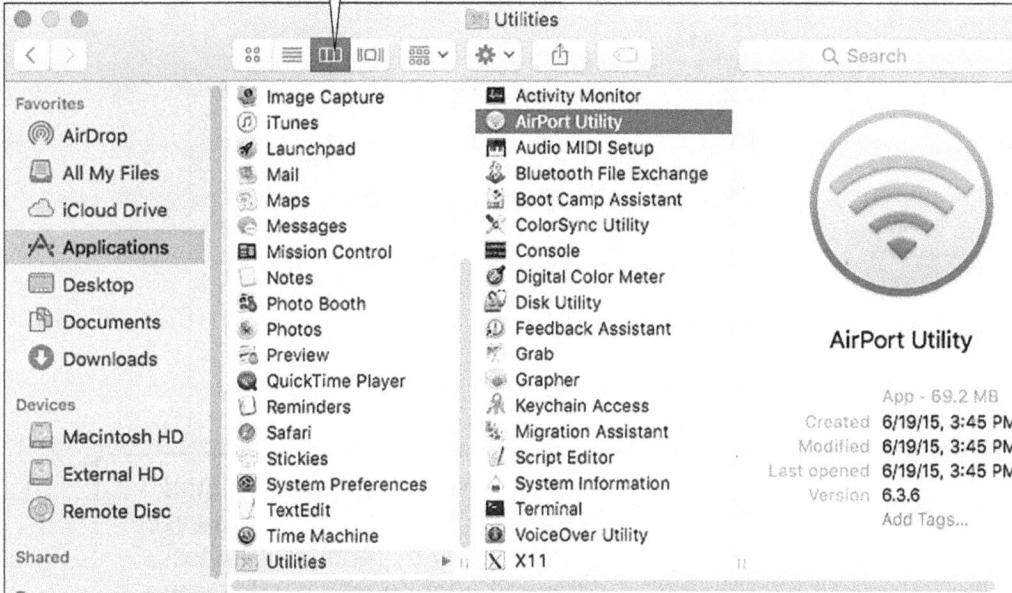

Cover Flow View
The Applications folder is selected from the Sidebar, and its contents are displayed as both a list, and either application icons or an image of the file content itself. This is a great way to get a quick preview of items in files such as pictures or text.

Reorganizing Files in Views

The Finder application gives you lots of options for reordering, sorting, and viewing your files and folders in any of the four layouts that we just saw. For example, if you want to sort your files by the date they were last opened rather than alphabetically by name, click on the Arrange button, then select the "Date Last Opened" option from the drop-down list as shown below.

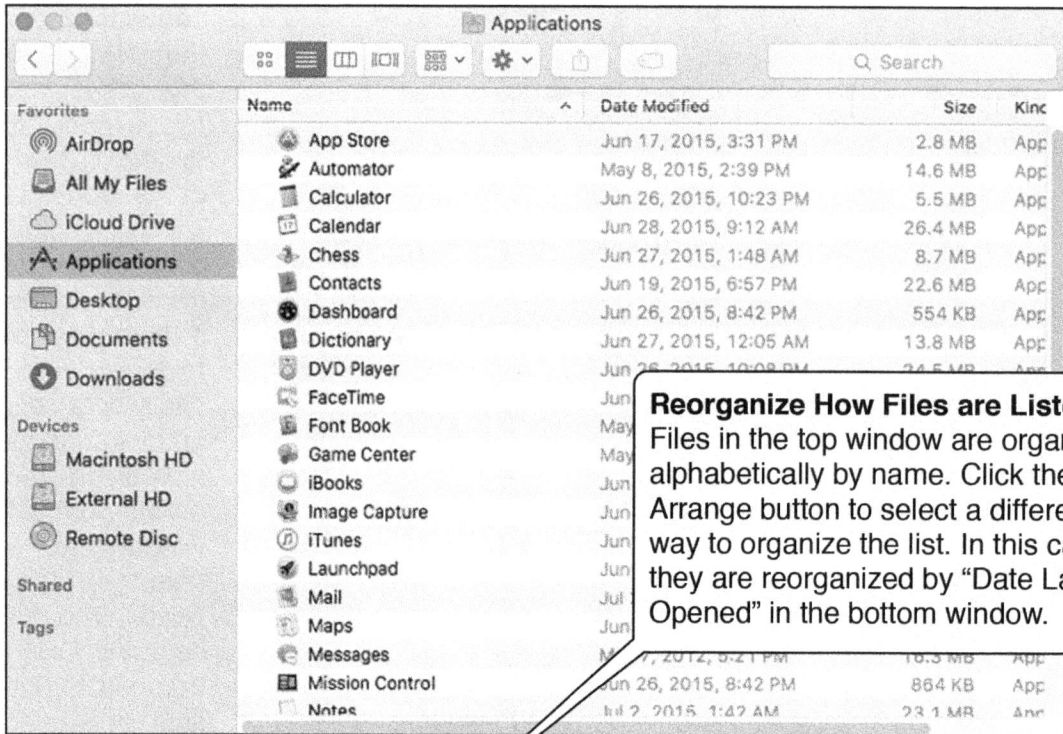

Reorganize How Files are Listed
Files in the top window are organized alphabetically by name. Click the Arrange button to select a different way to organize the list. In this case, they are reorganized by "Date Last Opened" in the bottom window.

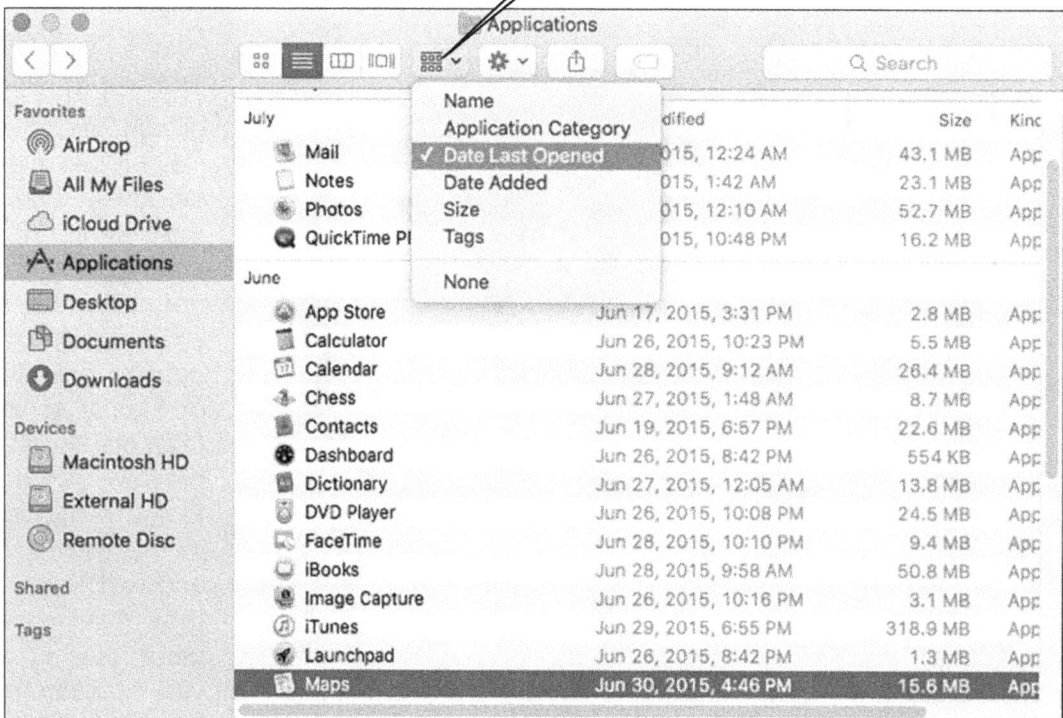

Staying Organized with Finder

Creating and Naming a New Folder

Folders are simply containers that hold other files or folders. For example, you may have photos of your vacations in Hawaii, California, and Maine. Each photo is a separate file. You can create three folders (Hawaii, California, and Maine) and put your photo files in each one. Then you can create another folder called Vacation Photos that will contain the three folders Hawaii, California, and Maine.

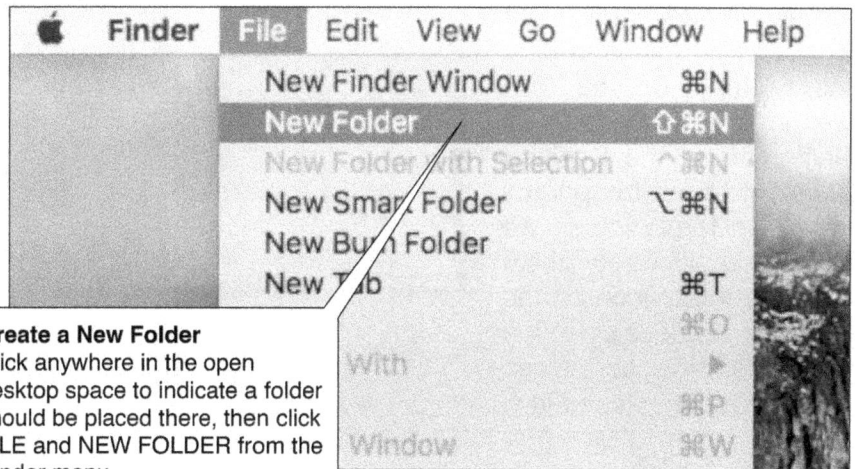

| 🍎 | Finder | File | Edit | View | Go | Window | Help |

New Finder Window ⌘N
New Folder ⇧⌘N
New Folder with Selection ^⌘N
New Smart Folder ⌥⌘N
New Burn Folder
New Tab ⌘T

Create a New Folder
Click anywhere in the open desktop space to indicate a folder should be placed there, then click FILE and NEW FOLDER from the Finder menu.

Follow these steps to create a new folder on the desktop:

1. Click anywhere on the open Desktop to indicate that this is where the new folder should be placed. Do not click in another window or on anything else, just the Desktop itself. This will activate the Finder application.

2. Go to the Finder menu bar in the upper left corner of the screen, click FILE, then NEW FOLDER from the drop-down menu. a new folder will appear on the Desktop. (Note that it may be in a different location on the desktop than what you see here.)

3. When the new folder is first created, you will see its name highlighted in a blue rectangle. Simply type in the name that you would like the folder to be called (in this case,

untitled folder

Naming a New Folder
When a Folder is first created, its name appears with a light blue background. This indicates that you can type in a new name. As you type, the background will become white.

California

California). As you type, the background behind the new name will become white.

4. Press the RETURN key or click outside the folder in the Desktop area again. Now the background behind the folder name will become transparent.

Putting Files in a Folder

Now that you have created a new folder, you'll want to put some things in it. In the example on the right we have some photos of California on the Desktop We want to put the photos in the California folder. We could simply drag them onto the folder icon on the Desktop, but let's open the California folder so we can see them being placed in it.

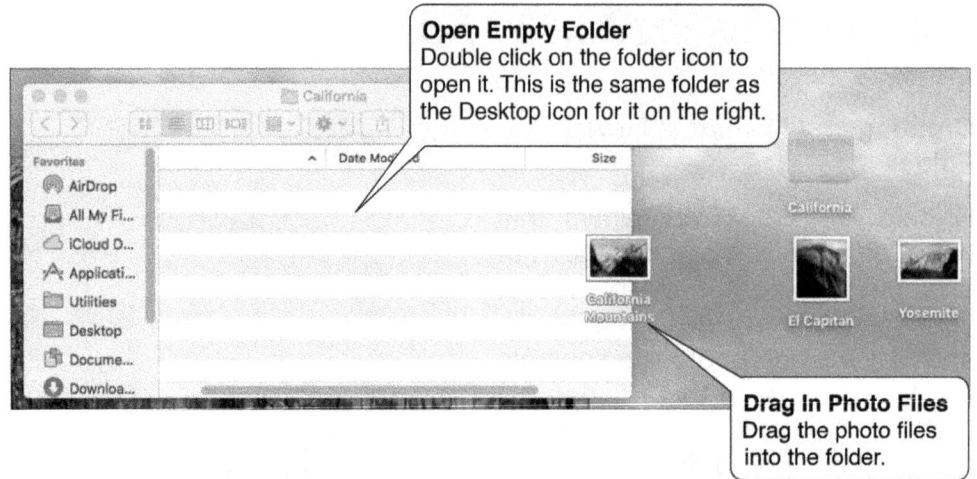

Open Empty Folder
Double click on the folder icon to open it. This is the same folder as the Desktop icon for it on the right.

Drag In Photo Files
Drag the photo files into the folder.

1. Double click on the folder that you would like to open (in this case, the California folder). A window will now appear with the folder name at the top. If this window is covering the photo files on the Desktop, simply click in the gray area at the top of the window and drag it over to a different location on the Desktop.

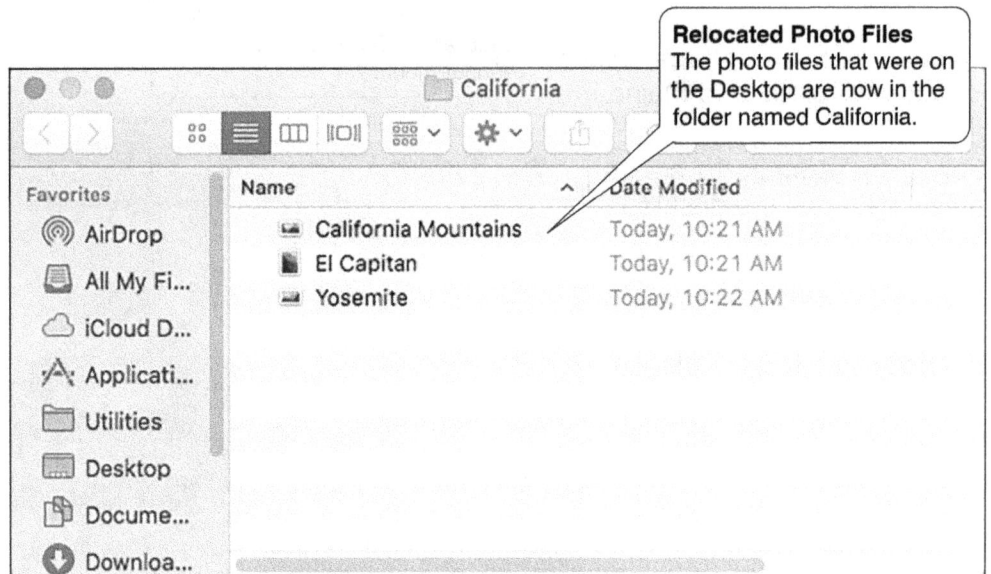

Relocated Photo Files
The photo files that were on the Desktop are now in the folder named California.

2. Click on the first photo file and drag it into the window that you've just created. Repeat this with the remaining files. (Hint: to select multiple files at the same time, hold down the shift key as you click on each file.) Now you'll see all of the photo files inside the California folder.

3. To close the folder, click on the red dot in the upper left corner. (Remember that the folder window must be active for the dot to appear red. If it isn't the active window, click on it once to make it active.)

Moving Folders Into Folders

Folders can be stored within other folders. For example, you may already have photos from other vacations stored in folders on your desktop. In the example on the right we have two other folders: Hawaii and Maine. Let's put

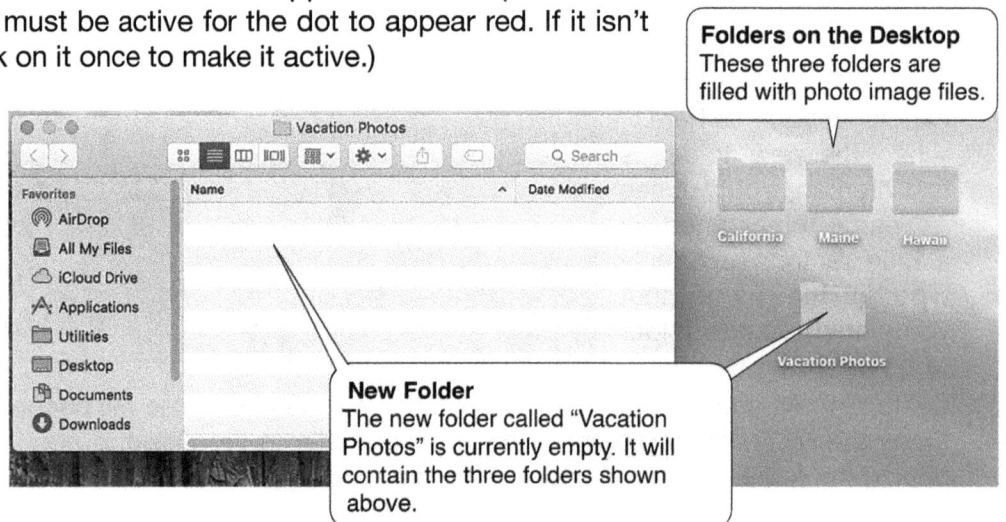

Folders on the Desktop
These three folders are filled with photo image files.

New Folder
The new folder called "Vacation Photos" is currently empty. It will contain the three folders shown above.

these two folders along with the California folder all in a single folder called Vacation Photos. To do this, follow these steps:

1. First we'll create another folder called Vacation Photos. Click in the open Desktop space, then select FILE and NEW FOLDER from the Finder menu. Name this folder Vacation Photos using the same steps from the previous example when you named a folder "California".
2. Double click on the Vacation Photos folder to open it. If it now covers your other items on the desktop, just click in the gray area at the top of the window and drag it to a new space on the desktop.
3. Drag the folders California, Maine, and Hawaii over into the Vacation Photos window. They will disappear from your Desktop and will now be show in the Vacation Photos folder.

Remaining Folders on the Desktop
The folders Maine and Hawaii are still on the Desktop and have not been moved into the Vacation Photos folder yet.

Folder Within a Folder
The folder California has been moved inside the folder Vacation Photos.

List View
Note that in order to see files and folders this way you must select List View.

Show Folder Contents
To see what's inside a folder, click on the triangle arrow so that it points down. The files (and other folders, if any) within will be listed beneath.

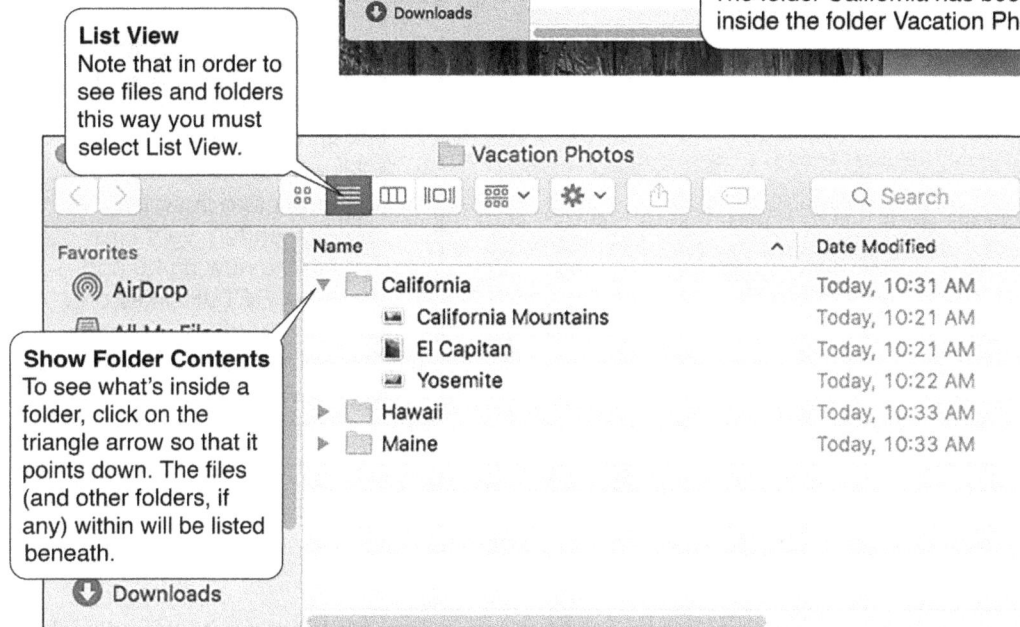

To see what's in any folder without opening a new window, select the List View button then look for the tiny triangle to the left of the folder name. This is actually a little arrow. Click on it so that it points down. The contents of the folder will now be shown. To close the listing, simply click on the little triangle again so that it points to the right.

Renaming Files and Folders

At some point you'll want to rename a file or folder. When you do, follow these steps:

1. Open a Finder window (Click on FINDER in the Dock to activate the Finder application, then NEW WINDOW in the Menu Bar at the top left).
2. Locate the file that you want to rename.
3. Click the file name once. The entire line will now appear with a dark blue background.
4. Click the file a second time. The name portion only of the line will now have a light blue background. (Note: if you do the second click too quickly, Finder will actually open the file. Make sure that you wait a second or two between the first and second clicks!)
5. Type in the new file name and press the RETURN key on your keyboard. The file name will now be highlighted in dark blue again.

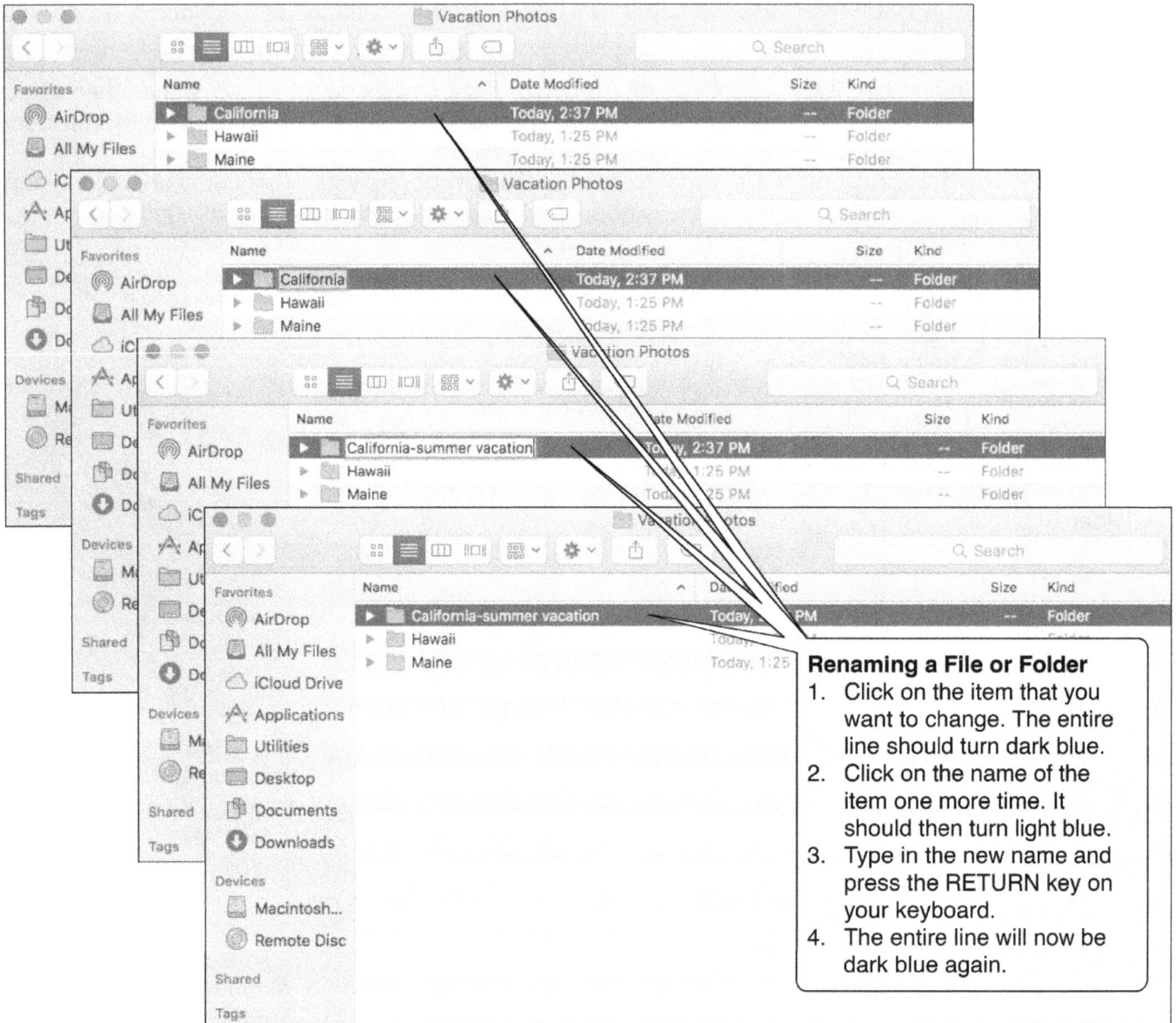

Renaming a File or Folder
1. Click on the item that you want to change. The entire line should turn dark blue.
2. Click on the name of the item one more time. It should then turn light blue.
3. Type in the new name and press the RETURN key on your keyboard.
4. The entire line will now be dark blue again.

Deleting Files and Folders

Deleting a file, folder, or even an entire application from your Mac is as easy as locating it in Finder, then dragging it to the Trash icon in the Dock. Note that by doing this, you haven't actually deleted anything. You've just moved it into the Trash folder, much like tossing something into your kitchen trash can in your house. You can drag multiple files into the Trash and leave them there. To see what you've thrown away, simply double click on the Trash icon.

To permanently get rid of the files in Trash you must empty the Trash can (again, like the trash can in your kitchen).

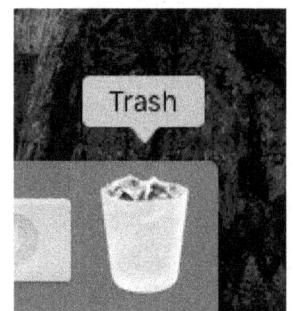

1. Click on FINDER in the Dock to activate the Finder application.
2. Click on the word FINDER in the Menu Bar (upper left of your screen), then click on EMPTY TRASH. Note that you also have a SECURE EMPTY TRASH option. This takes the deletion process one step further by removing the possibility of someone with special file recovery software

from getting your files back. This usually isn't necessary unless you're deleting items that contain private information, such as financial documents.

3. You will be given one last opportunity to cancel your file deletion with the "Are you sure...?" warning message. Click EMPTY TRASH if you're sure you want to delete the contents of the Trash can.

Empty Trash
Erases anything that you put in the Trash. You cannot undo this once it is done.

Secure Empty Trash
Erases items that you put in the Trash so that no one could retrieve them using special file recovery software. You cannot undo this once it is done.

Are you sure you want to permanently erase the items in the Trash?
You can't undo this action.

Cancel   Empty Trash

| Finder | File | Edit | View | Go | W |

About Finder

Preferences...   ⌘,

Empty Trash...   ⇧⌘⌫
Secure Empty Trash...

Services   ▶

Hide Finder   ⌘H
Hide Others   ⌥⌘H
Show All

Using Finder to Find Things

Searching with Finder

The whole point of Finder is to help you find things. It shows you exactly what you have on your computer and gives you quick access to any file or folder. But what if you can't remember where you put something? That's where the Search option comes in.

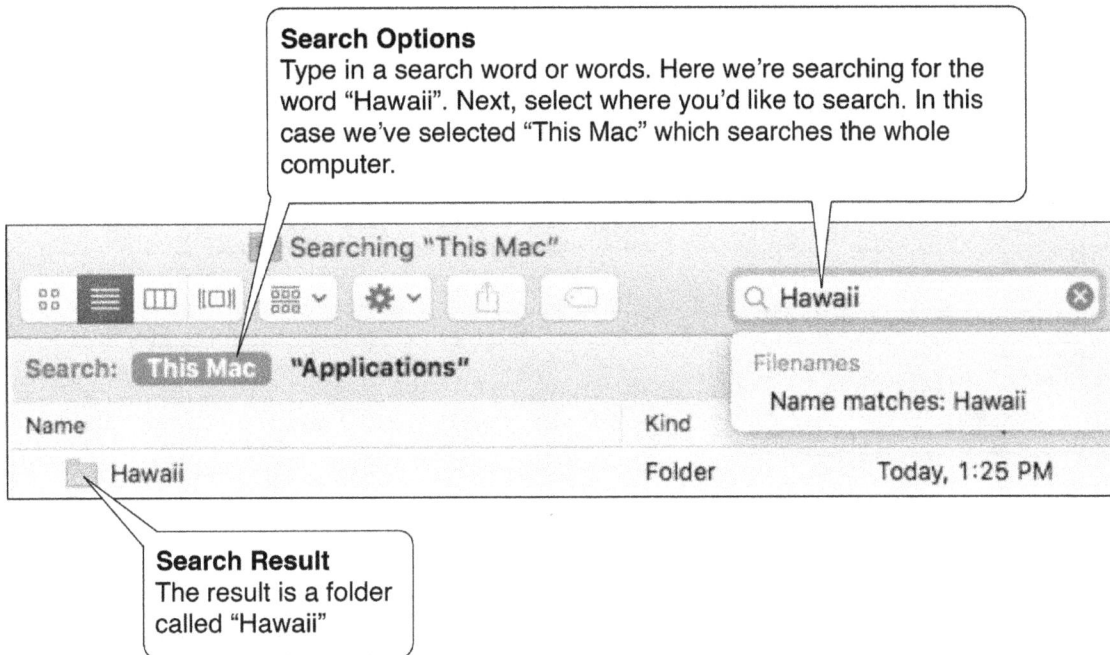

Search Options
Type in a search word or words. Here we're searching for the word "Hawaii". Next, select where you'd like to search. In this case we've selected "This Mac" which searches the whole computer.

Searching "This Mac"

Q Hawaii

Search: **This Mac** "Applications"

Filenames
Name matches: Hawaii

Name	Kind
Hawaii	Folder	Today, 1:25 PM

Search Result
The result is a folder called "Hawaii"

In the top right corner of every search window you'll see a magnifying glass icon within a search field where you can enter text. Click your cursor in that space and type in the word or words that you're searching for. As you type, you'll begin to see items appear that contain your search terms. For example, if you wanted to find where you put your Hawaii vacation photos, type in the word "Hawaii". You will now see a list of all items that contain the word "Hawaii".

Adding and Removing Items in the Sidebar Favorites

Apple provides you with some initial folders in the Sidebar, but you can add or remove anything to customize the list for easy access. When you add or remove something in this list, you're not actually changing its location on your Mac. You're just adding it to a "quick access" list. For example, you may want to access

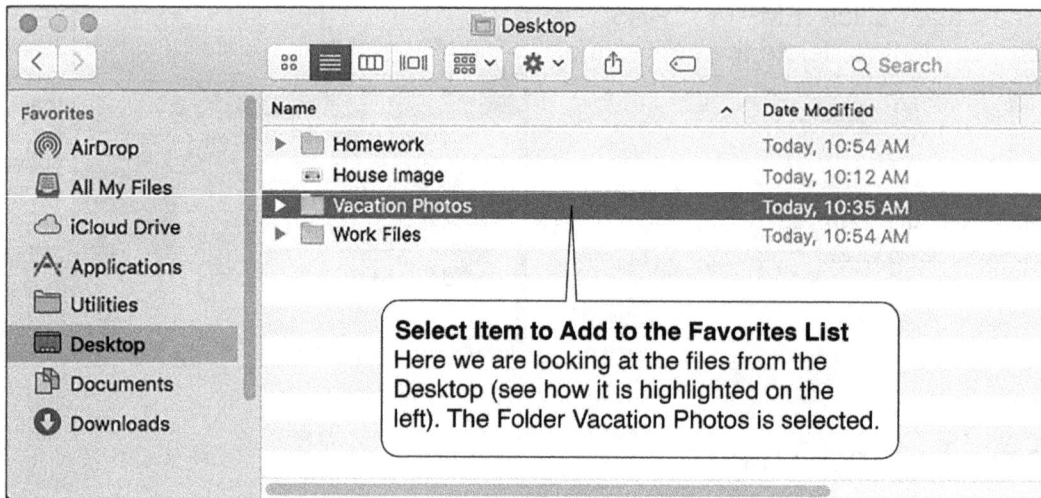

Select Item to Add to the Favorites List
Here we are looking at the files from the Desktop (see how it is highlighted on the left). The Folder Vacation Photos is selected.

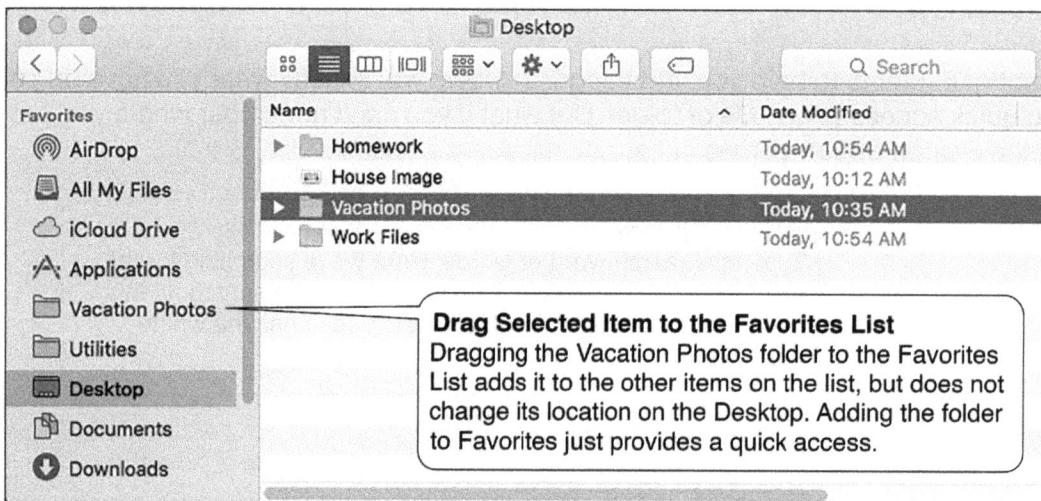

Drag Selected Item to the Favorites List
Dragging the Vacation Photos folder to the Favorites List adds it to the other items on the list, but does not change its location on the Desktop. Adding the folder to Favorites just provides a quick access.

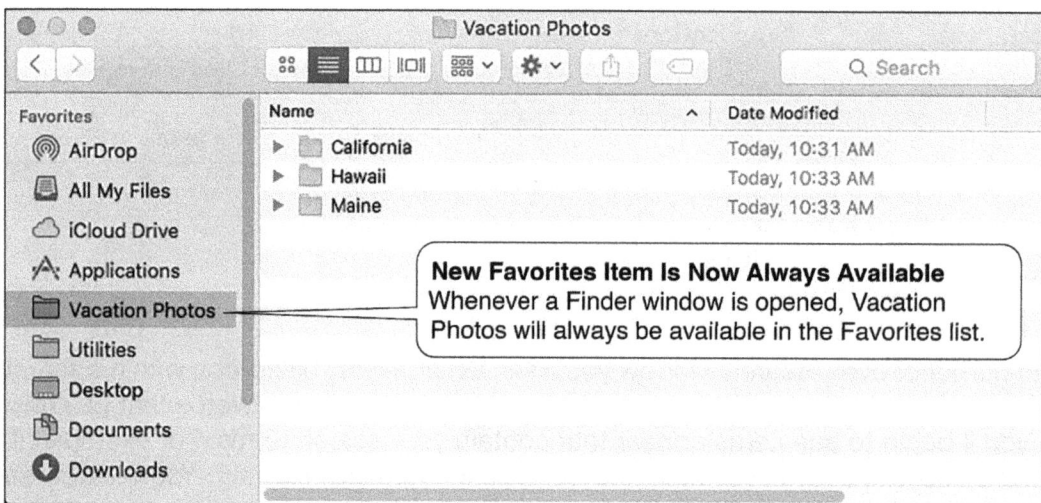

New Favorites Item Is Now Always Available
Whenever a Finder window is opened, Vacation Photos will always be available in the Favorites list.

your Vacation Photos folder frequently. You can easily add this folder to the Favorites list in the sidebar with these steps:

1. Open a Finder Window (Click on FINDER in the Dock, then NEW WINDOW in the Menu Bar).
2. Locate the item that you want to add to your Sidebar Favorites (in this case we'll add the Vacation Photos folder).
3. Drag the item over into the Sidebar space.
4. The item (the Vacation Photos folder) will now appear in the Favorites list.

To remove an item from the Sidebar, follow these steps:

1. Open a Finder Window (Click on FINDER in the Dock, then NEW WINDOW in the Menu Bar)
2. Locate the item that you want to remove from the Sidebar
3. Drag the item out of the Sidebar until an "x" appears beside the folder's icon, then let go. It will disappear and will no longer be shown in the Sidebar.

Remember that the folder still exists in its original location even after you remove it from the Favorites list in the Sidebar. The only thing that you've done here is take away the quick access to it.

Finder's "Quick Look" Option

Finder has a convenient tool for allowing you to see a file without actually opening it. It's called "Quick Look" and it's very easy to use:

1. Open a Finder window (Click on FINDER in the Dock, then NEW WINDOW in the Menu Bar)
2. Locate the file that you want to look at and click on it once to highlight it.
3. Press the Spacebar on your keyboard. A window will pop up showing the file's contents.
4. To close the Quick Look window, click on the "x" in the upper left corner of the window.

Show a File in Quick Look
Open a Finder window, click once on the file you want to see, then press the SPACEBAR on your keyboard.

A Quick Look Image Appears
A new window pops up showing a quick image of the file you have selected.

Note that using Quick Look is not the same as actually opening a file. You won't be able to edit the file contents in this view. It's just to give you, literally, a quick look!

Use Finder to Add an Application to the Dock

To add an application icon to the Dock, open Finder and go to the Applications folder. Locate the application that you want, and just drag it down into the Dock. To change the icon's location in the Dock, just drag it in the dock to the place where you want it. The other icons will separate to make room for it. To remove an icon from the Dock, drag it out of the dock onto the Desktop and it will disappear.

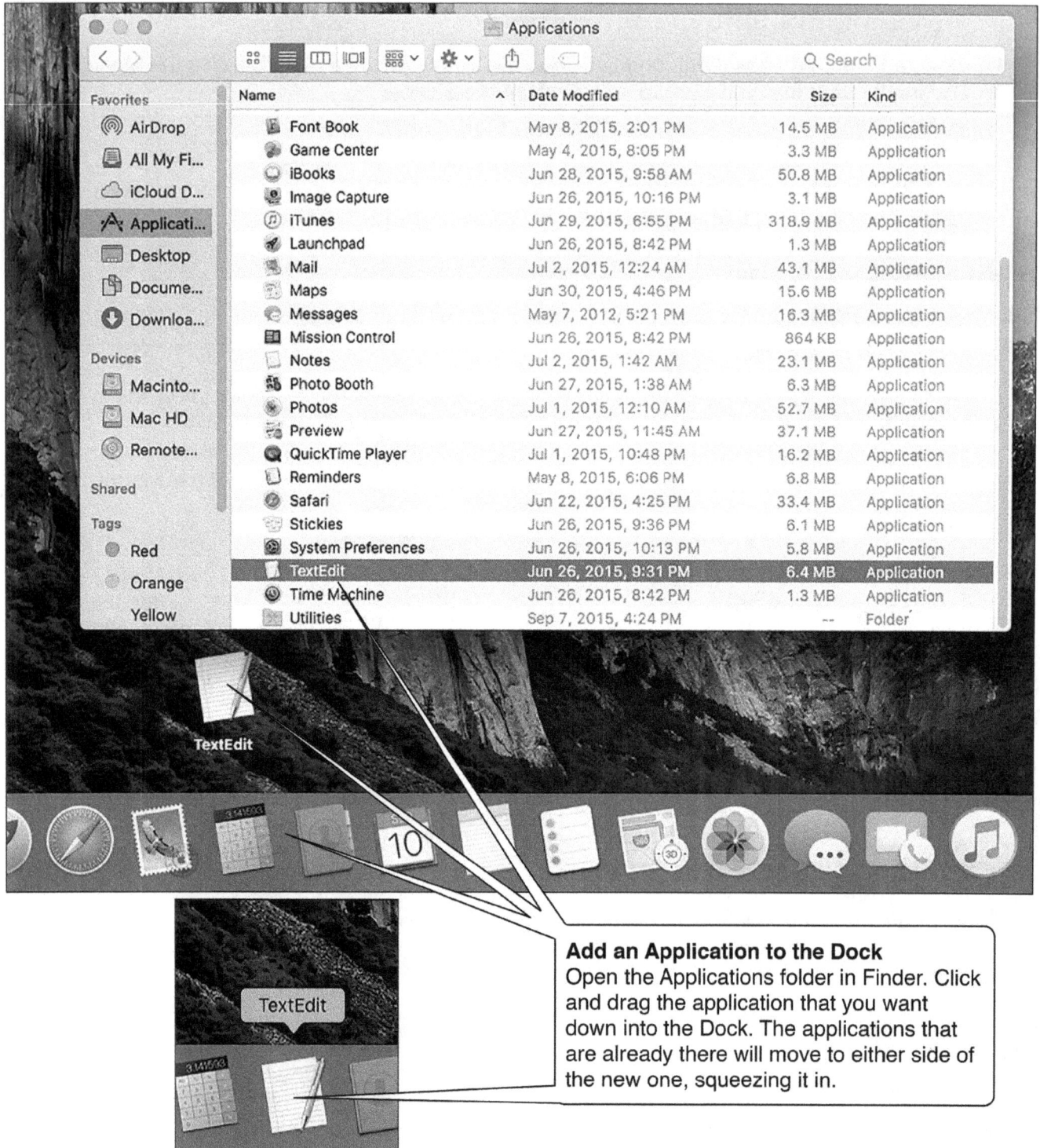

Add an Application to the Dock
Open the Applications folder in Finder. Click and drag the application that you want down into the Dock. The applications that are already there will move to either side of the new one, squeezing it in.

3 – SETTING YOUR SYSTEM PREFERENCES

What's Next in this chapter...

- Making Your Desktop Look the Way You Want
- Setting the Date and Time
- Energy Saving Settings
- General Preferences
- Changing the Sound Your Mac Makes
- Changing how the Mouse and Trackpad Work

System Preferences is a set of tools that allow you to control exactly how you want your Mac to look, sound, and operate. The settings in System Preferences let you change things such as your screen saver and desktop images, your mouse and keyboard controls, printer and scanner settings, and volume controls.

To access the System Preferences window, click on the Apple icon at the upper left of the corner of your screen in the Menu Bar, then select SYSTEM PREFERENCES.

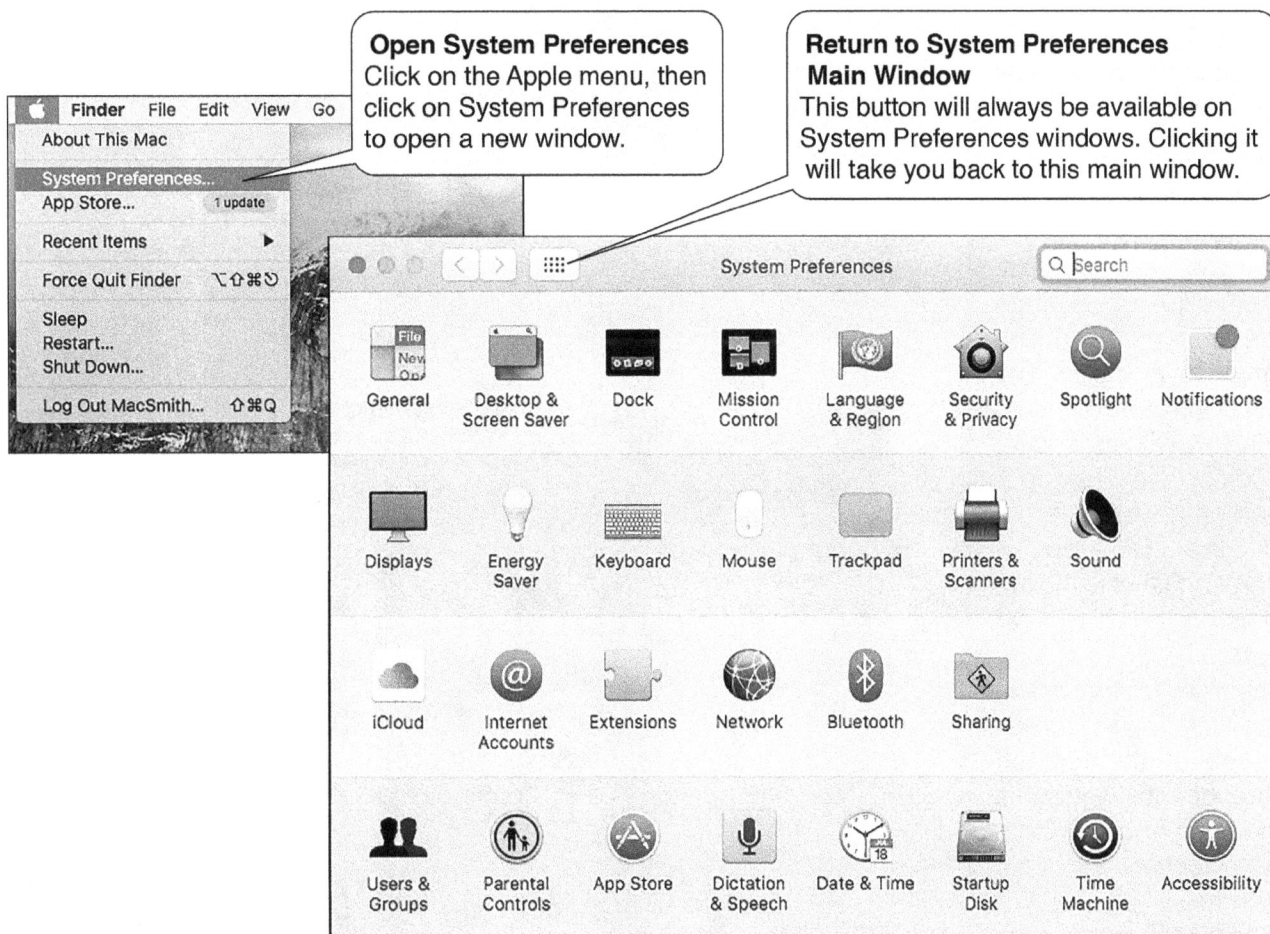

Open System Preferences
Click on the Apple menu, then click on System Preferences to open a new window.

Return to System Preferences Main Window
This button will always be available on System Preferences windows. Clicking it will take you back to this main window.

The System Preferences window shows icons for all of the different settings that you can use to set up and control your Mac. When you click on any of the icons, the System Preferences window will then display the specific controls for that group of settings. To return to the main System Preferences window, click on the checkerboard icon in the gray band at the top of the window.

21

Changing the Desktop Image

Perhaps one of the most fun things to do with your Mac is to customize it with your own images. You'll probably be spending a lot of time on your computer, so why not have it display images that you like?

Let's start with your Desktop. Remember that your Desktop is the entire area of your screen between the Menu Bar at the top and the Dock at the bottom. You can fill this area with an image, a solid color, or even images that rotate over an interval of time. Here's how:

Select System Preferences
Click on the Apple menu, then click on System Preferences to open a new window.

Open Desktop & Screensaver
Click on the Desktop & Screensaver icon. The window will change to show these options.

1. Click on the Apple icon at the upper left corner of your screen in the Menu Bar, then click on System Preferences in the drop-down menu. The System Preferences window will appear.
2. Click on the Desktop & Screen Saver icon.
3. In the Desktop & Screen Saver window, click on the DESKTOP button.
4. The item shown in the miniature screen image at the top left side of the window is the current option that is selected for your desktop.
5. Your Mac comes with a number of stock images as well as solid color display options. The list on the left side

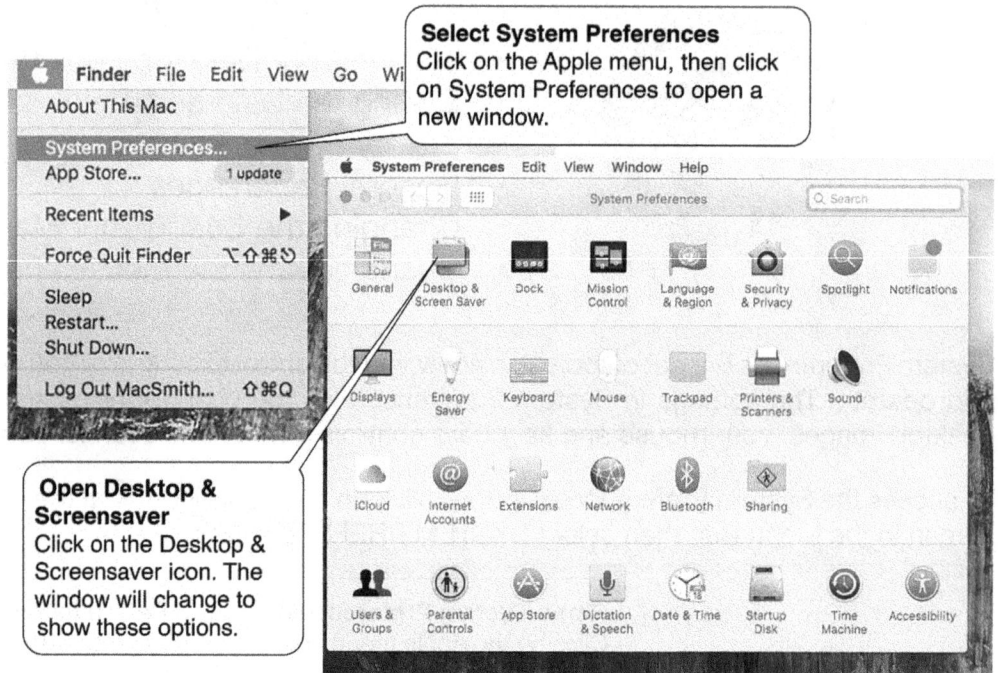

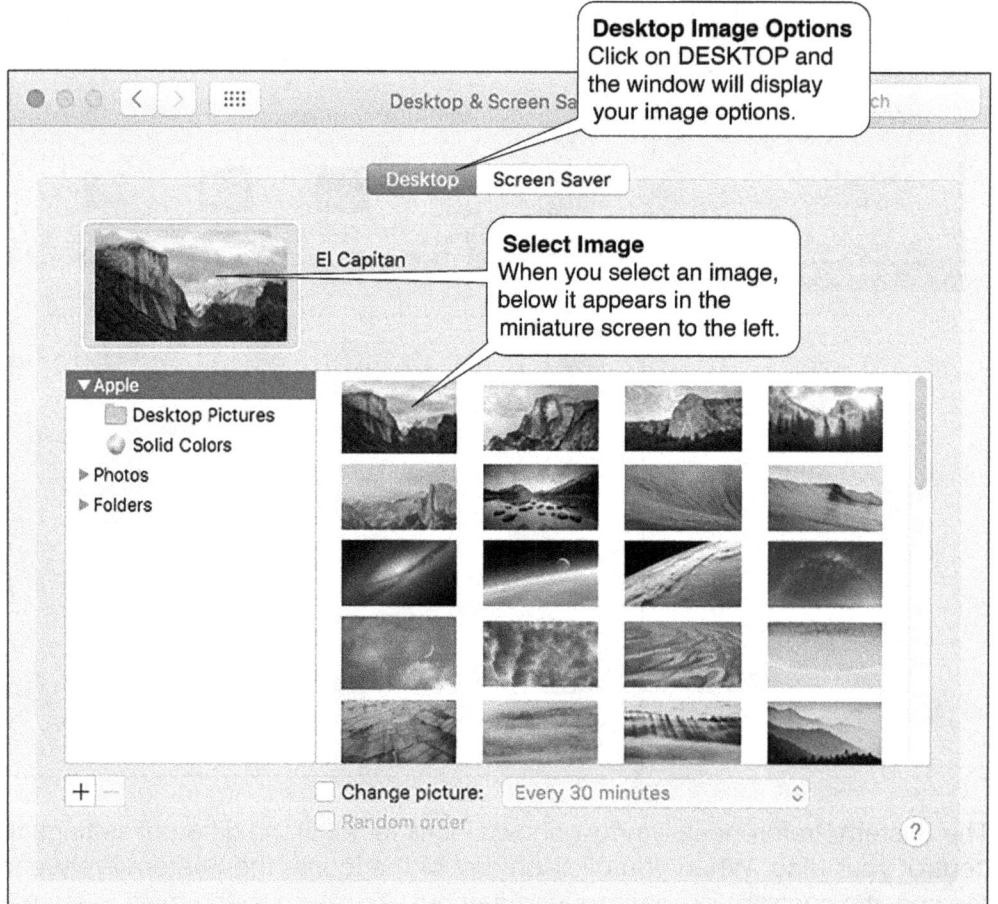

Desktop Image Options
Click on DESKTOP and the window will display your image options.

Select Image
When you select an image, below it appears in the miniature screen to the left.

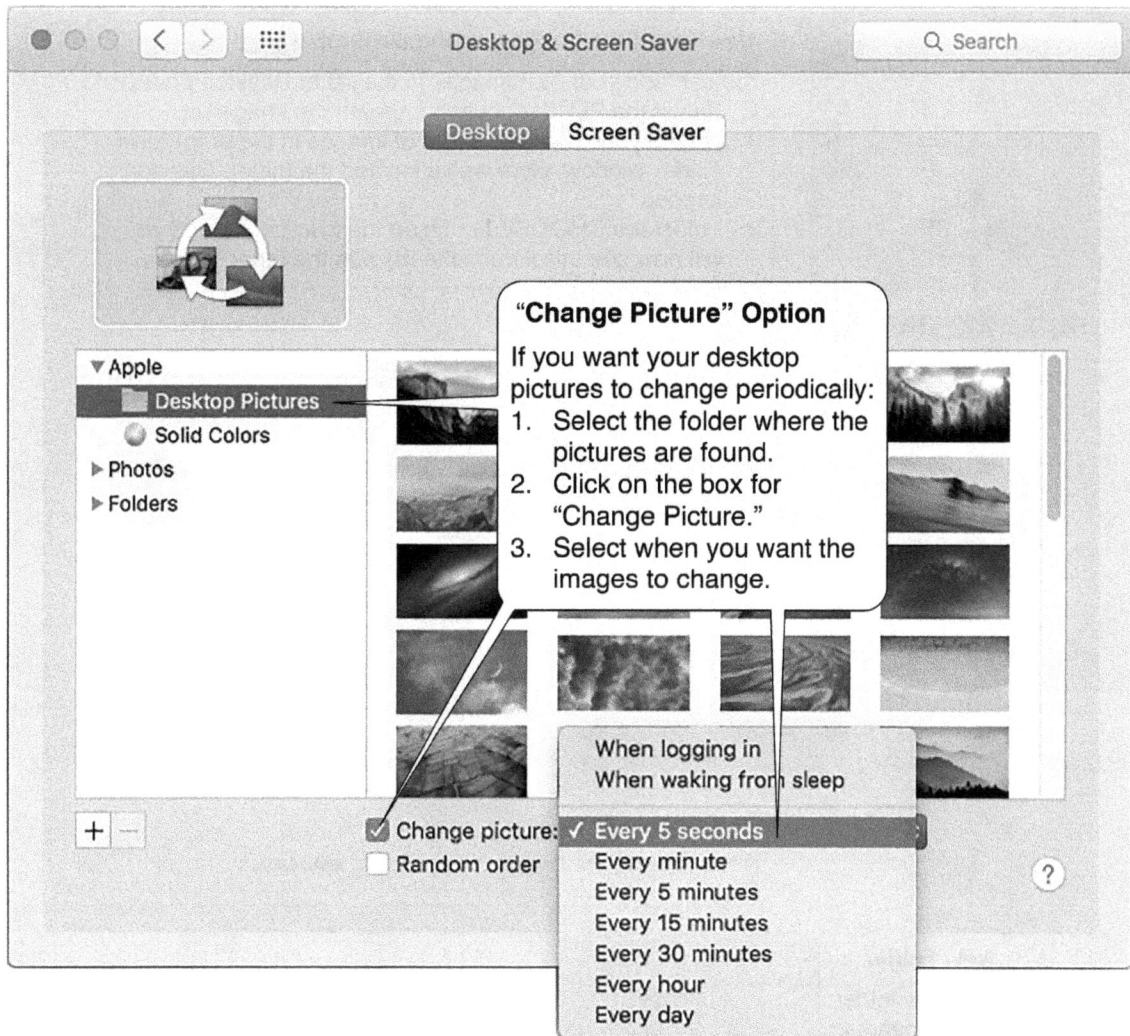

of the window shows the folders that contain these images and colors. Click on the little triangle pointer beside the Apple file name to see a drop-down list of the items in this folder: "Desktop Pictures" and "Solid Colors". Double click on the Desktop Pictures option to see the images in this folder.

6. Click on a picture that you like. It will appear in the miniature screen at the top of the window and will now be your Desktop image.

You can also select multiple images that change periodically with these steps:

1. Repeat steps 1-5 from the previous sequence, then select as many images as you like by holding down the SHIFT key on your keyboard while clicking on each image.
2. Check the box beside CHANGE PICTURE, and select the time interval from the pull-down menu.
3. Check the box beside RANDOM ORDER if you want the pictures to appear randomly.

You can use your own images for the Desktop as well. If you have them in your Photos app already, select "Pictures" from the list on the left of the window, then locate the image file or image folder that you want. If your images are located in a different folder, you can add it to the list:

1. Click the PLUS (+) button beneath the list. A drop-down Finder window will appear.
2. Locate the folder that contains your images. Either open it and select one image, or select the whole folder.
3. Your own images will now appear on the Desktop & Screen Saver window.

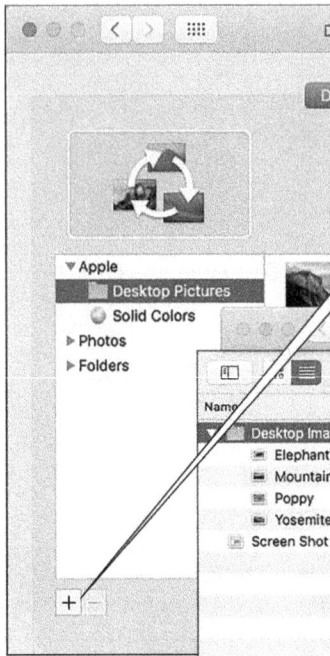

Use Your Own Images on the Desktop

You can add your own images to the list of Desktop photos:
1. Select the PLUS (+) button beneath the image list.
2. Locate your image or folder of images in the drop-down Finder window. Here we've located the folder "Desktop Images."
3. Select the CHOOSE button on the lower right, and you will now see this item in the list with the other images.

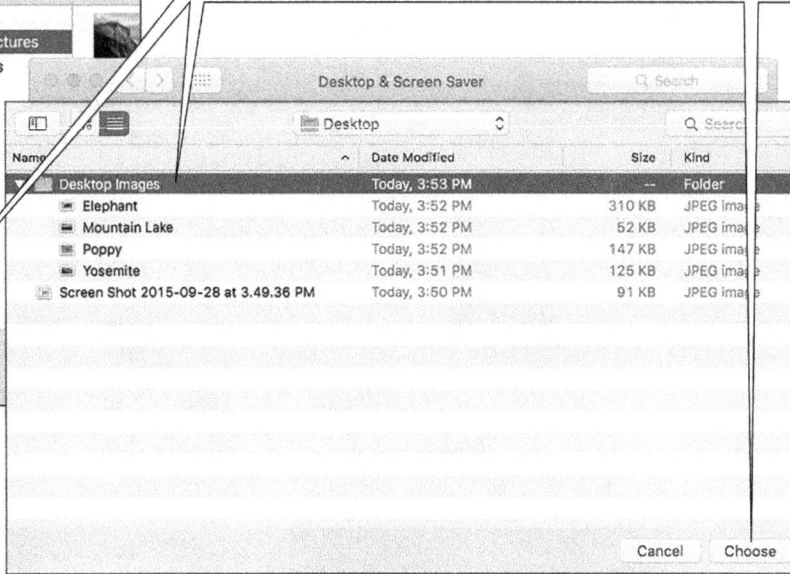

New Folder

The new folder now appears in the list. You can choose the entire folder, or select a single image.

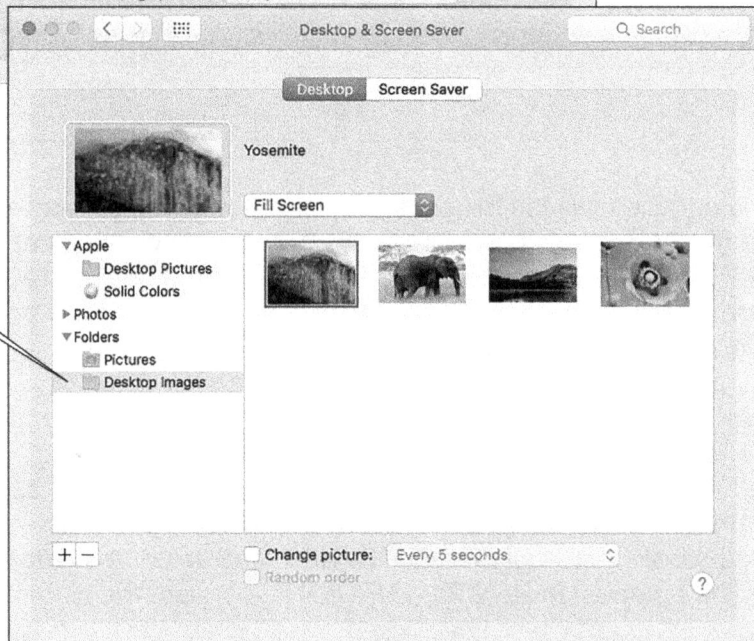

Setting Your Screen Saver

A Screen Saver is a moving image or series of moving images that appear after a set period of time that your Mac has been idle. The Screen Saver is actually a hold-over from the old days when computers used a different kind of monitor. Those monitors had luminescent phosphors that could permanently burn an image into the screen if held there for too long, which is why a Screen Saver always moves. Today computer monitors don't use phosphors, so technically we don't really need Screen Savers, but people still use them both for privacy and for fun.

To set the Screen Saver on your Mac, use these steps:

1. Click on the Apple icon at the upper left corner of your screen in the Menu Bar, then click on System Preferences in the drop-down menu. The System Preferences window will appear.
2. Click on the Desktop & Screen Saver icon.
3. In the Desktop & Screen Saver window, click on the SCREEN SAVER button at the top of the window.
4. In the space on the left side of the window you have a series of different motion options for your Screen

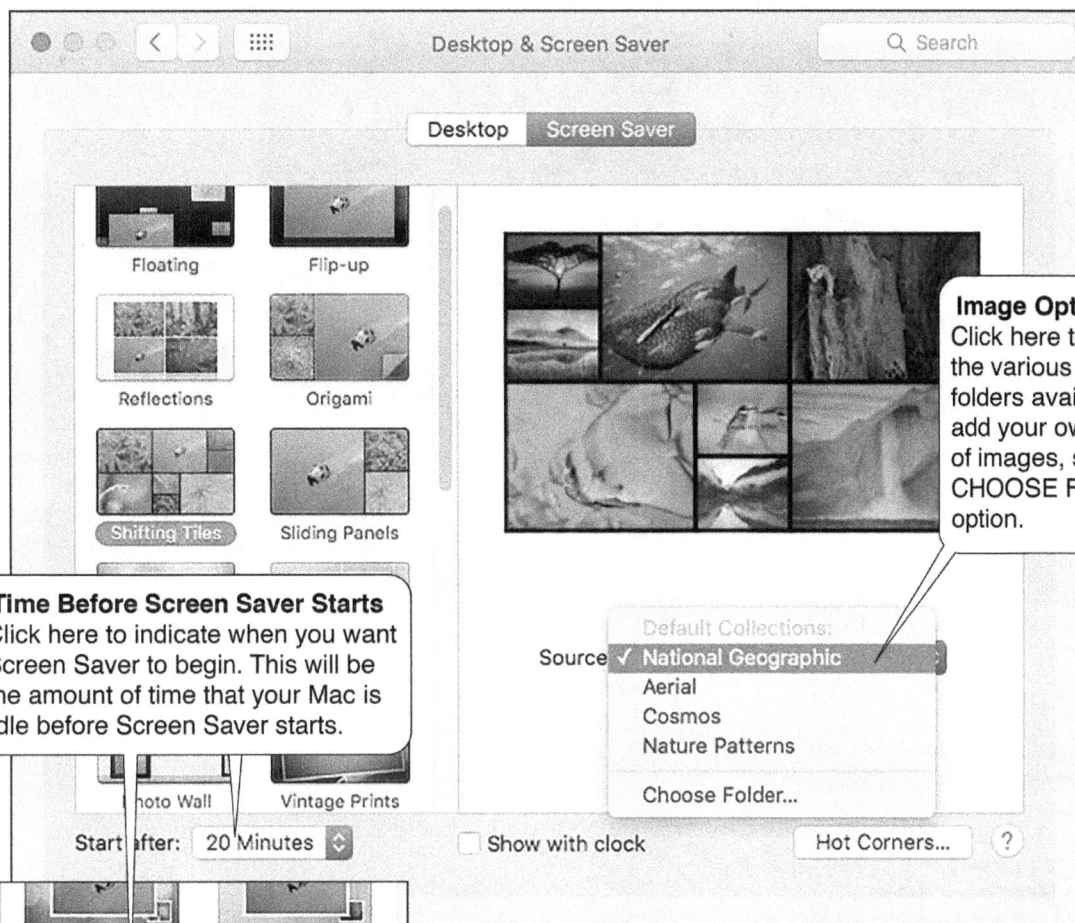

Image Options
Click here to access the various image folders available. To add your own folder of images, select the CHOOSE FOLDER option.

Time Before Screen Saver Starts
Click here to indicate when you want Screen Saver to begin. This will be the amount of time that your Mac is idle before Screen Saver starts.

Saver. Click on any of these to see how it looks in the small screen preview display on the right.

5. Beneath the small screen preview display on the right side of the window is a drop-down menu called SOURCE. Click on this to select a folder containing the images that you would like to put in your Screen Saver. (Note: If you need to put images in a folder for the Screen Saver and can't remember how, skip back to Chapter 2 and review the section called "Putting Files in a Folder".)
6. Choose the amount of time that your Mac will wait before starting the Screen Saver by selecting a time interval from the START AFTER pull-down menu at the bottom of the window on the left.

Changing the Size and Action of the Dock Icons

The dock provides quick access to many useful applications on your Mac, and you'll find yourself using the icons over and over. In Chapter 1 we reviewed some basic information about how the Dock works. Here, let's look at how to customize it so that you can use it more efficiently.

1. Click on the Apple icon at the upper left corner of your screen in the Menu Bar, then click on System Preferences in the drop-down menu. The System Preferences window will appear.
2. Click on the Dock icon. The Dock window will appear.

Icon Size
Use the slider to change the size of all of the icons in your Dock.

Icon Magnification
This option will change the size of the Dock icons as you hover over them with your cursor. Check the box, then use the slider to set the size that you want. The image above shows how the icons increase in size.

Zoom or Minimize Windows
To make windows either increase in size or minimize when you double-click on the title bar (the darker gray bar at the top), check the box and select the ZOOM or MINIMIZE options.

Shrink Windows with Genie or Scale
Select whether windows will visually squeeze down to an icon as they are minimized (GENIE) or will simply shrink to an icon (SCALE).

Change Minimized Window Icon
When windows are minimized they usually appear as a tiny image of whatever they contain. This option keeps the file name but shows an icon of the application used instead.

Animate Opening Applications
Check this option to make application icons bounce a few times when they are being opened.

Show Indicators
This option will show a little black dot beneath the Dock icon of any application that is open.

Hide and Show Dock
Checking this option will make the Dock disappear. It will only reappear when you place the cursor at the bottom of the screen.

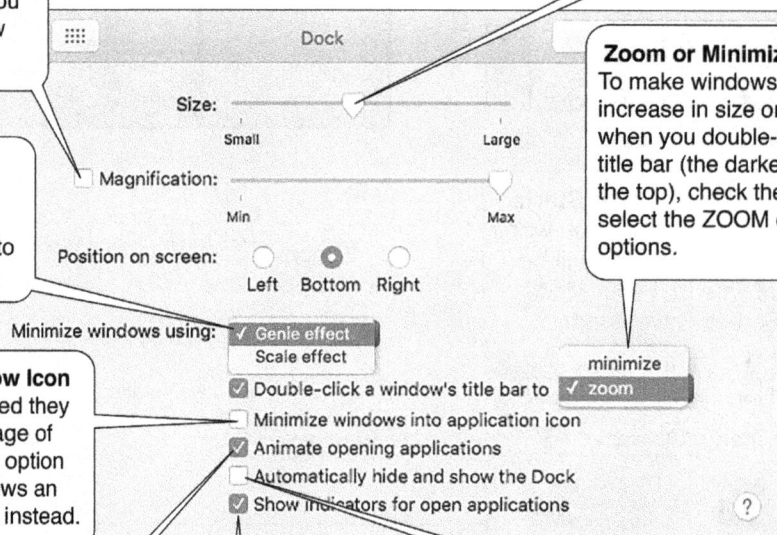

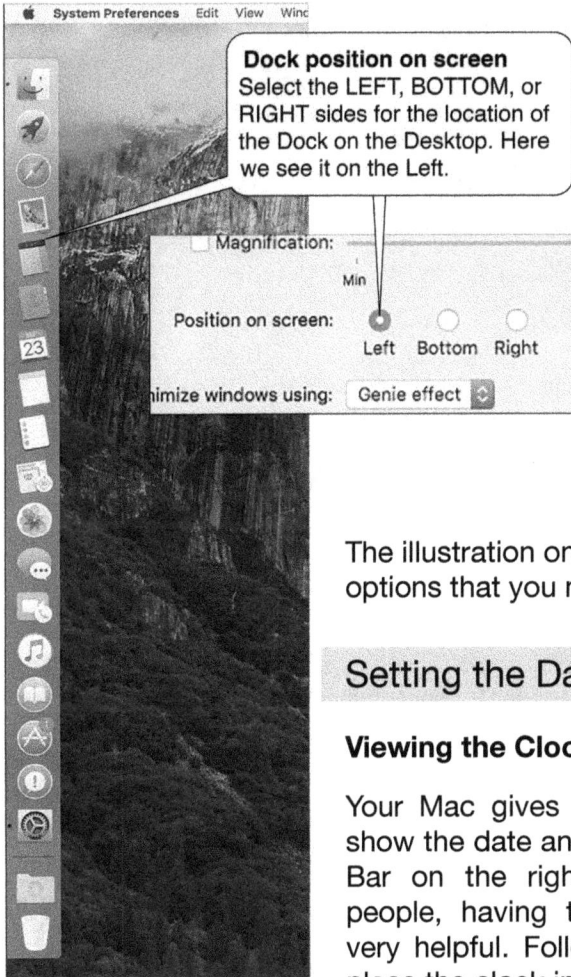

Dock position on screen
Select the LEFT, BOTTOM, or RIGHT sides for the location of the Dock on the Desktop. Here we see it on the Left.

3. The SIZE slidebar lets you change the size of the icons that appear in the Dock. (Note that your screen has a limit to the space it can use, so sometimes icons will automatically become smaller just to fit everything in!)
4. MAGNIFICATION alters an icon's size when you hover your cursor over it. Check this box if you want to use this option.
5. Most people prefer the Dock at the bottom of the screen, but you can position it on the left or right by selecting one of the POSITION options.
6. Choose how you want to MINIMIZE (or maximize) a window with the next drop-down menu. Select GENIE EFFECT to make the window appear to squeeze down into (or out of) a tiny space, or SCALE EFFECT to allow windows to simply become larger or smaller.

The illustration on the previous page provides a description of other Dock icon options that you might want to use.

Setting the Date and Time

Viewing the Clock

Your Mac gives you the option to show the date and time in the Menu Bar on the right side. For most people, having the clock there is very helpful. Follow these steps to place the clock in the Menu Bar and for the initial viewing setup:

1. Click on the Apple icon at the upper left corner of your screen in the Menu Bar, then click on System Preferences in the drop-down menu. The System Preferences window will appear.
2. Click on the Date & Time icon.
3. Select either the analog or digital clock options. Analog is the most basic. It removes access to the other options and simply shows an old-fashioned clock face in the menu bar. Selecting the digital option will provide access to the additional features.
4. Check the boxes for the additional features that you would like to see in the Menu Bar including a seconds display, a 24-hour clock, and an AM/PM display.

Show Items in Menu Bar
Click this box to show the clock, date, and even the day of the week in the Menu Bar.

Select Time and Date Options
Select the Digital clock, then choose the options that you want to see in the Menu Bar above.

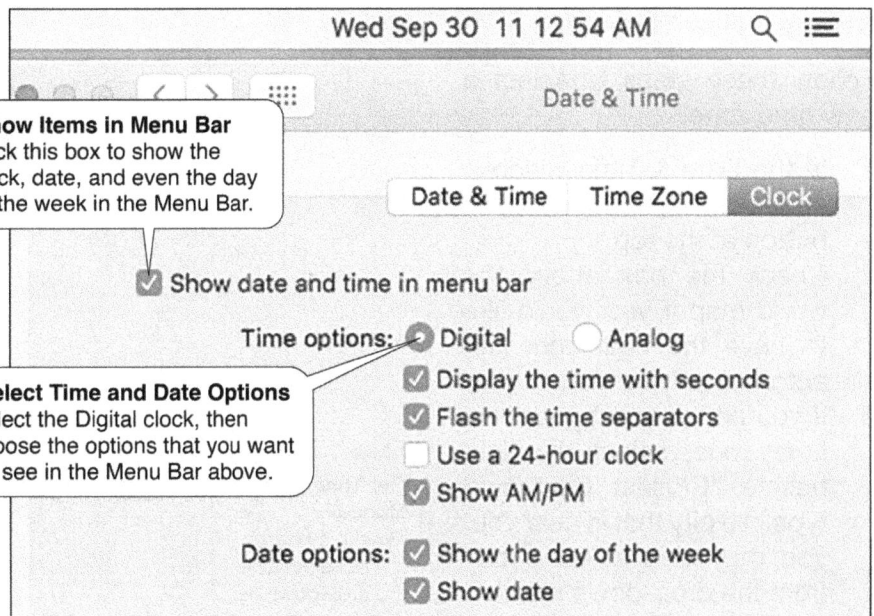

Date & Time | Time Zone | Clock

☑ Show date and time in menu bar

Time options: ◉ Digital ○ Analog
☑ Display the time with seconds
☑ Flash the time separators
☐ Use a 24-hour clock
☑ Show AM/PM

Date options: ☑ Show the day of the week
☑ Show date

Changing the Date and Time

Setting the date and time on your Mac is pretty simple. In addition, Apple lets you customize your clock, even to the point of adding audible time announcements throughout the day with customized voices.

To reset just the date and time, follow these steps:

1. Click on the Apple icon at the upper left corner of your screen in the Menu Bar, then click on System Preferences in the drop-down menu. The System Preferences window will appear.
2. Click on the Date & Time icon.
3. In the Date & Time window, click on the Date & Time button at the top.

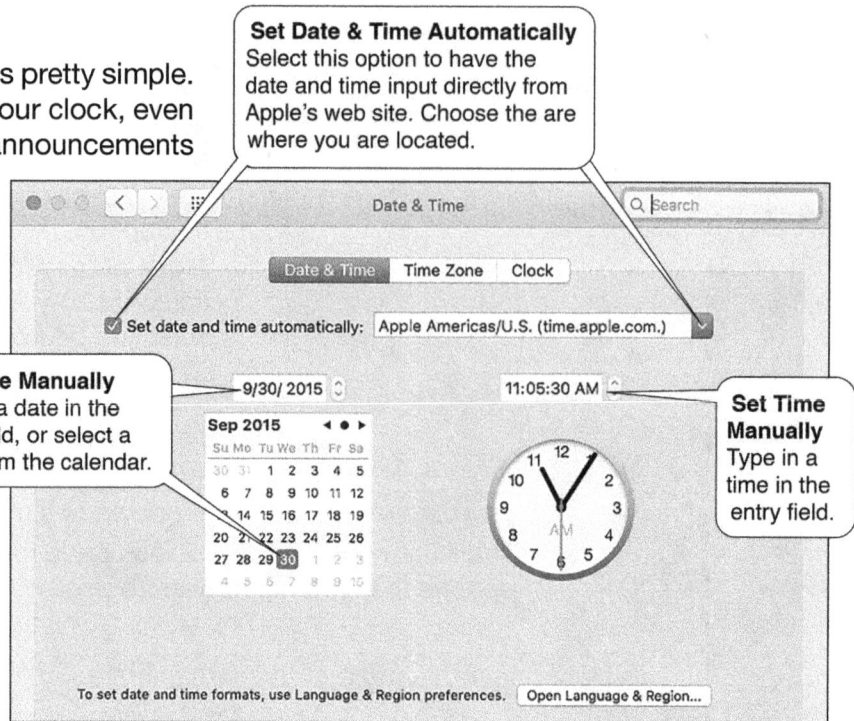

Set Date & Time Automatically
Select this option to have the date and time input directly from Apple's web site. Choose the are where you are located.

Set Date Manually
Type in a date in the entry field, or select a date from the calendar.

Set Time Manually
Type in a time in the entry field.

4. If you prefer to have the date and time set automatically, check the box for "Set date and time automatically". This option accesses the correct time from Apple's web site. Click on the pull-down menu to select Apple's site in the Americas, Europe, or Asia.
5. To reset the date, either type in a date in the DD/MM/YYYY format in the space provided, or select a date from the calendar. Use the tiny arrows at the top right of the calendar to move backward and forward through the months.
6. To reset the time, type in the new time on the digital clock with the HH:MM:SS and AM-PM format, or click the tiny up and down arrows to the right of the digital clock.

Setting a New Time Zone

Follow these steps to select a new time zone:

1. In the Date & Time window, click on the Time Zone button at the top.
2. Check the box above the world map if you would like to have the time zone set automatically for you.
3. If you prefer to set your own time zone, select the field beside "Closest City" and type in a city that is near you. You may also select a city from the drop-down menu.

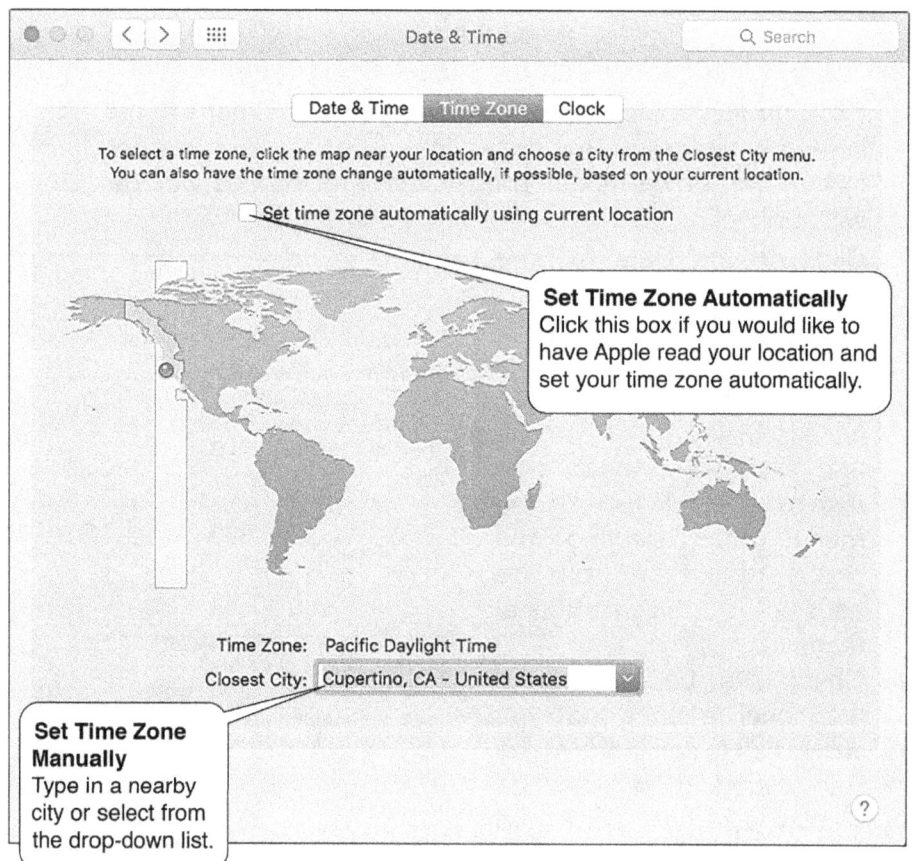

Set Time Zone Automatically
Click this box if you would like to have Apple read your location and set your time zone automatically.

Set Time Zone Manually
Type in a nearby city or select from the drop-down list.

Announcing the Time

Another feature of the clock, available in both analog and digital modes, is an audible time announcement. Here's how to set it up:

1. In the Date & Time window, click on the Time Zone button at the top, then check the box for "Announce the time" at the bottom of the window.
2. Choose how often the announcement should be made: every quarter, half, or full hour.
3. Click on the button CUSTOMIZE VOICE. A drop-down window will appear.
4. You may now choose the voice that you would like to hear, the rate that the voice is spoken, and the volume for the announcement. Click the PLAY button to hear each of the options, then click OK when you have chosen one.

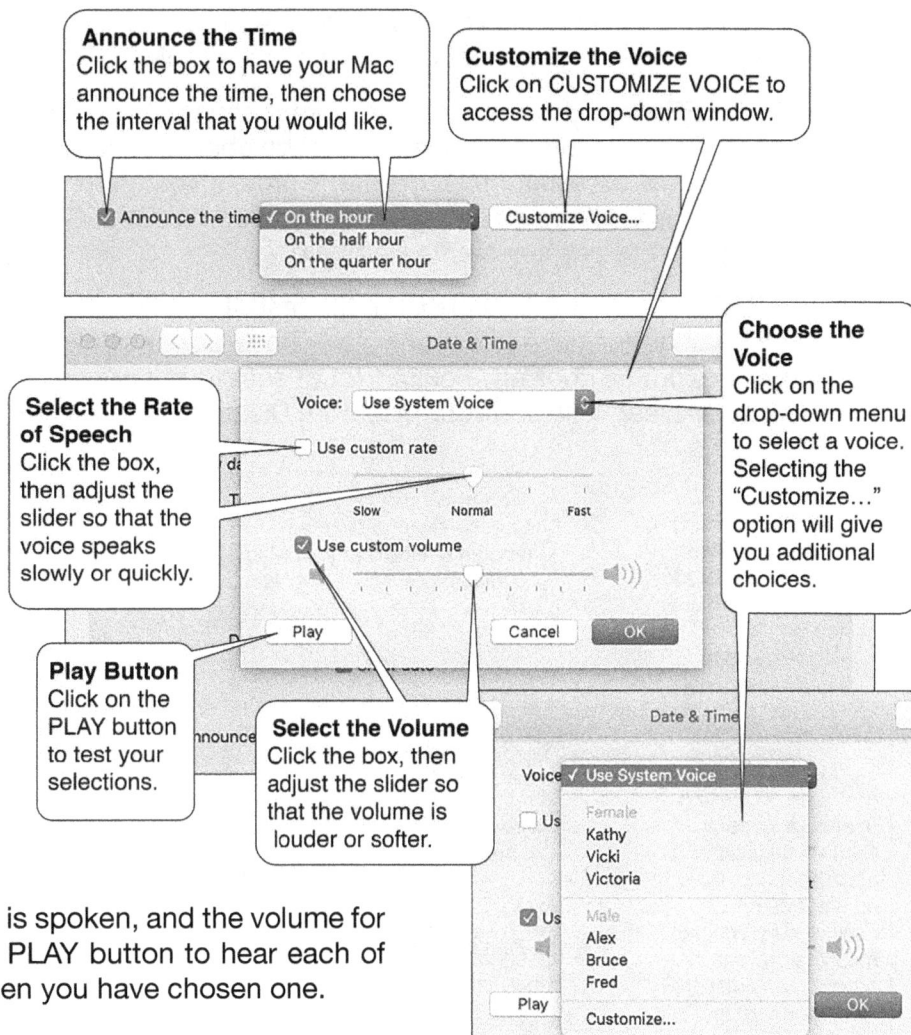

Announce the Time
Click the box to have your Mac announce the time, then choose the interval that you would like.

Customize the Voice
Click on CUSTOMIZE VOICE to access the drop-down window.

Choose the Voice
Click on the drop-down menu to select a voice. Selecting the "Customize..." option will give you additional choices.

Select the Rate of Speech
Click the box, then adjust the slider so that the voice speaks slowly or quickly.

Play Button
Click on the PLAY button to test your selections.

Select the Volume
Click the box, then adjust the slider so that the volume is louder or softer.

Energy Saving Settings

Your options for Energy Saver will differ depending on the kind of Mac that you have. We'll look at desktop machine (for example, iMac or Mac Mini) options first, then the laptop (for example, MacBook Pro or MacBook Air) options after.

Before we go any further, let's clarify what it means for a computer to go to sleep. When you shut down a computer, everything inside will power off. No processing will happen, nothing will appear on the screen, and you won't be able to do anything with it until you power it on again. In Sleep mode, your Mac is still powered on, but various aspects of it (that you set up) will no longer be running until it wakes up.

Energy Saver on a Desktop Mac

To open the Energy Saver window, follow these steps:

1. Click on the Apple icon at the upper left corner of your screen in the Menu Bar, then click on System Preferences in the drop-down menu. The System Preferences window will appear.
2. Click on the Energy Saver icon.
3. Review the options discussed here to determine how you would like to set up your Mac.

The Energy Saver options for desktops can seem a bit overwhelming at first. Let's look at them as they appear on the window. The two most basic options are COMPUTER SLEEP and DISPLAY SLEEP.

COMPUTER SLEEP shuts down all of the major functions of your Mac, including the display. This option will save the most power. Outside entities will not be able to communicate with your Mac, however, unless you provide additional access for this. In other words, if you are on a network and someone else wants a file on your Mac, they won't be able to get it until you come out of Computer Sleep mode. To wake up your Mac again, simply press any key on the keyboard.

DISPLAY SLEEP blacks out the display, but the rest of your Mac is still operating and alert. If you're on a network, it will still be available to anyone else. Since displays take up a large percentage of your Mac's overall power, this option does save quite a lot of energy, but not as much as the Computer Sleep option. As with Computer Sleep, to wake your Mac from Display Sleep, simply press any key on the keyboard.

Hard Disk Sleep
Click on this box to allow the hard disk to sleep when it is not being used.

Computer Sleep
Use the slider to set the amount of time that your Mac is idle before it goes to sleep.

Display Sleep
Use the slider to set the amount of time that your Mac is idle before the display goes to sleep. Your Mac will continue to process anything that it's working on, but the screen will be black.

Network Access
Click on this box to allow your Mac to wake up if it is being accessed by another machine on your network. An additional window will appear with more information.

Automatic Restart
As it states, your machine will restart after a power failure if you check this option.

Energy Saver

Computer sleep:
1 min   15 min   1 hr   3 hrs Never

Display sleep:
1 min   15 min   3 hrs Never

☑ Put hard disks to sleep when possible
☑ Wake for network access
☐ Start up automatically after a power failure

Restore Defaults

Schedule... (?)

Schedule Start Up or Wake Times
1. Click the SCHEDULE button to access the drop-down window.
2. Click the box for "Start up or wake".
3. Select the drop-down menu to indicate the days that your Mac should wake.
4. Select the drop-down day menu and time to indicate when your Mac should start.
5. Click the OK button.

Energy Saver

☑ Start up or wake   Every Day ⬍ at 12:00 AM ⬍
☐ Sleep   Every Day ⬍ at 12:00 AM ⬍

(?)   Cancel   OK

Energy Saver

☐ Start up or wake   Every Day ⬍ at 12:00 AM ⬍
☑ ✓ Sleep   Every Day ⬍ at 12:00 AM ⬍
    Restart
    Shut Down

(?)   Cancel   OK

Schedule Sleep, Restart or Shut Down Times
1. Click the SCHEDULE button to access the drop-down window.
2. Click the box beside "Sleep"
3. Click on "Sleep" and select the SLEEP, RESTART, or SHUTDOWN option.
4. Select the drop-down menu to indicate the days when your selection should happen.
5. Select the drop-down day menu and time to indicate when your Mac should start.
6. Click the OK button.

The other Energy Saver options allow you to control various aspects of Computer Sleep and Display Sleep:

- **Network Access** - Remember how Computer Sleep shuts down the major functions of your Mac and doesn't allow others on your network access? Checking this box enables access again. If someone on your network wants to connect to your computer while it is in sleep mode, this now allows them to do so. Your computer will wake up while they are accessing it, then go to sleep again at the preset time that you indicated with your Computer Sleep slide bar.

- **Power Button for Sleep** - Some people like the option of pressing the power button once (without holding it down for several seconds) to put their Macs to sleep. Checking off this option enables that functionality.

- **Reduce Brightness** - Checking this option will cause your screen to dim for several seconds before it goes to sleep. It serves as a brief warning that the sleep mode is about to happen. If you don't want it to sleep yet, just press any key on the keyboard or wiggle the cursor on the screen. Any interaction with the Mac will keep it from sleeping.

- **Automatic Restart** - When your Mac has shut down due to a power failure, checking this option will enable it to restart again once the power is restored

The last option with Energy Saver is the Schedule button. Clicking on this brings up a window allowing you to schedule specific times when you want your Mac to either wake up or go to sleep. This option is often useful in an office setting when someone is working a regular schedule and would like their Mac to be on (or off) at certain times of the day or night.

Energy Saver on a Laptop Mac

If your Mac is a laptop, you will see different Energy Saver options than you would for a desktop machine. These options appear on two separate windows: BATTERY and POWER ADAPTER. Battery options apply when your laptop is not plugged in, and is operating from the power of the battery. Power Adapter options apply when your laptop is plugged in.

Energy Saver: Battery - Many of these options function in the same way as they did for a desktop machine.

- **Computer Sleep** - This option shuts down all of the major functions of your Mac, including the display. This option will save the most power. Outside computers will not be able to communicate with your Mac, however, unless you provide additional access for this. In other words, if you are on a network and someone else wants a file on your Mac, they won't be able to get in until you come out of Computer Sleep mode. To wake up your Mac again, simply press any key on the keyboard.

- **Display Sleep** - This option blacks out the display, but the rest of your Mac is still operating and alert. If you're on a network, it will still be available to anyone else. Since displays take up a large percentage of your Mac's overall power, this option does save quite a lot of energy, but not as much as the Computer Sleep option. As with Computer Sleep, to wake your Mac from Display Sleep, simply press any key on the keyboard.

- **Hard Disk Sleep** - This sleep option puts your hard disk to sleep when it is not in use. Some laptops have hard disks with spinning components (like an old-fashioned record player) so this option stops them to save energy. Many newer machines have solid-state hard disks with no moving parts, so this option would be irrelevant for those.

- **Dim Display on Battery Power** - Checking this option will cause your display to be slightly dimmer when you are using it on battery. Since the display uses a large percentage of your Mac's power, this will help to lengthen battery time.

Display Sleep
Use the slider to set the amount of time that the display is idle before it goes to sleep. Your Mac will continue to process anything that it's working on, but the screen will be black.

Computer Sleep
Use the slider to set the amount of time that your Mac is idle before it goes to sleep.

Hard Disk Sleep
Click on this box to allow the hard disk to sleep when it is not being used.

Dim Display on Battery Power
This option dims your Mac's screen slightly when you are on battery power. This uses less energy and allows the battery charge to last longer.

Battery Status in Menu Bar
Click on this box to show what is happening with the battery. If it is connected to a power supply and the battery is charging it will have this icon:

If your Mac is running off the battery, it will show the amount of charge remaining. Here the icon shows that it is fully charged:

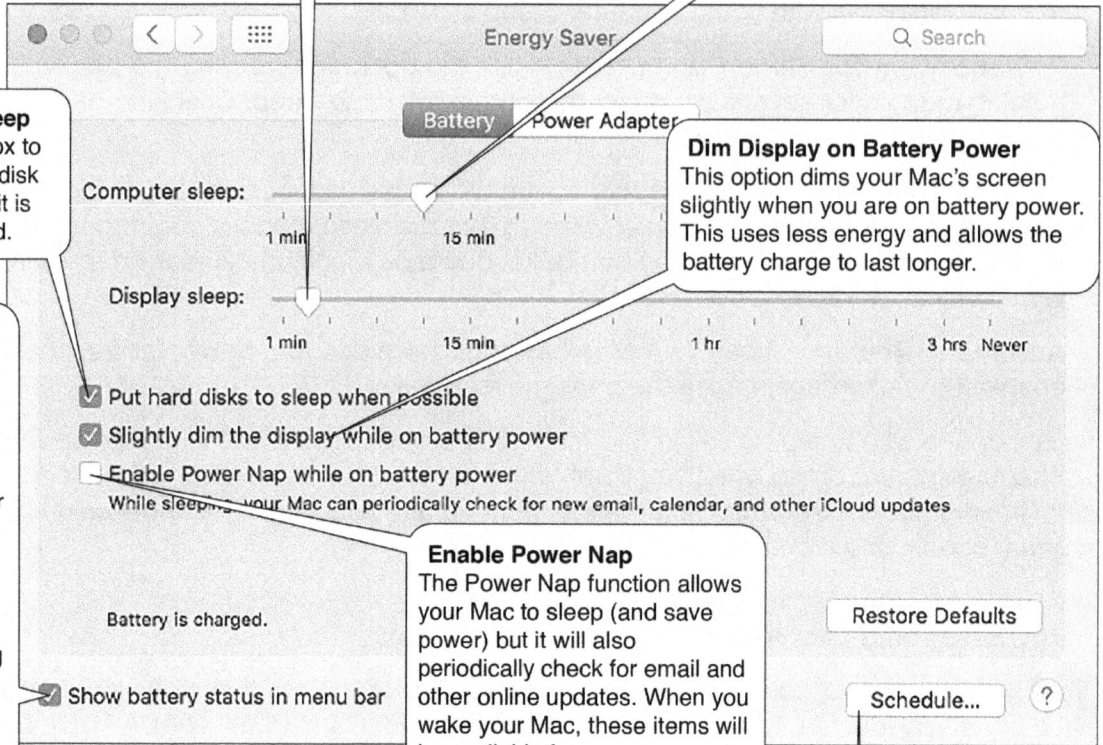

Enable Power Nap
The Power Nap function allows your Mac to sleep (and save power) but it will also periodically check for email and other online updates. When you wake your Mac, these items will be available for you.

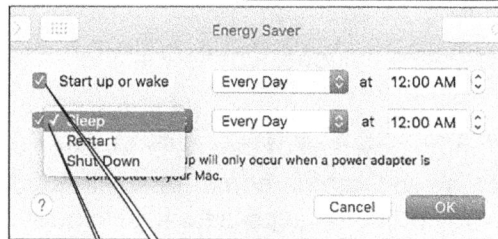

Energy Saver

Q Search

Battery   Power Adapter

Computer sleep:

1 min   15 min

Display sleep:

1 min   15 min   1 hr   3 hrs Never

☑ Put hard disks to sleep when possible
☑ Slightly dim the display while on battery power
☐ Enable Power Nap while on battery power
   While sleeping your Mac can periodically check for new email, calendar, and other iCloud updates

Battery is charged.

Restore Defaults

☑ Show battery status in menu bar

Schedule...   ?

Energy Saver

☑ Start up or wake   Every Day ◊ at 12:00 AM ◊
☑ Sleep   Every Day ◊ at 12:00 AM ◊
   Restart
   Shut Down   up will only occur when a power adapter is
                      connected to your Mac.

?   Cancel   OK

Schedule Wake and Sleep Times

Click the SCHEDULE button to access the drop-down window.

These steps will set Start Up or Wake:
1. Click the box for "Start up or wake"
2. Select the drop-down menu to indicate the days that your Mac should wake.
3. Select the drop-down menu to indicate the time that your Mac should wake.

These steps will set Sleep, Restart, or Shutdown:
1. Click the box beside "Sleep"
2. Select the SLEEP, RESTART, or SHUTDOWN option from the dropdown menu beside the checkbox.
3. Select the drop-down menu to indicate the days when your selection should happen.
4. Select the drop-down menu to indicate the time that your selection should happen.

- **Enable Power Nap** - When your laptop is in Power Nap mode it will go to sleep, but awaken periodically to check email and other online updates. When you wake it from Power Nap, these items will be available for you. This saves time for you because you won't need to wait for the system to download lots of new things when you wake it up.

- **Battery Status in Menu Bar** - Checking this option places a battery icon on the menu bar in the upper right corner of the screen. It will display the status of your laptop battery's charge while it is running on the battery. If your laptop is plugged in, this icon will have a small lightening bolt through it indicating that the battery is charging.

As with the desktop Mac, the last option is the Schedule button. Clicking on this brings up a window allowing you to schedule specific times when you want your Mac to either wake up or go to sleep. This option is often useful in an office setting when someone is working a regular schedule and would like their Mac to be on (or off) at certain times of the day or night.

> **Wake for Wi-Fi Access**
> Also referred to as "Wake on Demand," this option will allow your laptop to be brought out of sleep mode when someone else on your network is trying to access your Mac.

Energy Saver: Power Adapter - Mac laptops have only one difference between the Battery and Power Adapter windows. The Battery window allows you to dim the screen to save energy. The Power Adapter window has replaced this option with WAKE FOR WI-FI ACCESS. This option is also called "wake on demand." It allows your laptop to come out of sleep mode when someone is trying to access it over a network. This works much like the "Wake for Network Access" option on a desktop machine.

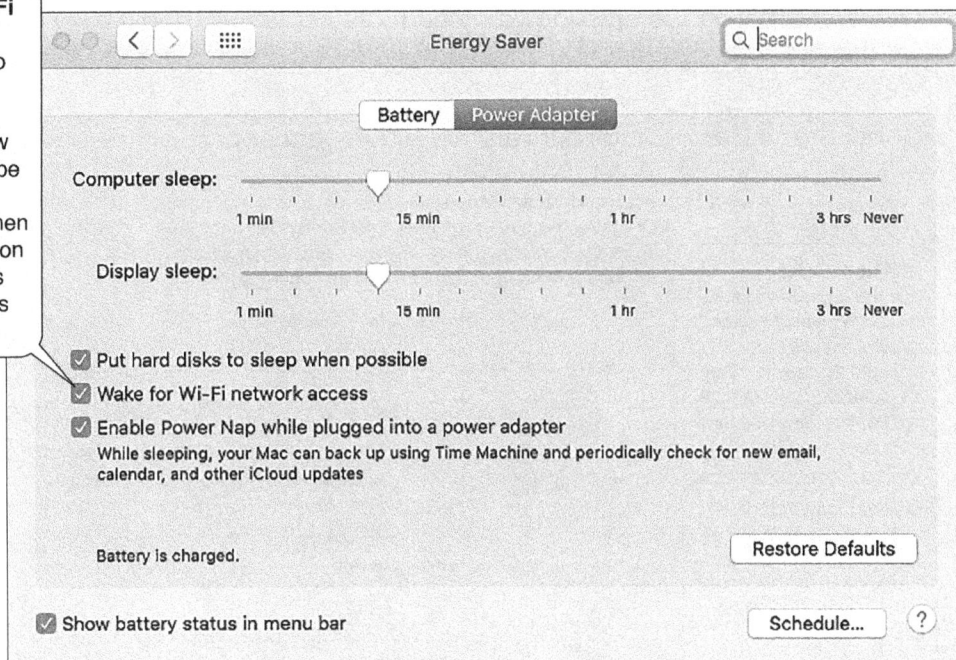

General Preferences

The General Preferences options apply to many different windows, buttons, menus and applications. Usually you'll set these up once then forget about them. Follow these steps to open the General Preferences window:

1. Click on the Apple icon at the upper left corner of your screen in the Menu Bar, then click on System Preferences in the drop-down menu. The System Preferences window will appear.
2. Click on the General Preferences icon.
3. Review the options discussed here to determine how you would like to set up your Mac.

33

- **Appearance** - This option allows you to select either a blue or graphite gray default color for various items, including some buttons, check boxes, menus and windows.

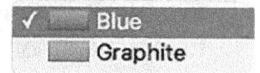

✓	Blue
	Graphite

- **Dark Menu Bar and Dock** - Checking this box will change the background of the menu bar and dock from semi-transparent to a darker opaque. Some people find it easier to see this way.

- **Automatically Hide and Show Menu Bar** - Checking this box will keep the menu bar hidden. It will drop down only when you move your cursor to the very top of the screen.

- **Highlight Color** - Click on the drop-down menu and choose from the various options to select a highlight color used when you select items. For example, if you choose blue for the highlight color, any item you select in Finder will appear with a blue background.

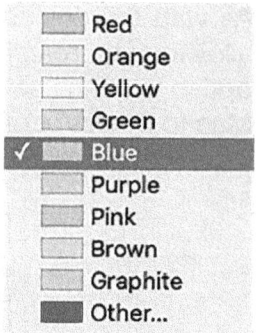

	Red
	Orange
	Yellow
	Green
✓	Blue
	Purple
	Pink
	Brown
	Graphite
	Other...

- **Sidebar Icon Size** - The Sidebar is the list of items on the left side of a Finder window. Click on the drop-down menu to select small, medium, or large icons for this list. The size that you choose will affect the items in the Mail sidebar as well.

- **Show Scroll Bars** - Scroll bars are the sliders that appear on the bottom or side

Highlight Color
Use the drop-down list to choose a highlight color for applications that highlight items when they are selected (for example, highlighting files selected in Finder).

Hide and Show Menu Bar
Checking this box keeps the Menu Bar hidden until you hover the cursor at the top of the screen. When you move the cursor away, the Menu Bar will disappear again.

Appearance
Use the drop-down list to select a blue or gray default color for various system items such as buttons, check boxes, menus and windows.

Sidebar Icon Size
Use the drop-down list to select the size of the text that appears in the Finder window sidebar and the Mail sidebar.

Dark Menu Bar and Dock
Checking this changes the backgrounds of the Dock and Menu Bar from semi-transparent to dark opaque.

Show Scroll Bars
The sliders that appear on the bottom or side of a window are scroll bars. Select "Always" if you would like them to appear all the time. The other selections will enable them as the cursor moves.

Default Web Browser
Select the web browser that you prefer from the drop-down list. Whenever you click on a web page link, it will open in the browser that you choose here.

Ask to Keep Changes
Apple will keep all of your changes anyway when you close a document, but if you'd like to be asked, check here.

Click in Scroll Bar
Select whether you would like to jump to the next page of the material in a window by clicking anywhere in the scroll bar, or if you'd rather jump to the location that corresponds to the place on the scroll bar. (For example, clicking on the middle of the scroll bar would bring you to the middle of the material you're scrolling through.)

Recent Items
Select the number of items you would like to see listed when you are opening files. They will appear in order beginning with the one most recently used.

Use LCD Font Smoothing
Checking this option reduces the appearance of jagged edges on some fonts.

Close Windows when Quitting
Checking this box will close all of the windows (and the files that they contain) in an application before the application itself quits. When you open the application again you will need to open the files in their windows again. If the box is not checked, the windows will automatically re-open with the application.

General

Appearance: Blue — For Buttons, Menus, and Windows
☐ Use dark menu bar and Dock
☐ Automatically hide and show the menu bar

Highlight color: Blue
Sidebar icon size: Medium

Show scroll bars: ● Automatically based on mouse or trackpad
○ When scrolling
○ Always

Click in the scroll bar to: ● Jump to the next page
○ Jump to the spot that's clicked

Default web browser: Safari (9.0)

☐ Ask to keep changes when closing documents
☑ Close windows when quitting an app
When selected, open documents and windows will not be re when you re-open an app.

Recent items: 10 Documents, Apps, and Servers

☑ Use LCD font smoothing when available

of a window that allow you to see the things that are beyond the window frame. If you have a mouse or trackpad that allows "gestures" (hand movements that control the computer) and don't want to see scroll bars until they are needed, select "Automatically based on mouse or trackpad." If you simply want the scrollbars to appear only when you begin to scroll, select "when scrolling." If you always want to see the scroll bars, select "Always." Most people prefer the last option.

- **Click in the Scroll Bar To** - Scrolling through long documents can get tedious. Apple gives you the option of either clicking anywhere in the scroll bar to jump to the next page, or clicking in the scroll bar to jump further along into the document (for example, clicking at the bottom of the scroll bar jumps to the end of the document.)

- **Default Web Browser** - Apple preloads Safari as the default browser, but many people prefer something different such as Google Chrome or Firefox. If you have downloaded a different browser and would like it to be the default whenever a web site is opened automatically, click on the drop-down menu in the option and select your preferred browser.

- **Ask to Keep Changes When Closing Documents** - It isn't actually necessary to check this box because Apple automatically saves any unsaved changes when you close a document. If you want to be asked anyway, check the box.

- **Close Windows When Quitting An Application** - Remember that quitting out of an application and closing windows are two different things. When you quit an application without closing the windows that you've been using in it, they will automatically reappear the next time that you open the application. If you close the windows before quitting the application, you will need to open them again once the application has been reopened. Click this box if you want the windows to be automatically closed when you quit the application (which means that you would need to reopen them the next time if you need them).

- **Recent Items** - The items that you've used recently are listed when you click on the Apple icon in the upper left corner. Select the drop-down menu and choose the number of items that you want to see. This also applies to the number of items in other app menus. For example, if you choose 30 items, a program such as Text Edit would show the last 30 files that you opened, allowing you to select any of them quickly rather than searching for them through a Finder window.

- **Use LCD Font Smoothing When Available** - To reduce jagged edges on some fonts, check this option.

Changing the Sound Your Mac Makes

Changing the sound that your Mac makes is a nice way of customizing the system. One of the easiest sounds to change is the Alert sound, the one that the computer makes when it's trying to get your attention. Use these steps:

1. Click on the Apple icon at the upper left corner of your screen in the Menu Bar, then click on System Preferences in the drop-down menu. The System Preferences window will appear.
2. Click on the Sound icon.
3. The Sound window will appear. Click on the SOUND EFFECTS button at the top.
4. Notice that there are two separate volume sliders. ALERT VOLUME applies to the Alert sound only. OUTPUT VOLUME applies to all sound that your Mac makes. Make sure that the MUTE box is not checked

in the Output Volume section. If it is checked, simply click on it again to uncheck it. Slide the Output Volume up to a level that you can hear easily.
5. Slide the Alert Volume to the level that you prefer.
6. Select any of the ALERT SOUNDS from the list in the Sound window. Each sound will play once when you select it as a demonstration. If you want to keep the sound as your alert, just leave it selected.
7. If you would like to have your Mac make this sound when you do other things (for example, when you empty trash), select the "Play user interface effects" checkbox.

Alert Volume
This volume affects only the Alert Sound, when the computer is trying to get your attention. This volume is separate from the overall Output Volume setting for all other sounds your Mac makes.

Alert Sound
Click the Sound Effects button, then select an Alert sound. This sound will play each time the computer wants to get your attention.

Sound Output
Usually the "Selected sound output device" will be your Mac's built-in speakers. If you have external speakers or headphones, you can select another option by clicking the dropdown list here.

User Interface Sound Effects
Checking this box will enable your Mac to play the specific sounds that are built-in for the user interface (for example, the sound made when you empty the trash).

Output Volume
This is the volume for all sounds coming from your Mac, except the Alert Sound. Use the slider to increase or decrease the volume.

Sound   Q Search

Sound Effects   Output   Input

Select an alert sound:

Name	Type
Basso	Built-in
Blow	Built-in
Bottle	Built-in
og	Built-in

Play sound effects through: Selected sound output device

Alert volume: 🔈 ————————🔻——— 🔊))

☑ Play user interface sound effects
☐ Play feedback when volume is changed

Output volume: 🔈 ———————🔺——— 🔊)) ☑ Mute

☐ Show volume in menu bar

Play Feedback
Check this box to allow your Mac to beep back the current volume each time you make an adjustment.

Show Volume in Menu Bar
Check this box by clicking on it to make the sound control appear in the Menu Bar at the upper right corner of your screen.

Mute
Checking this box will turn off all sound coming from your Mac.

Changing How the Mouse and Trackpad Work

Your mouse or trackpad are among the primary ways that you interact with your Mac. Making them function in a way that's easy and intuitive for you makes your experience on your Mac more enjoyable. (Note that the Mouse and Trackpad functionalities will be different depending on the kind of system you're using, so the options may not appear exactly as you see them in the examples here.)

There are four basic functionalities to think about when controlling how your cursor moves on the screen:
• Tracking Speed - how quickly the cursor moves across the screen when you move your mouse or slide your finger on the trackpad.
• Scrolling Speed - how quickly the material moves up or down in a window when you scroll through.
• Scroll Direction - Whether the screen material moves up or down according to how you move the mouse scrolling wheel or your fingers on the trackpad.
• Double-Click Speed - how quickly you click twice in succession on an item in order to select it.

Scroll direction can be confusing. Apple defines the "Natural" scroll direction as the reverse of what many people intuitively consider natural. Apple's "Scroll Direction-Natural" means that if you want to scroll *down* in a document, you wind the mouse scrolling wheel down, or slide your fingers on the track pad up in a bottom-to-top direction. To make the scrolling action on your Mac function in a more intuitive manner (in other words, to make the screen items move up when you move your fingers up on the trackpad or wind the mouse scrolling wheel from top to bottom), make sure that the SCROLL DIRECTION NATURAL box is not checked. We'll look at this next for both a mouse and a trackpad.

If you are using a mouse, follow these steps to change the three cursor speed options and the scroll direction:

1. Click on the Apple icon at the upper left corner of your screen in the Menu Bar, then click on System Preferences in the drop-down menu. The System Preferences window will appear.
2. Click on the Mouse icon. The Mouse window will appear.
3. Move the Tracking Speed slider to either a slower or faster level, then move your mouse. You'll see the cursor traveling either more slowly or quickly across the screen. Set a speed that's comfortable for you.
4. Move the Scrolling Speed slider to a comfortable speed as you did with the Tracking Speed slider.
5. Move the Double-Click Speed slider to your preferred speed of double-clicking.
6. Make sure that there is no check in the "Scroll Direction: Natural" box if you want the screen to move in the same direction that your scroll wheel on the mouse is moving. (If this box is checked, click on it once to remove the check.)

Tracking Speed
Use the slider to adjust the speed that the cursor moves on the screen when you move your mouse.

Scroll Direction
"Natural" means that the material in the window moves up when you move your scroll wheel up. (Note: Most people do not check this box because it's the reverse of what they feel is "natural".)

Double Click Speed
Use the slider to adjust how quickly you prefer to click twice on an item when selecting it.

Scrolling Speed
Use the slider to adjust the speed that the material moves up or down when you scroll in a window.

Primary Mouse Button
Usually the primary mouse button (the one that you use the most to select things) is on the left, but you may prefer it to be the right button, especially if you're left handed.

If you are using a trackpad, you'll have some different options for controlling the cursor:

1. Click on the Apple icon at the upper left corner of your screen in the Menu Bar, then click on System Preferences in the drop-down menu. The System Preferences window will appear.
2. Click on the Trackpad icon. The Trackpad window will appear.
3. Select the POINT AND CLICK button at the top of the Trackpad window.
4. Move the Tracking Speed slider to either a slower or faster level, then slide your finger across the trackpad. You'll see the cursor traveling either more slowly or quickly across the screen. Set a speed that's comfortable for you.
5. The trackpad does not have a double-click speed option. Instead it allows you to set whether you want to click on, or select, something by tapping the trackpad with either one or two fingers. Check the box for the method that you prefer.
6. Click on the SCROLL & ZOOM button at the top of the Trackpad window.
7. If you prefer to have the screen scroll in the same direction that you are moving your finger on the trackpad, uncheck the box for "Scroll Direction Natural".

Look Up & Data Detectors
Checking this option allows you to look up a word in the dictionary or perform quick tasks with certain kinds of data by tapping on the item with three fingers on the trackpad.

Tap to Click
Checking this option allows you to tap the trackpad with one finger to select an item instead of clicking on it.

Secondary Click
Checking this option allows you to tap the trackpad with two fingers on an item to perform the same function as a CONTROL+Click (holding down the Control button on your keyboard while clicking).

Tracking Speed
Use the slider to adjust the speed that the cursor moves on the screen when you move your finger on the trackpad.

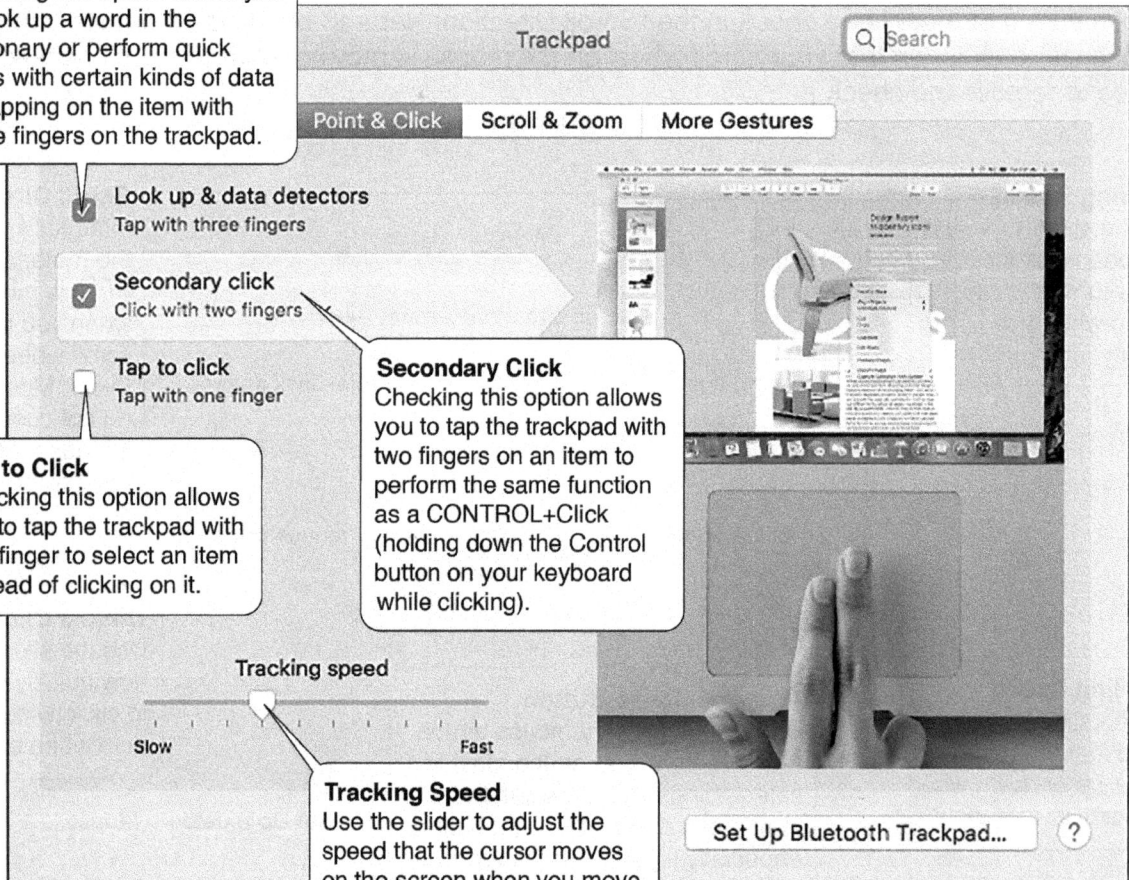

8. The Trackpad does not have a scrolling speed option, but it does give you several other options for zooming and manipulating what you see on the screen. Watch the demonstrations for these and select any that you think will be helpful.
9. Click on the MORE GESTURES button at the top of the window.
10. Apple gives you lots of different ways to access things on your screen using the trackpad. Some people like to use these as shortcuts, but others find them unhelpful. If you do not want to use the gestures indicated, simply uncheck the boxes.

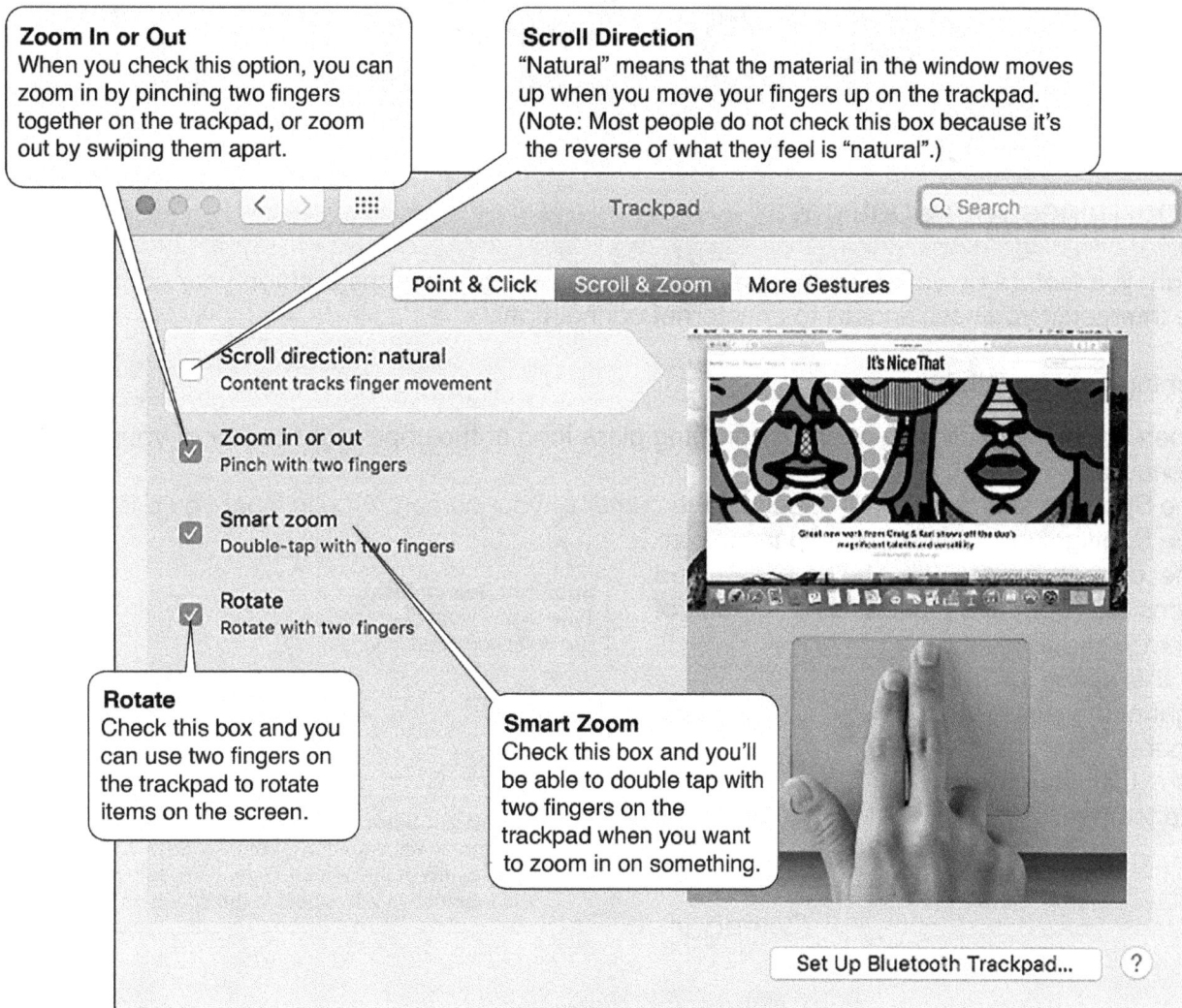

Zoom In or Out
When you check this option, you can zoom in by pinching two fingers together on the trackpad, or zoom out by swiping them apart.

Scroll Direction
"Natural" means that the material in the window moves up when you move your fingers up on the trackpad. (Note: Most people do not check this box because it's the reverse of what they feel is "natural".)

Point & Click   Scroll & Zoom   More Gestures

Scroll direction: natural
Content tracks finger movement

Zoom in or out
Pinch with two fingers

Smart zoom
Double-tap with two fingers

Rotate
Rotate with two fingers

It's Nice That

Rotate
Check this box and you can use two fingers on the trackpad to rotate items on the screen.

Smart Zoom
Check this box and you'll be able to double tap with two fingers on the trackpad when you want to zoom in on something.

Set Up Bluetooth Trackpad...   ?

4 – ORGANIZING AND ACCESSING THINGS

What's Next in this chapter...

- Spotlight
- Launchpad
- Dashboard
- Mission Control

Finding Things with Spotlight

Spotlight is a feature on your Mac that helps you to quickly locate items both on your computer or even on the Internet (if you have access to an Internet connection).

Searching with Spotlight

1. Open Spotlight by clicking on the magnifying glass icon at the upper right corner of your screen in the Menu Bar.
2. The Spotlight search field will appear in the center of your screen. Type in what you'd like to find.
3. The Spotlight search field will expand in size.
4. The column on the left shows the related items that Spotlight located. Click on any of them to see a preview in the space on the right of the window.
5. Double click on the item that you would like to open.

Spotlight Search Field
Type in any word or phrase to find what you need to locate.

Q Spotlight Search

Spotlight Search Results
A window will drop down from the Search Field listing the results of the search. Select any item on the left and its information will appear in the space on the right.

Q Calendar

TOP HIT
- Calendar - External HD

APPLICATIONS
- Calendar - Volumes

DEFINITION
- calendar

SYSTEM PREFERENCES
- Internet Accounts - System

FOLDERS
- Calendar Sync Changes
- C2D067FF-8858-4709-89DD-7E5...
- 8DD79084-2FC0-40B3-A978-98A...

MAIL & MESSAGES
- Re: Join my "Home" calendar?
- Re: Join my "Home" calendar?
- Re: Join my "Home" calendar?
- Re: Join my "Home" calendar?

JUL
17

Calendar
Version: 8.0

Kind Application
Size 26.4 MB
Created 6/28/15
Modified 6/28/15

Removing Spotlight Search Categories

You can remove any of the categories that Spotlight searches. For example, if you only want Spotlight to search your Mac, you can opt out of the Internet search option. Use these steps to remove categories:

1. Click on the Apple icon at the upper left corner of your screen in the Menu Bar, then click on System Preferences in the drop-down menu. The System Preferences window will appear.
2. Click on the Spotlight icon. The Spotlight window will appear.
3. Click on the SEARCH RESULTS button.
4. Click on any of the items in the list to remove the check mark. Spotlight will not search that category if it is not checked.
5. You can also change the order that the Spotlight search results appear by dragging any of the categories up or down within the list.

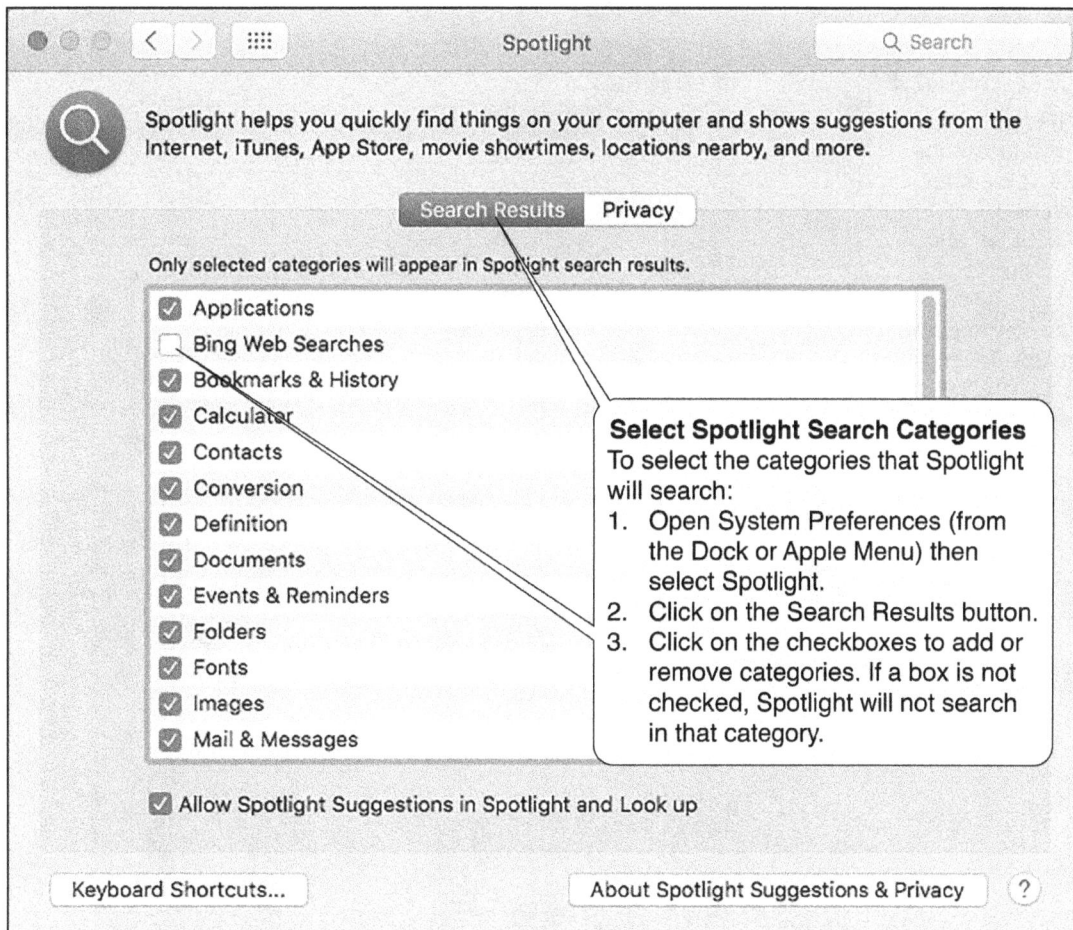

Select Spotlight Search Categories
To select the categories that Spotlight will search:
1. Open System Preferences (from the Dock or Apple Menu) then select Spotlight.
2. Click on the Search Results button.
3. Click on the checkboxes to add or remove categories. If a box is not checked, Spotlight will not search in that category.

You can also prevent Spotlight from searching specific items on your Mac. Not only is this helpful for privacy, but it also is a good option if you have folders that contain many files that would take a great deal of time to search. Here's how:

1. Click on the Apple icon at the upper left corner of your screen in the Menu Bar, then click on System Preferences in the drop-down menu. The System Preferences window will appear.
2. Click on the Spotlight icon. The Spotlight window will appear.

3. Click on the PRIVACY button.
4. Click the plus sign at the bottom left corner of the window.
5. A drop-down finder window appears. Locate and click on any of the items that you do not want Spotlight to search.
6. To remove an item from the Privacy list, select it, then click the minus button at the lower left corner of the window. The item will disappear from the list.

Define Where Spotlight Cannot Search

If you don't want Spotlight to search certain folders, select them through Privacy:

1. Open System Preferences (from the Dock or Apple Menu) then select Spotlight.
2. Click on the Privacy button.
3. Click on the plus (+) sign.
4. In the drop-down Finder window, navigate through and locate the folder that you do not want searched.
5. Select the folder, and press the Choose button.
6. The folder now appears in the Privacy list and will not be searched
7. To remove it from the list, select it, then press the minus (-) button.

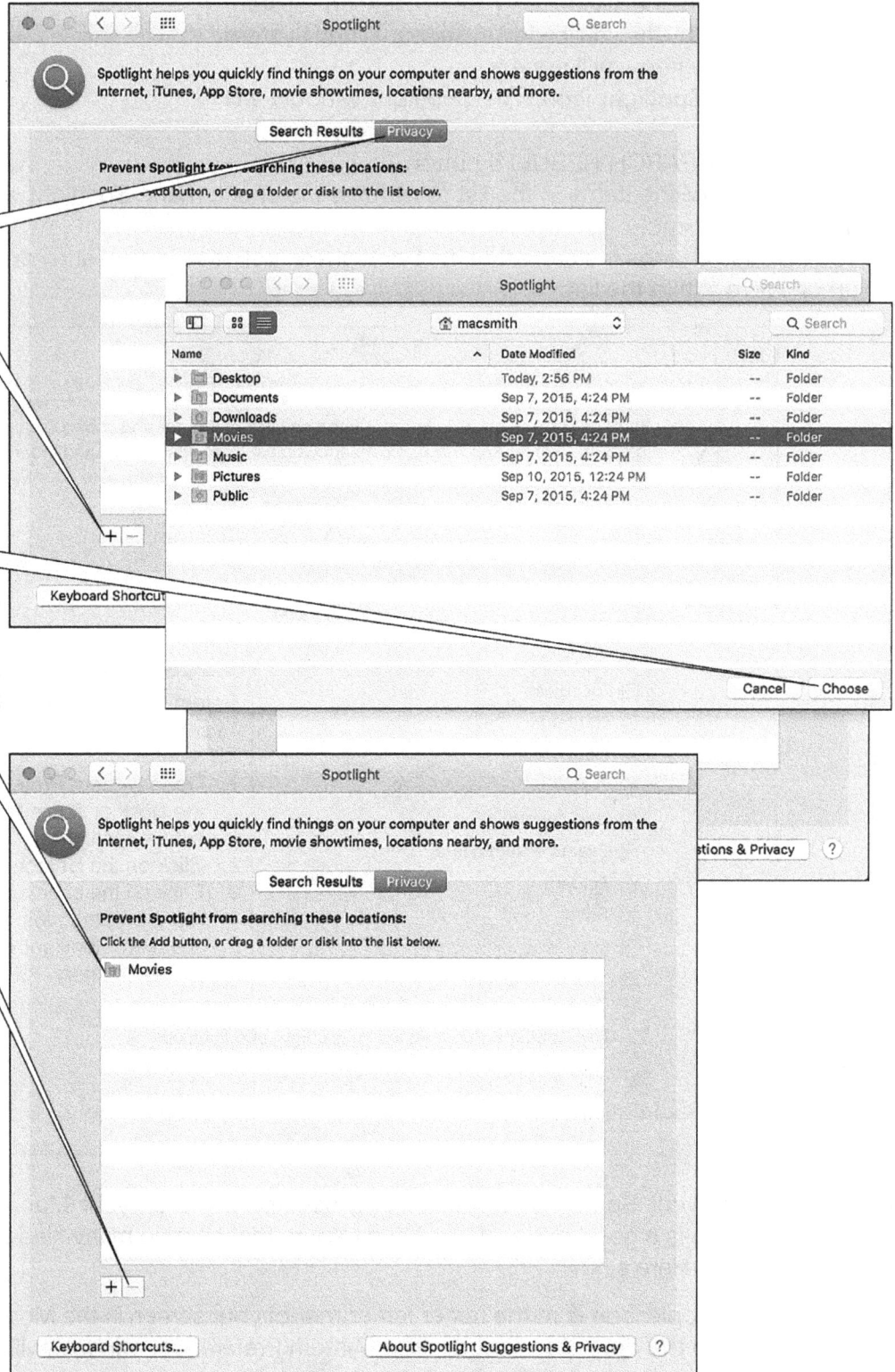

Using Launchpad to Access Apps

You might remember that all of your apps are located in a folder called Applications. Launchpad is a quick and easy way to access all of those apps without using Finder to open the folder and scroll through everything.

To open Launchpad, click on its icon in the Dock. If you don't see it there, open Finder, select the Applications folder, then double click on Launchpad from there. (Remember, if you want to add it to your dock, just drag the icon down to the Dock from Finder.)

When you open Launchpad, the screen background will become blurry and you'll see many icons appear. These are all of the apps that are available on your Mac. Click on one and it will immediately open that application.

Launchpad Screens
Launchpad shows all of your Apps on multiple screens if needed. The dots at the bottom show the screen that you're on. Click on another dot to go to that screen.

Launchpad - First Screen
The bright dot on the left indicates that this is the first screen.

Multiple screens of icons can be accessed by selecting the white dots at the bottom of the screen (each one corresponds to a separate screen of icons). If you are using a trackpad, you can also page through by swiping with two fingers right or left. If you don't see any dots at the bottom, all your icons are on the screen that you're viewing.

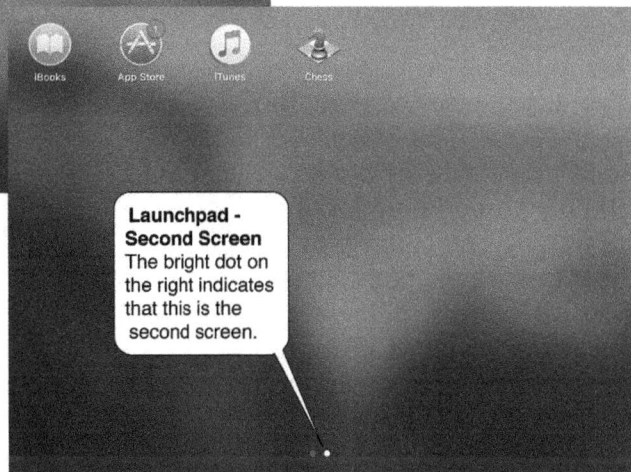

Launchpad - Second Screen
The bright dot on the right indicates that this is the second screen.

Some of the apps may be grouped in folders. To open a folder and access its apps, simply click on the folder first, then click on the app.

If you want to add an app to a folder, just click on it and drag it into the folder. If you want to remove an app from a folder, first open the folder, then drag the app icon outside of the folder area. The folder will close and the app icon will now appear with the others.

Adding an Item to a Launchpad Folder
1. Select the item that you want to add to an existing folder.
2. Drag the item into the folder.
3. The folder will now contain the new item.

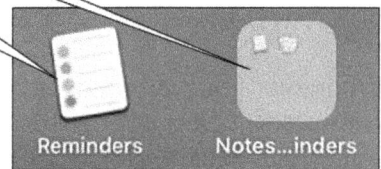

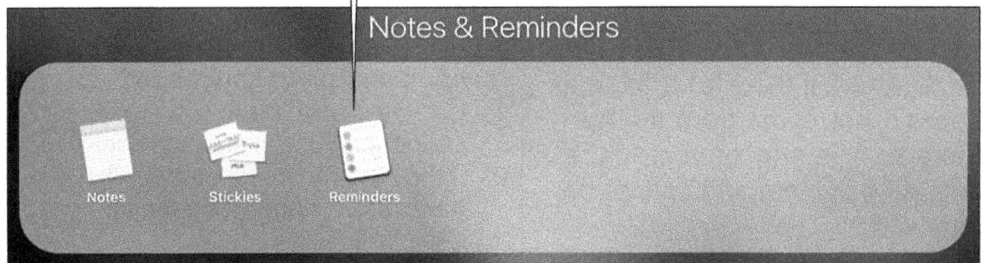

Reminders   Notes...inders

Notes & Reminders

Notes   Stickies   Reminders

To create a new folder, drag one app over another. A folder will automatically be created containing both apps. Now you can drag in other apps to the folder as well.

To delete a folder, simply drag out all of its apps. When the last one is removed, the folder will disappear.

Change a Launchpad Folder Name
1. Open Launchpad and click on the folder that you want to change.
2. When the folder opens, click on the name. The background will turn light blue.
3. Type in the new name.
4. Click outside the folder to return to the Launchpad screen. The folder will now show the new name.

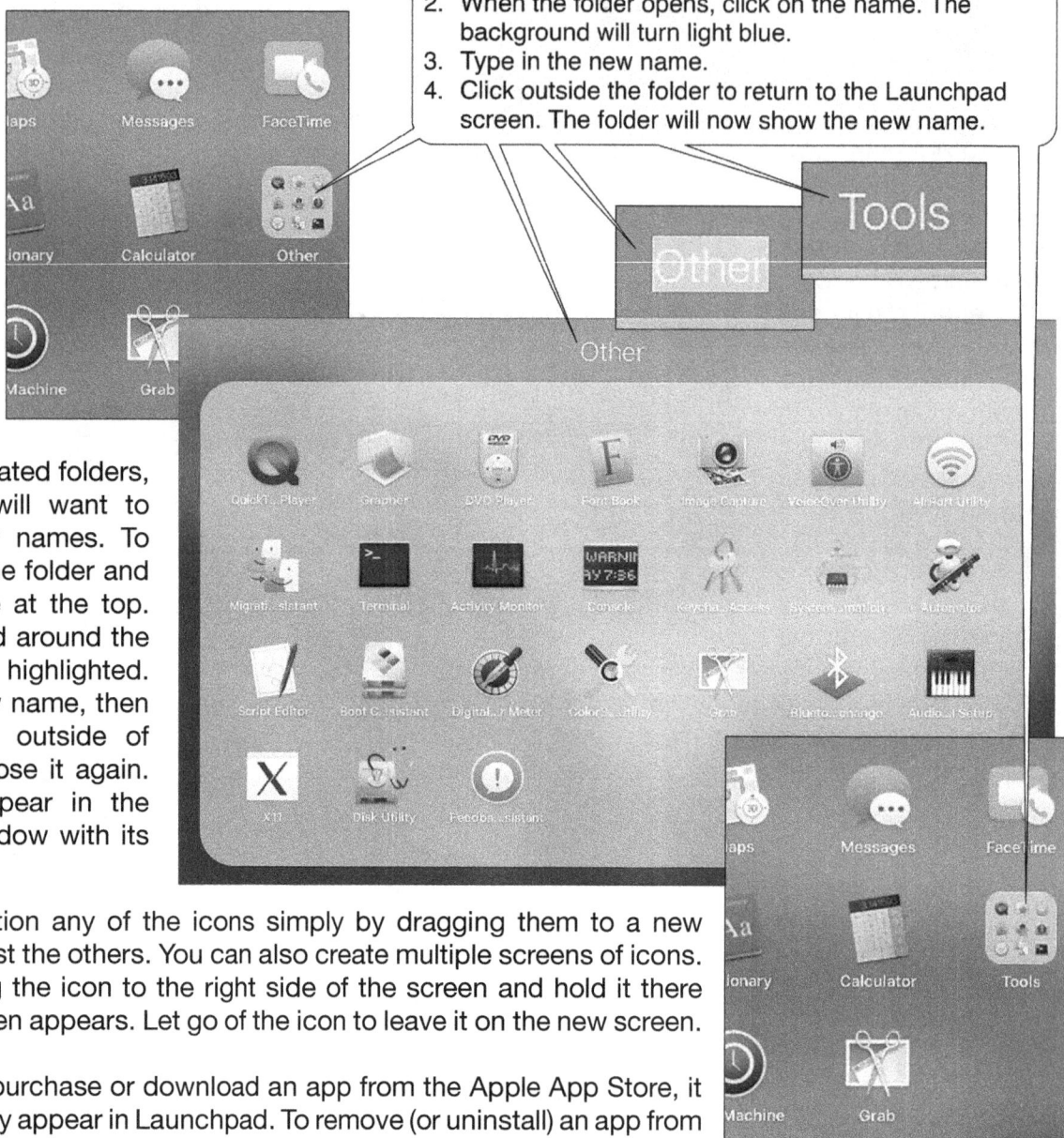

Tools

Other

Other

After you've created folders, you probably will want to give them new names. To do this, open the folder and select its name at the top. The background around the name will be highlighted. Type in the new name, then click anywhere outside of the folder to close it again. It will now appear in the Launchpad window with its new name.

You can reposition any of the icons simply by dragging them to a new location amongst the others. You can also create multiple screens of icons. To do this, drag the icon to the right side of the screen and hold it there until a new screen appears. Let go of the icon to leave it on the new screen.

Whenever you purchase or download an app from the Apple App Store, it will automatically appear in Launchpad. To remove (or uninstall) an app from your Mac, click and hold its icon until it jiggles and a small "x" appears at its upper left corner. Click on the "x" and the app (and its icon) will be removed. If there is no "x", the app did not come from the App Store or it is part of your Mac's operating system and cannot be removed.

To exit Launchpad without opening an app, click anywhere in the screen space outside of the icons, or press the ESCAPE ("esc") key on your keyboard.

Deleting an App in Launchpad
1. Click and hold the App in Launchpad until it starts to jiggle.
2. If the App can be deleted it will have an "X" above it on the left.
3. Click on the "X".
4. You will be prompted with a window asking if you are sure you want to delete the App. Click DELETE.

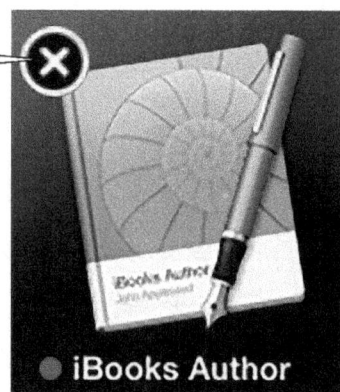

iBooks Author

Accessing Tools with Dashboard

Dashboard gives you quick access to items that you may use multiple times a day. This might include a calculator, the weather report, stock market reports, or a notepad. The items that you can place on the Dashboard are mini applications called widgets. Follow these steps to use the Dashboard:

1. Click the Dashboard icon in the Dock. (If it isn't in the Dock, open the Applications folder in Finder, locate Dashboard, and drag it down into the Dock).

2. The widgets that you currently have available will appear on the screen. To use any of them, simply click on them.

3. To add a new widget, click on the plus sign (+) in the lower left corner of the screen. Many new widget options will appear. To add one to your Dashboard, simply click on it.

4. Some widgets are customizable. These will have a small info button (a letter "i") on

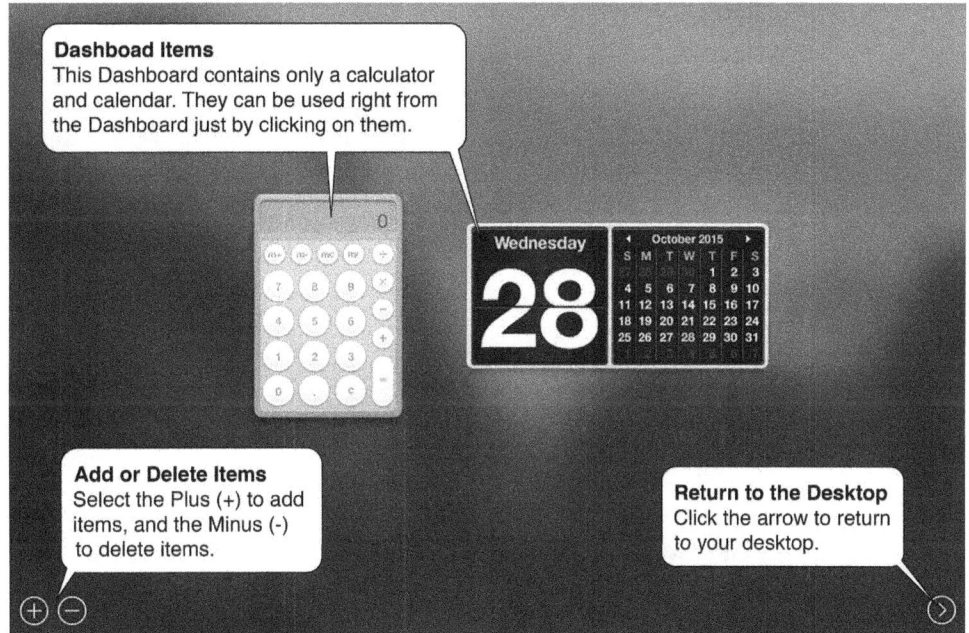

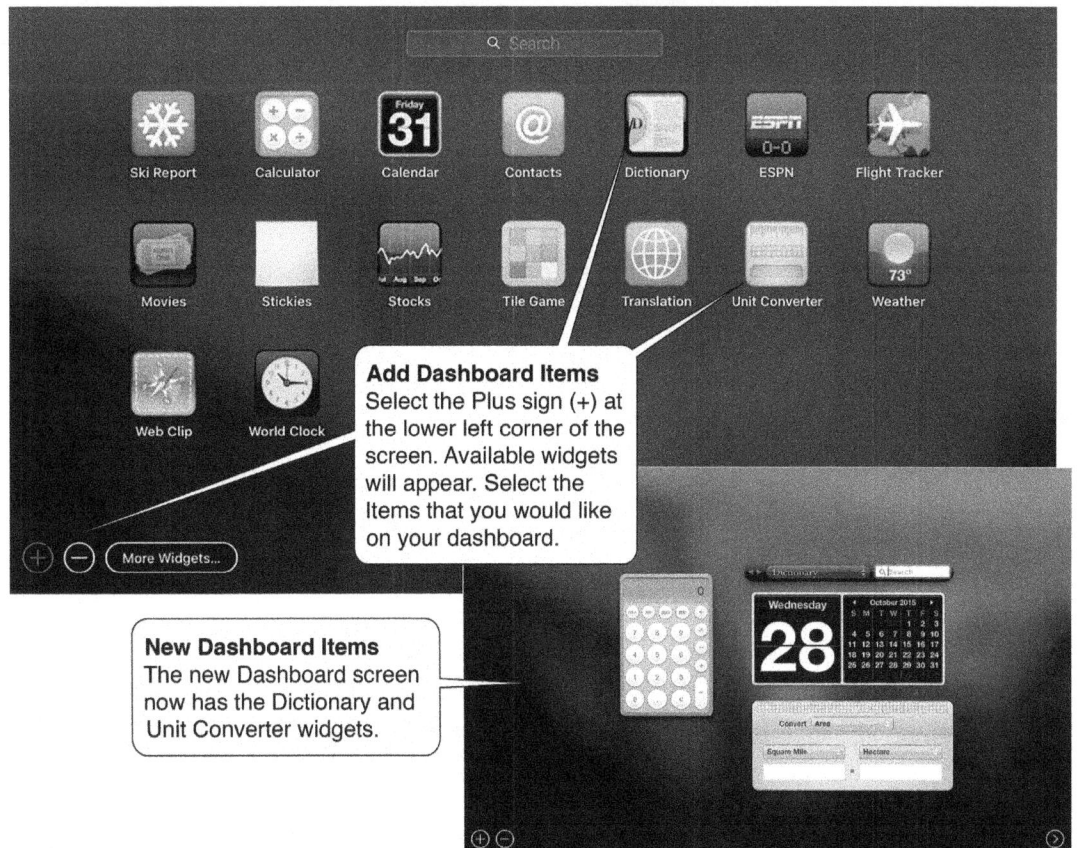

Dashboad Items
This Dashboard contains only a calculator and calendar. They can be used right from the Dashboard just by clicking on them.

Add or Delete Items
Select the Plus (+) to add items, and the Minus (-) to delete items.

Return to the Desktop
Click the arrow to return to your desktop.

Ski Report   Calculator   Calendar   Contacts   Dictionary   ESPN   Flight Tracker

Movies   Stickies   Stocks   Tile Game   Translation   Unit Converter   Weather

Web Clip   World Clock

More Widgets...

Add Dashboard Items
Select the Plus sign (+) at the lower left corner of the screen. Available widgets will appear. Select the Items that you would like on your dashboard.

New Dashboard Items
The new Dashboard screen now has the Dictionary and Unit Converter widgets.

Delete Dashboard Item
Select the Minus sign (-) at the lower left corner of the screen. A circle with a small "x" will appear on each item. Click on the "x" and the item will disappear.

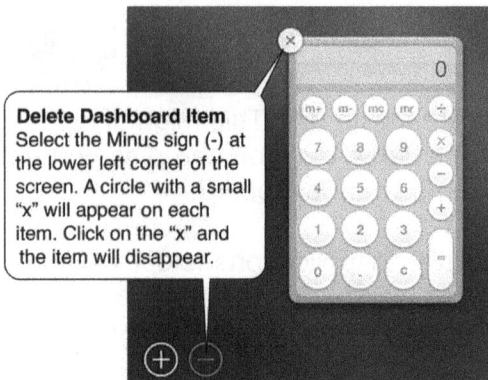

them. Click this button, and the options for customizing will appear.

5. To delete a widget, select the minus sign (-) at the lower left corner of the screen. Each widget icon will now have an "x" in the upper left corner. Click on the "x" and the icon will disappear.

6. To return to your regular desktop, click the arrow at the lower right of the screen. You can also press the Escape key ("esc") on your keyboard to return to your desktop.

Accessing Windows with Mission Control

Mission Control is an app that allows you to see everything that's on your desktop and even organize it into different desktop views called Spaces. To access Mission Control, click on its icon in the Dock.

Smaller versions of all of the windows that are currently open will appear separately. Click on one, and everything will enlarge to full size again, with your selected window at the front.

Use Mission Control to See Everything on your Desktop
1. Click the Mission Control icon in the Dock
2. All of the windows that were overlapping on your Desktop will shrink in size and be shown separately.
3. Click on the window that you want to use. The desktop will return to the way it looked before (with overlapping windows) but the one that you selected will now be shown in front of the others.

Mission Control has an optional function called Spaces. A Space is a copy of your desktop that contains certain windows and applications that you specify. Imagine a room that has multiple desks. You can place items on each desk, then move from one desk to the next to work on each group of items. If you need something from one desk that is currently on another desk, you simply move it over. Each Space is essentially like a separate desk, which means that each Space is a separate Desktop on your Mac.

Using the Spaces aspect of Mission Control can be helpful if you are using a Mac with a smaller screen, which can become cluttered very quickly. You can keep many different windows and applications open, yet still access them easily. For example, you could put your email and Internet browser on one desktop Space, your photo viewing and editing files and applications on another desktop Space, and a word processing project on a third desktop Space. Each time you access one of the Spaces the desktop would contain only those items on it and would appear far less cluttered with open windows.

To access your Spaces, click on Mission Control in the Dock. Move your cursor up to the top of the screen. The different desktop Spaces will appear. You will always have one Space which is the initial desktop that you see when you start your Mac. Here's how to create additional Spaces, move between Spaces, and delete Spaces:

1. Move the cursor to the very top of the desktop. A light blue band containing the image of a miniature desktop window will appear. This is your first Space.
2. Click on the plus sign on the right side of the light blue band. A second Space will appear.

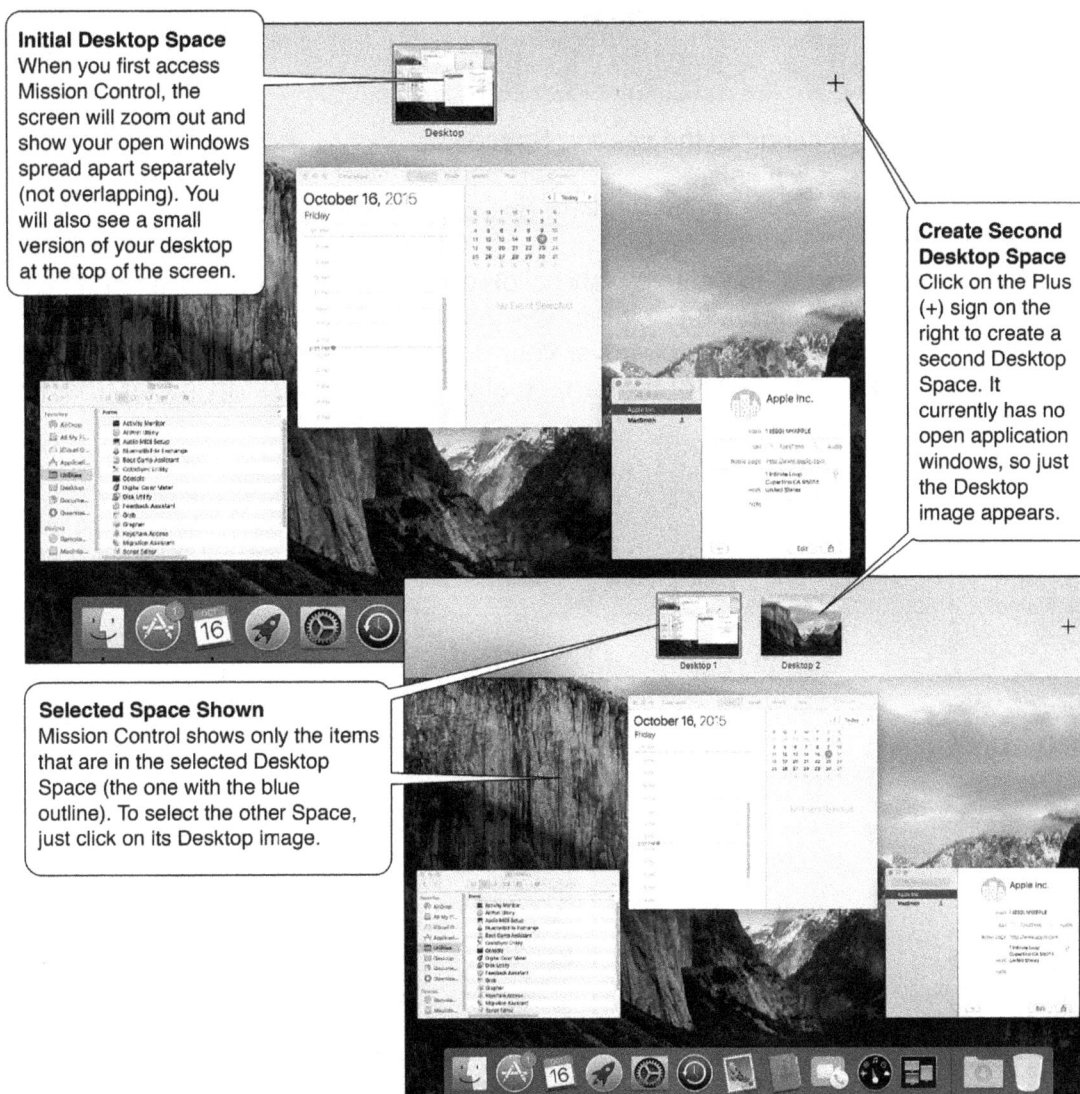

Initial Desktop Space
When you first access Mission Control, the screen will zoom out and show your open windows spread apart separately (not overlapping). You will also see a small version of your desktop at the top of the screen.

Create Second Desktop Space
Click on the Plus (+) sign on the right to create a second Desktop Space. It currently has no open application windows, so just the Desktop image appears.

Selected Space Shown
Mission Control shows only the items that are in the selected Desktop Space (the one with the blue outline). To select the other Space, just click on its Desktop image.

Put Items in Second Desktop Space
1. Select the Desktop 1 Space icon. (It will have a blue outline around it when selected.)
2. Click on the item that you want to place in the Desktop 2 Space, and drag it up on top of the Desktop 2 icon. In this example, we're moving Calendar from Desktop 1 to Desktop 2.

3. Drag any windows or applications to the second Space.
4. Click on either Space, and it will enlarge.
5. To access a different Space while you're working on your computer, go back to Mission Control (the icon in the Dock) and click on it.
6. Move your cursor to the top of the display, and click on the Space that you need. It will enlarge to become your new working desktop.
7. To delete a Space, open Mission Control, hover your cursor over the Space until an X appears in the top left corner, then click on the X. All of the items that were on the desktop in that Space will transfer back to the original desktop Space.

Desktop 1
Now when you are in Mission Control and you select Desktop 1, only those windows appear.

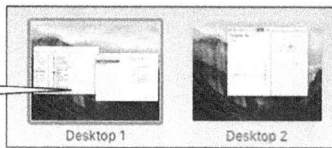

Desktop 2
When you go back to Mission Control and select Desktop 2, only the items that you placed there will appear.

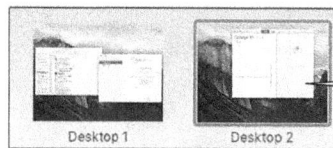

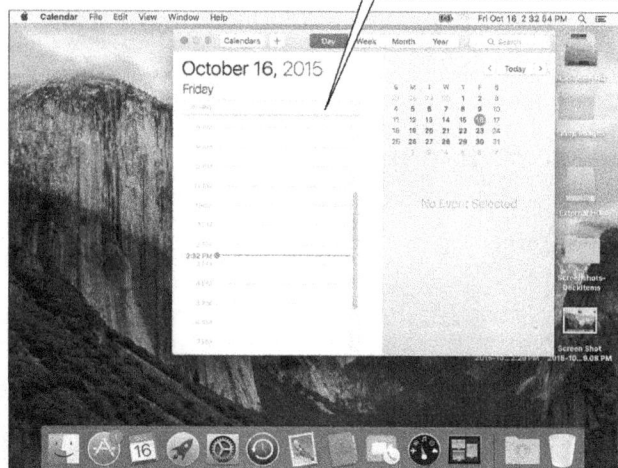

5 – CONNECTING YOUR MAC WITH THE OUTSIDE WORLD

What's Next in this chapter...

- Connecting Other Devices to Your Mac
- Printers and Scanners
- Setting Up Email to Access in Mac Mail
- Setting up Internet Access through a Network

Connecting Other Devices to Your Mac

Wired Devices

Most Macs will have at least some of the ports shown on the right. Whenever you plug something into your Mac, the machine will usually recognize it right away. For example, if you plug in an external hard drive through a USB port, an icon for the drive will appear on your desktop, and the drive will be shown in Finder. If you plug in speakers to the headphone port, you'll be able to go to SOUND in System Preferences and see them listed there.

Newer laptops may have only one port available on the entire machine. This is called a USB-C port and can be used for power or any other kind of connection. You'll need to buy separate adapters to connect most other devices to it, however. For example, to connect a USB device to the USB-C port, you'll need a USB-C-to-USB Adapter. There are many kinds of adapters available, so make sure that you're getting the right one.

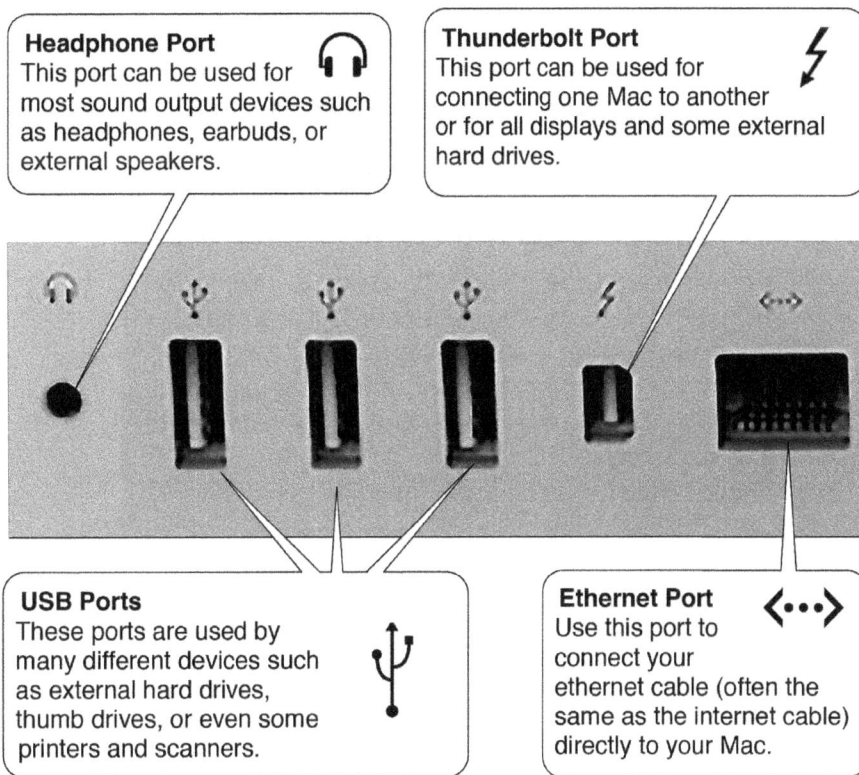

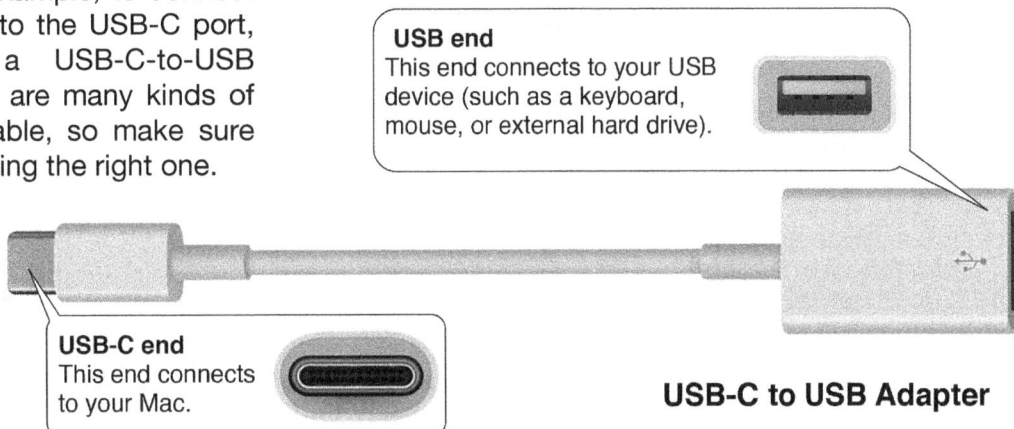

Headphone Port
This port can be used for most sound output devices such as headphones, earbuds, or external speakers.

Thunderbolt Port
This port can be used for connecting one Mac to another or for all displays and some external hard drives.

USB Ports
These ports are used by many different devices such as external hard drives, thumb drives, or even some printers and scanners.

Ethernet Port
Use this port to connect your ethernet cable (often the same as the internet cable) directly to your Mac.

USB end
This end connects to your USB device (such as a keyboard, mouse, or external hard drive).

USB-C end
This end connects to your Mac.

USB-C to USB Adapter

Wireless Devices and Bluetooth

The most important thing to remember about any wireless device is that it always needs an energy source to communicate with your Mac. Usually, this source is a battery of some kind. Sometimes batteries are rechargeable but sometimes they need to be replaced whenever they lose their charge. Make sure that you read the instructions that come with any wireless device and know the kind of battery (and how to recharge it if necessary) that your devices uses.

Many wireless devices work using a connector device called a dongle. The dongle typically connects to a USB port on your Mac and sends a signal to the wireless device. Follow the manufacturer's instructions that came with the device to set these up.

Bluetooth is another kind of wireless system. Your Mac is set up to connect with Bluetooth devices through System Preferences. Many of the newer Macs come with wireless keyboards, mice, or trackpads. Follow these steps to set up Bluetooth devices.

1. Click on the Apple icon at the upper left corner of your screen in the Menu Bar, then click on System Preferences in the drop-down menu. The System Preferences window will appear.
2. Click on the Bluetooth icon. The Bluetooth window will appear.
3. Make sure that the Bluetooth device is turned on. You may need to put the device in "discovery mode" as well so that your Mac can find it. Follow the manufacturer's instructions for the device to set up discovery mode.
4. Make sure that your Mac has Bluetooth turned on using the Button just below the large Bluetooth icon.
5. Your Mac will scan for devices and show all that it finds in a list. Locate the device that you would like to use and click the PAIR button.
6. You should now be able to use the wireless Bluetooth device.

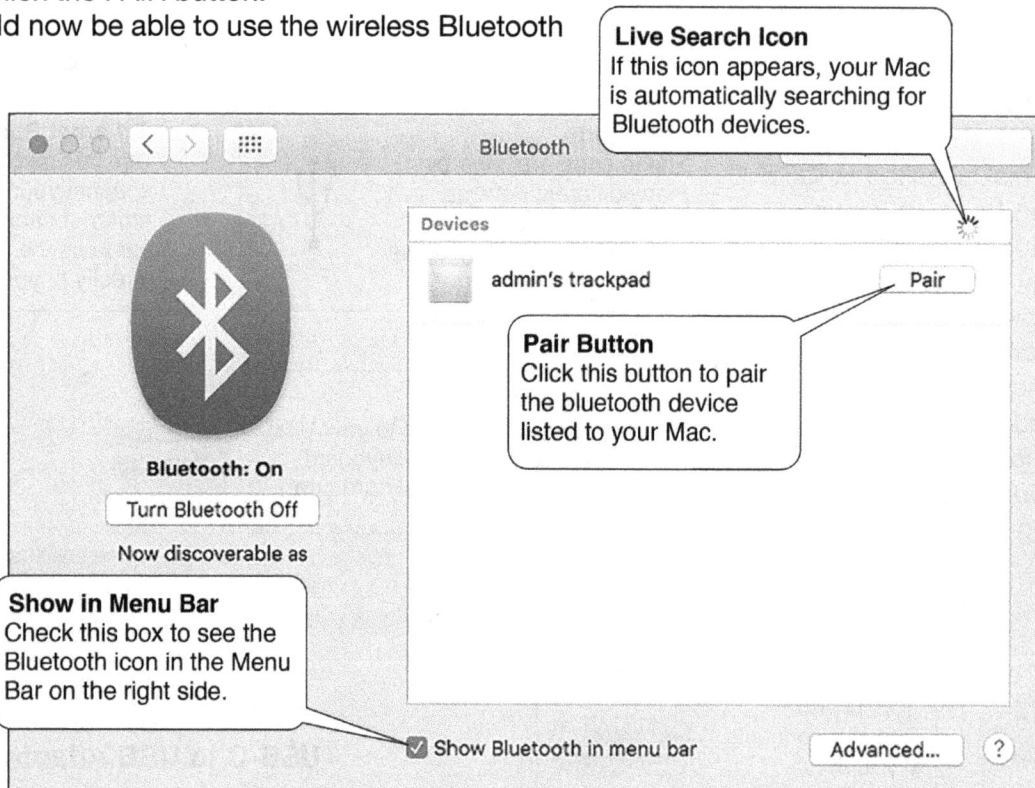

Live Search Icon
If this icon appears, your Mac is automatically searching for Bluetooth devices.

Pair Button
Click this button to pair the bluetooth device listed to your Mac.

Show in Menu Bar
Check this box to see the Bluetooth icon in the Menu Bar on the right side.

Clicking the ADVANCED button on the Bluetooth window will provide a drop-down menu with a few more options. The first two enable Bluetooth Setup Assistant which will walk you through the Bluetooth connection process for your keyboard, mouse or trackpad. If you're having difficulty making things work, select these two check boxes and restart your Mac. If it doesn't detect any of these devices, it will prompt you with instructions.

The third option on this window allows you to wake up your Mac more easily. By selecting this option you will be able to wake up your machine by pressing a key on the wireless keyboard or clicking the mouse or trackpad. If this box is not checked, your Bluetooth devices will not be able to wake your Mac from sleep mode.

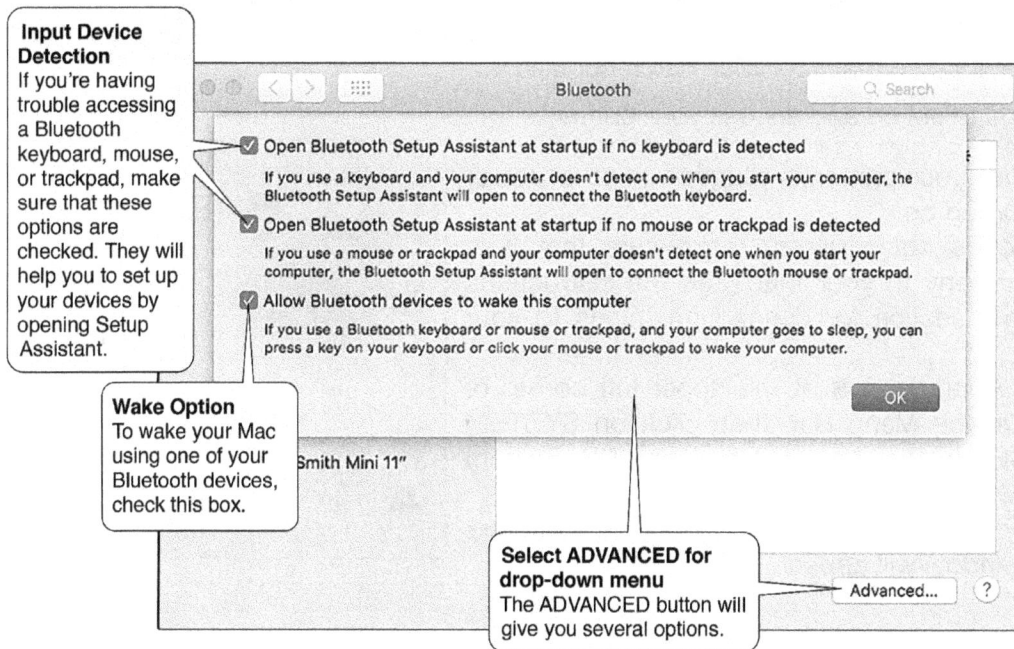

Input Device Detection
If you're having trouble accessing a Bluetooth keyboard, mouse, or trackpad, make sure that these options are checked. They will help you to set up your devices by opening Setup Assistant.

Wake Option
To wake your Mac using one of your Bluetooth devices, check this box.

Bluetooth

☑ Open Bluetooth Setup Assistant at startup if no keyboard is detected
If you use a keyboard and your computer doesn't detect one when you start your computer, the Bluetooth Setup Assistant will open to connect the Bluetooth keyboard.

☑ Open Bluetooth Setup Assistant at startup if no mouse or trackpad is detected
If you use a mouse or trackpad and your computer doesn't detect one when you start your computer, the Bluetooth Setup Assistant will open to connect the Bluetooth mouse or trackpad.

☑ Allow Bluetooth devices to wake this computer
If you use a Bluetooth keyboard or mouse or trackpad, and your computer goes to sleep, you can press a key on your keyboard or click your mouse or trackpad to wake your computer.

OK

Smith Mini 11"

Select ADVANCED for drop-down menu
The ADVANCED button will give you several options.

Advanced... ?

You might want to give your Bluetooth devices more logical names, such as "iMac Mouse" or "Mac Mini Keyboard." To do this, hold down the CONTROL key and select the device's name from the list in the Bluetooth window. A window will drop down allowing you to rename the device. It will now appear on the list with its new name.

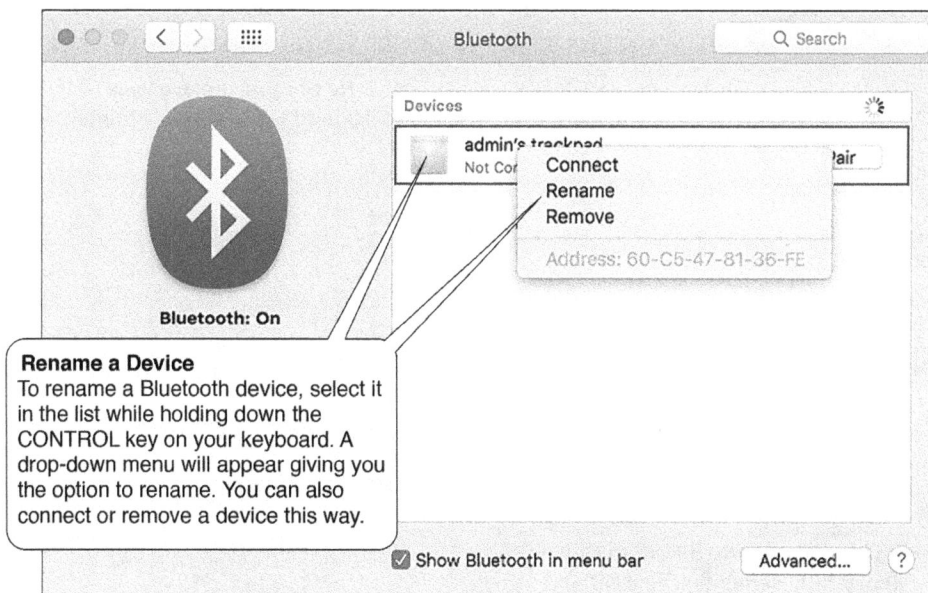

Bluetooth   Q Search

Devices

admin's trackpad
Not Con   Connect
           Rename   air
           Remove

Address: 60-C5-47-81-36-FE

Bluetooth: On

Rename a Device
To rename a Bluetooth device, select it in the list while holding down the CONTROL key on your keyboard. A drop-down menu will appear giving you the option to rename. You can also connect or remove a device this way.

☑ Show Bluetooth in menu bar   Advanced... ?

The steps for setting up either a new printer or a new scanner are quite similar to each other. We'll start with setting up a printer first, then take a quick look at scanners.

Printers

Printers can be wireless or wired. If you have a wireless printer, make sure that it is connected to your Mac properly so that the computer can recognize it. Some wireless devices come with a dongle that plugs in to one of your Mac's ports and acts as the communication relay. Other devices are Bluetooth, so follow the steps in the previous section to access these. The documentation that came with your printer should explain how to set it up so that your Mac can recognize it.

Follow these steps to set up and access your printer.

1. Make sure that your printer is plugged in to a power source and turned on.
2. If your printer is not wireless, make sure that it is connected properly to your Mac.(See the instructions in the previous section for connecting things to your machine.)
3. Click on the Apple icon at the upper left corner of your screen in the Menu Bar, then click on SYSTEM PREFERENCES in the drop-down menu. The System Preferences window will appear.
4. Click on the PRINTERS & SCANNERS icon. The Printers & Scanners window will appear.

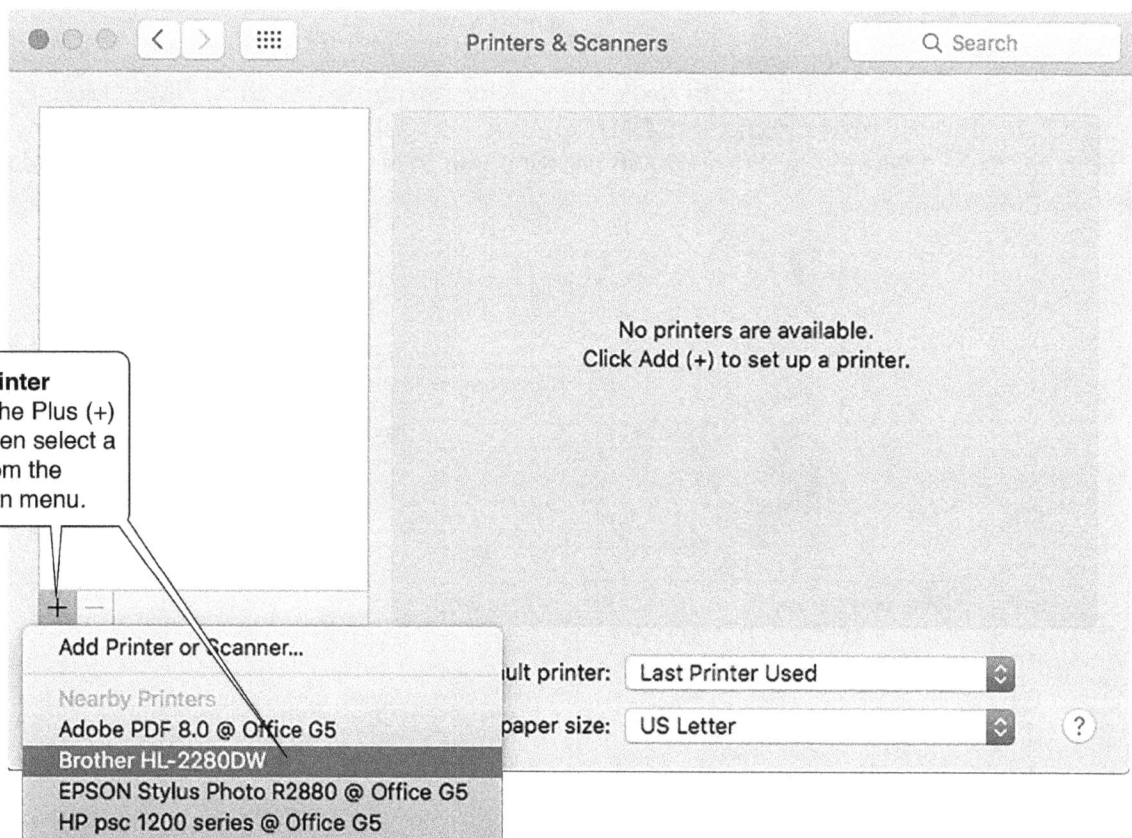

Add a Printer
Click on the Plus (+) button, then select a printer from the drop-down menu.

No printers are available.
Click Add (+) to set up a printer.

Add Printer or Scanner...

Nearby Printers
Adobe PDF 8.0 @ Office G5
Brother HL-2280DW
EPSON Stylus Photo R2880 @ Office G5
HP psc 1200 series @ Office G5

ult printer: Last Printer Used

paper size: US Letter

5. From the Printers & Scanners window, click on the Plus (+) to access a drop-down menu that lists available printers. Locate your printer and click on it.
6. The printer that you selected will now appear in the list area on the left side of the window.

After you've set up access to your printer, you might want to change some of the default settings. One important setting is paper size:

1. Click on the Apple icon at the upper left corner of the screen, then select SYSTEM PREFERENCES. From this window, select PRINTERS & SCANNERS.
2. From the Printers & Scanners window, select the printer that you're using from the list on the left.
3. Click on the up-down arrow to access the drop-down menu for default paper size.
4. Select the paper size that you would like to set as your default.

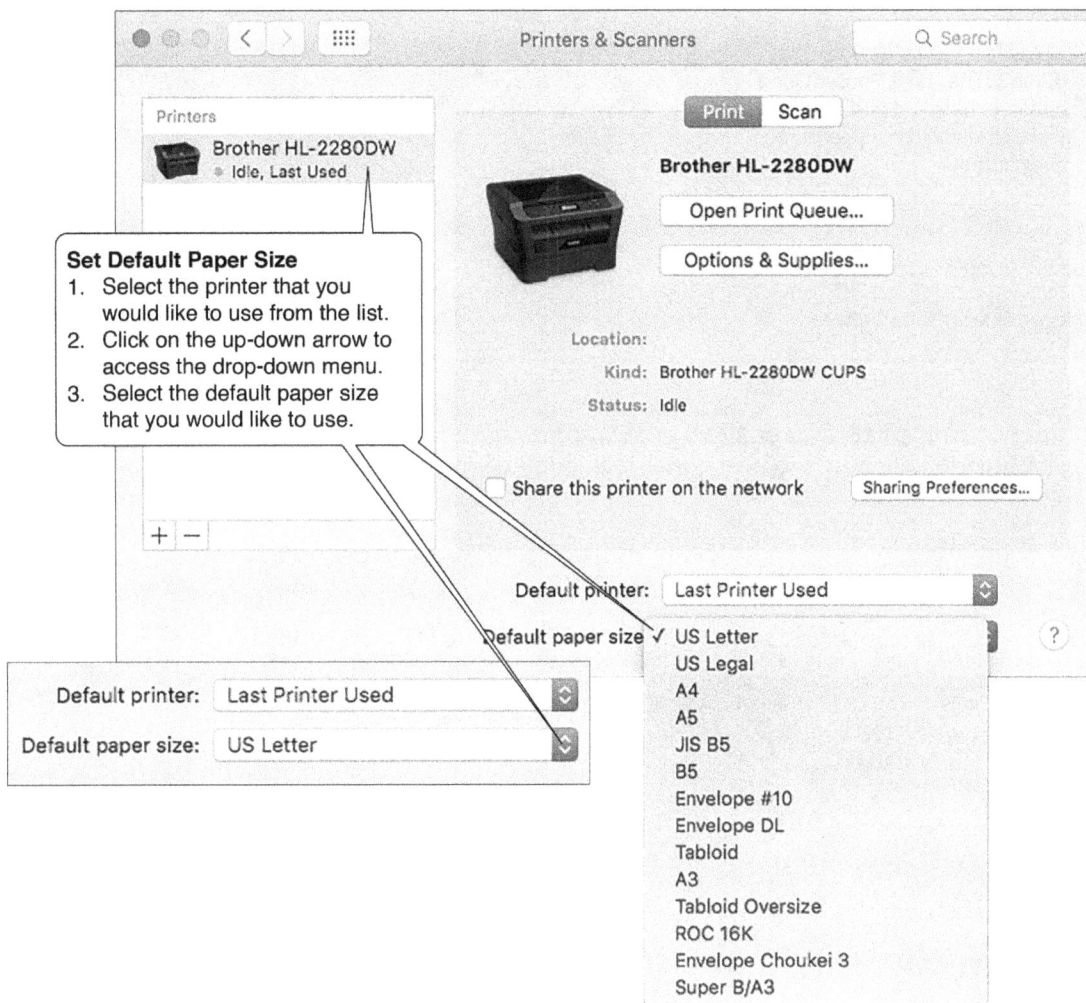

Many homes and offices have access to more than one priner To set a particular printer as your default, follow these steps:

1. Click on the Apple icon at the upper left corner of the screen, then select SYSTEM PREFERENCES. From this window, select PRINTERS & SCANNERS.
2. From the Printers & Scanners window, select the printer that will be your default from the list on the left.
3. To the right of "Default Printer", click on the up-down arrow to access additional options from the drop-down menu.
4. Select your preferred printer. If you use the same printer repeatedly, it may be helpful to simply select the "Last Printer Used" option.

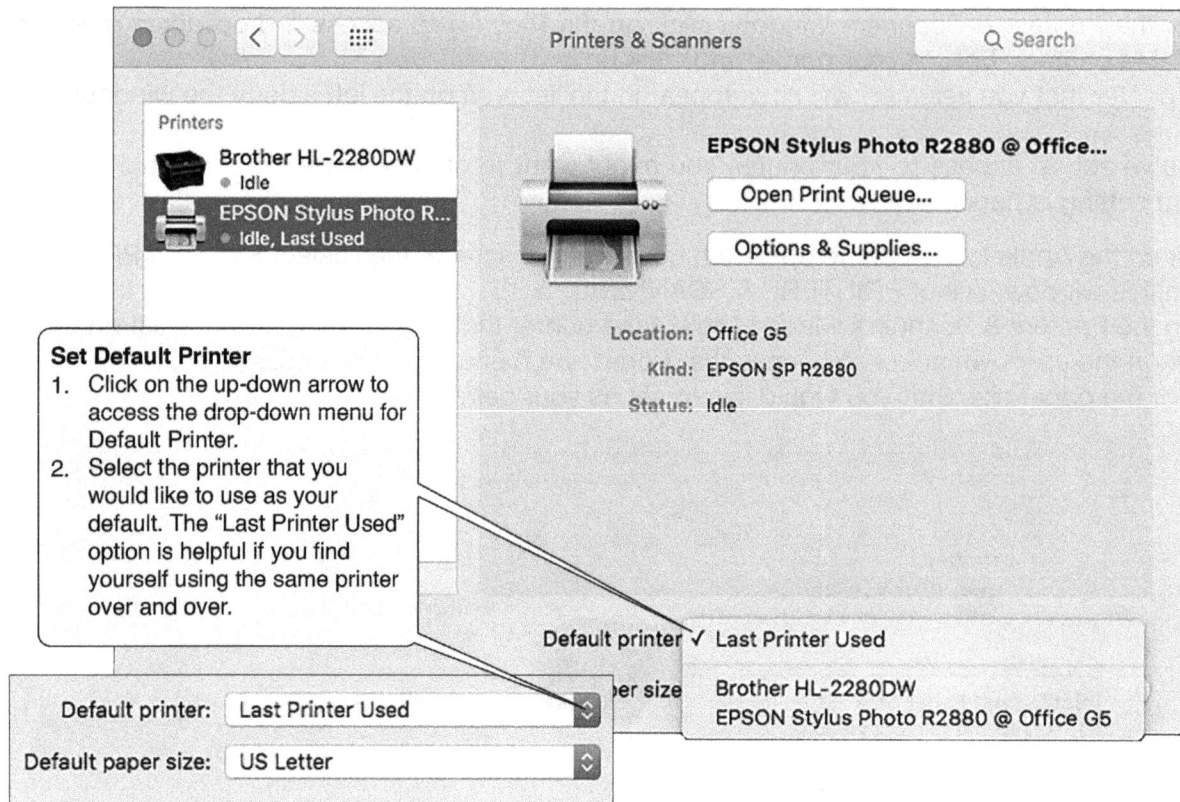

Set Default Printer
1. Click on the up-down arrow to access the drop-down menu for Default Printer.
2. Select the printer that you would like to use as your default. The "Last Printer Used" option is helpful if you find yourself using the same printer over and over.

Deleting a printer from the list is as easy as adding one. elect the printer that you want to delete, then click on the minus (-) button. A drop-down window will ask if you're sure. If you are, click DELETE PRINTER.

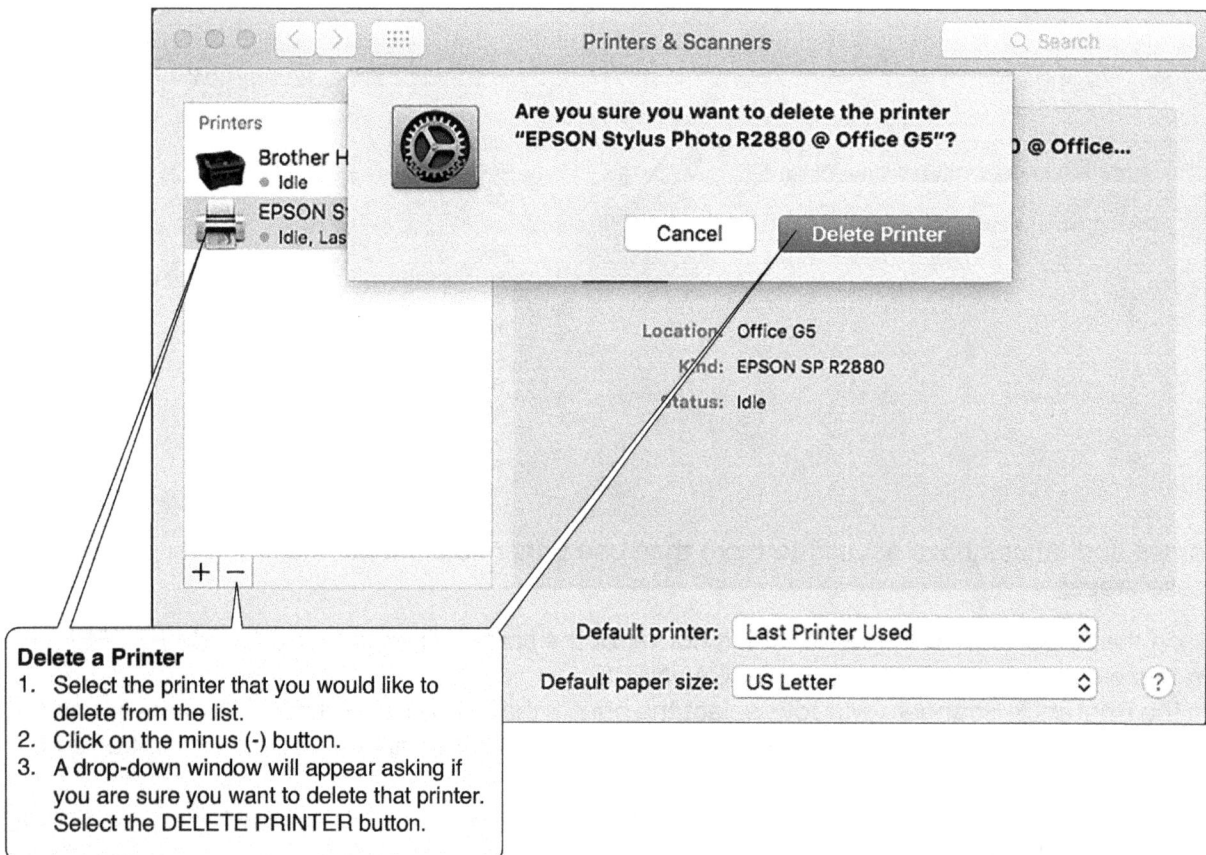

Delete a Printer
1. Select the printer that you would like to delete from the list.
2. Click on the minus (-) button.
3. A drop-down window will appear asking if you are sure you want to delete that printer. Select the DELETE PRINTER button.

Scanners

Like printers, scanners can be wireless or wired. Some are also part of an all-in-one unit that includes the printer and scanner together. The first step to accessing the scanner is to make sure that it is turned on and connected to your Mac. If you have a wireless scanner, make sure that it can communicate with your Mac properly so that the computer can recognize it. Some wireless devices come with a dongle that plugs in to one of your Mac's ports and acts as the communication relay. Other devices are Bluetooth, so follow the steps in the previous section to access these. The documentation that came with your scanner should explain how to set it up so that your Mac can recognize it.

Add a Scanner
Click on the Plus (+) button, then select a scanner (or all-in-one printer that includes a scanner) from the drop-down menu.

+ −

Add Printer or Scanner...

Nearby Printers
Adobe PDF 8.0 @ Office G5
Brother HL-2280DW
EPSON Stylus Photo R2880 @ Office G5
HP psc 1200 series @ Office G5

Adding a new scanner follows the same steps as adding a new printer. Open the Printers & Scanners window from System Preferences, select the Plus (+) button, then select your scanner. If you're unsure of the steps, look back at the procedure for adding a new printer earlier in this section.

Accessing a Scanner
1. Select the scanner that you would like to use.
2. Click the SCAN button.
3. Click the OPEN SCANNER button.

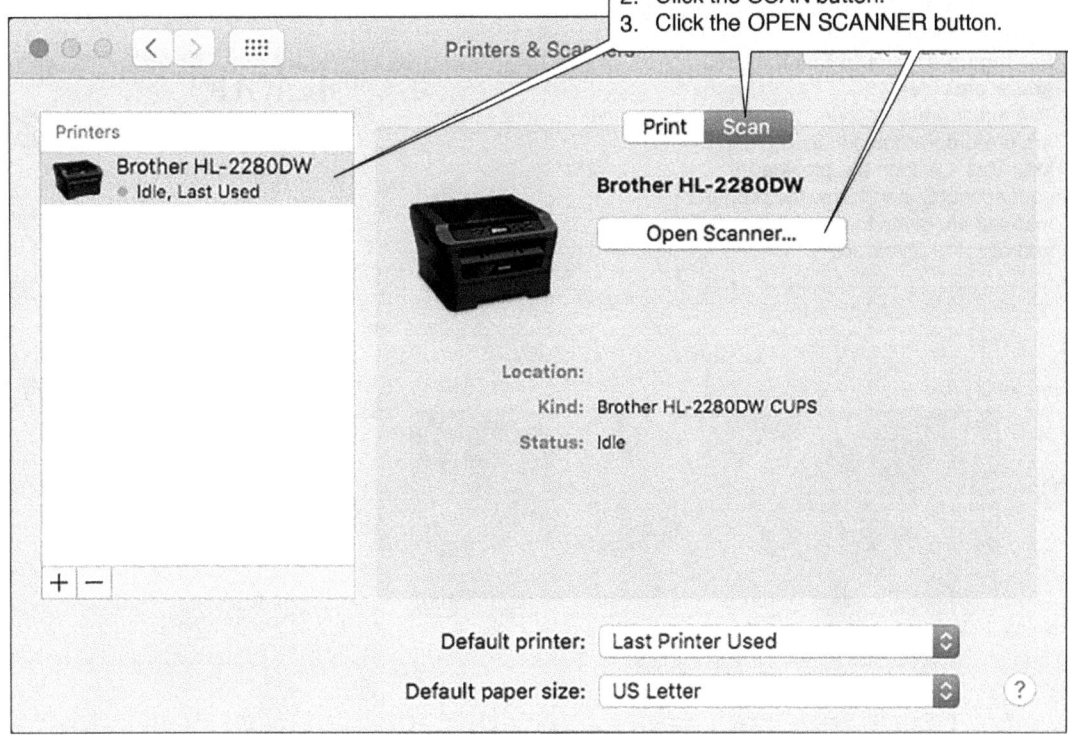

Printers & Scanners

Printers

Brother HL-2280DW
● Idle, Last Used

Print   Scan

Brother HL-2280DW

Open Scanner...

Location:
Kind: Brother HL-2280DW CUPS
Status: Idle

+ −

Default printer: Last Printer Used

Default paper size: US Letter   ?

Once the scanner is set up you can access it for scanning. To do this, follow these steps:

1. Click on the Apple icon at the upper left corner of the screen, then select SYSTEM PREFERENCES. From this window, select PRINTERS & SCANNERS.
2. From the Printers & Scanners window, select the scanner that you would like to use.
3. Click the SCAN button.
4. Click the OPEN SCANNER button.
5. A new window will open with the scanner commands that are specific to your model. Follow the manufacturers instructions from this point on to scan an item.

One troubleshooting tip to note for printers or scanners is that if you're having trouble with one, delete it from the list on the left side of the PRINTERS & SCANNERS window (the one that you accessed from System Preferences), then add it again. This will often clear up any difficulties.

Setting Up Access to an Email Account in Mac Mail

It's important to know that your Mac will provide access to an existing email account through Mac Mail (the icon that looks like a postage stamp), but you must first set up an account through a system provider. There are many different account providers available, including Google (Gmail), Yahoo, AOL, or your Internet service provider such as TimeWarner or Comcast. Before you can use your Mac to access mail, choose one of these providers and set up an account with an email address and password. Each account setup is a bit different, so contact the provider to make sure you do this properly.

Setting up access to Email from a major provider
The major email account providers are pre-programmed in to Apple's Mac Mail. Click on the provider of your account, then follow the prompts that you are given to enter your email address and password.

Internet Accounts sets up your accounts to use with Mail, Contacts, Calendar, Messages, and other apps.

iCloud

Exchange

Google

Sign in

Let this Mac access your mail and other Google Account data

Enter your email

More options   NEXT

Google

Cancel

Once you have your email address and password, Apple makes it very easy to set up email access through your Mac's preloaded Mail app. Most of the major Internet mail system providers have been built into your Mac's system. To access these and set up Mail, follow these steps:

1. Click on the Apple icon at the upper left corner of the screen, then select System Preferences. From this window, select Internet Accounts.

2. A list of account options will appear in the Internet Accounts window. Select the company that hosts your email account. If you're using a provider not listed, select "Add Other Account" and skip to step 4.

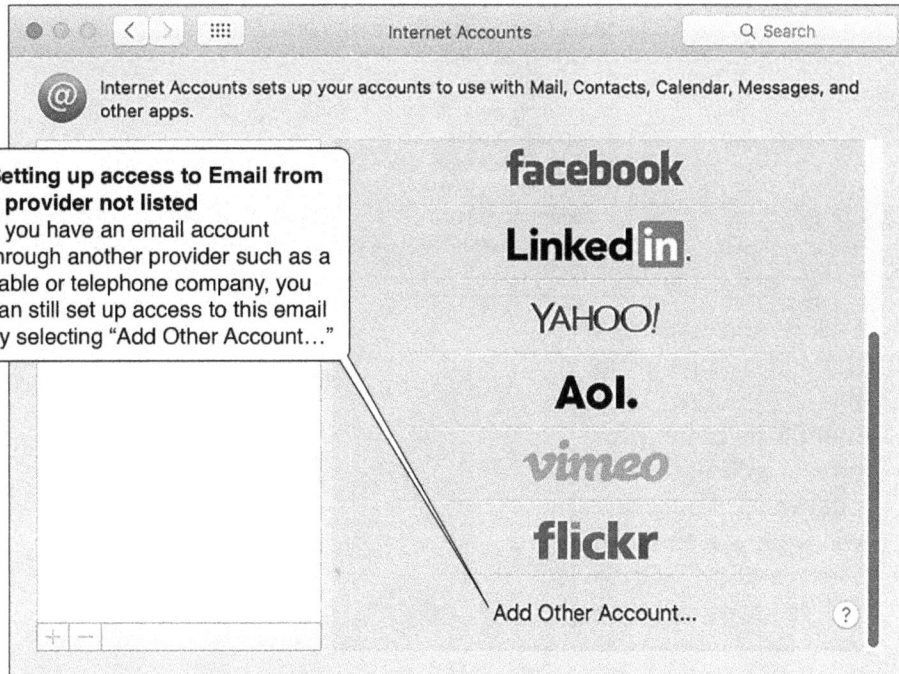

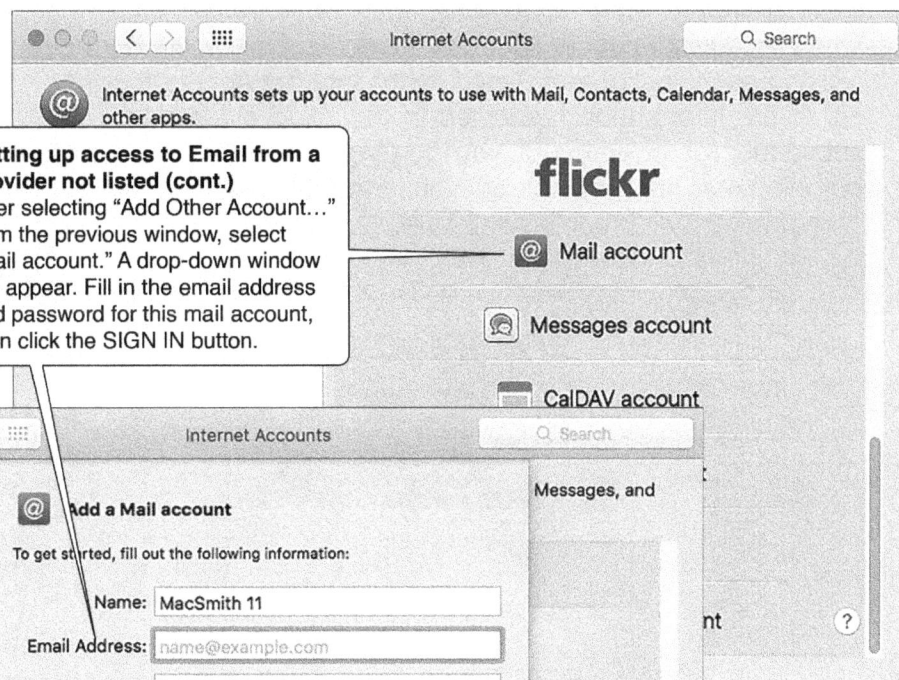

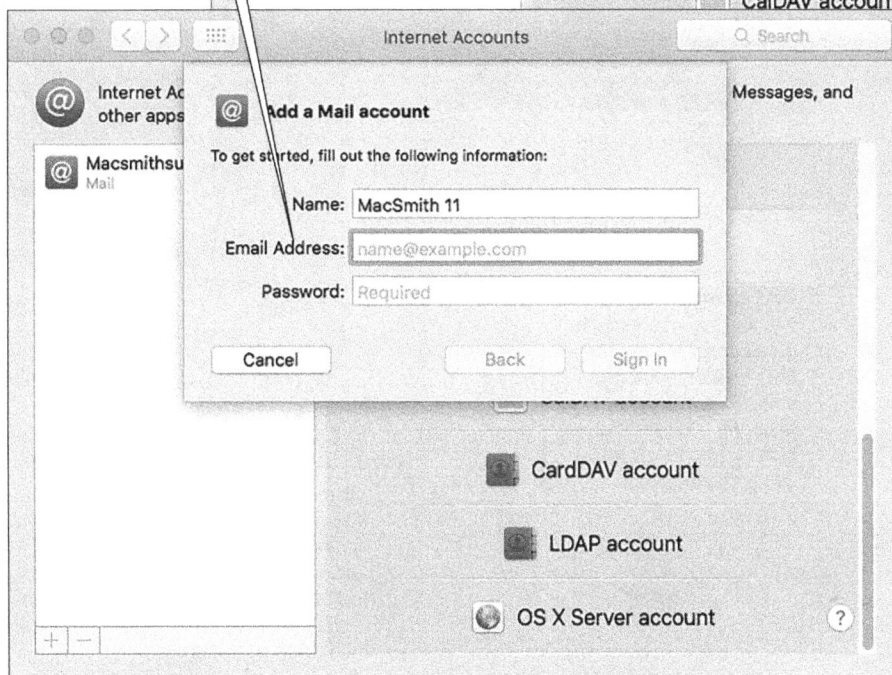

Setting up access to Email from a provider not listed
If you have an email account through another provider such as a cable or telephone company, you can still set up access to this email by selecting "Add Other Account…"

Setting up access to Email from a provider not listed (cont.)
After selecting "Add Other Account…" from the previous window, select "Mail account." A drop-down window will appear. Fill in the email address and password for this mail account, then click the SIGN IN button.

Add a Mail account
To get started, fill out the following information:

Name: MacSmith 11
Email Address: name@example.com
Password: Required

Cancel   Back   Sign In

Setting Incoming and Outgoing Servers
If your Mac needs this information, you will be prompted with this window. Check with your email account provider and they'll give you the address for each.

Internet Accounts   Q Search

Messages, and

Email Address: Macsmith@macsmithsupport.com

User Name: Automatic

Password: ••••••••

Account Type: IMAP

Incoming Mail Server: mail.example.com

Outgoing Mail Server: mail.example.com

Cancel   Back   Sign In

CardDAV account

LDAP account

OS X Server account

3. Follow the prompts that are given in the subsequent menus to enter your email address and password. Your Mac will walk you through the setup. Once you're done, skip to Step 6.

4. If you did not see your provider listed and clicked "Add Other Account" you will find additional options listed on the Internet Accounts window. Click on the "Mail account" option.

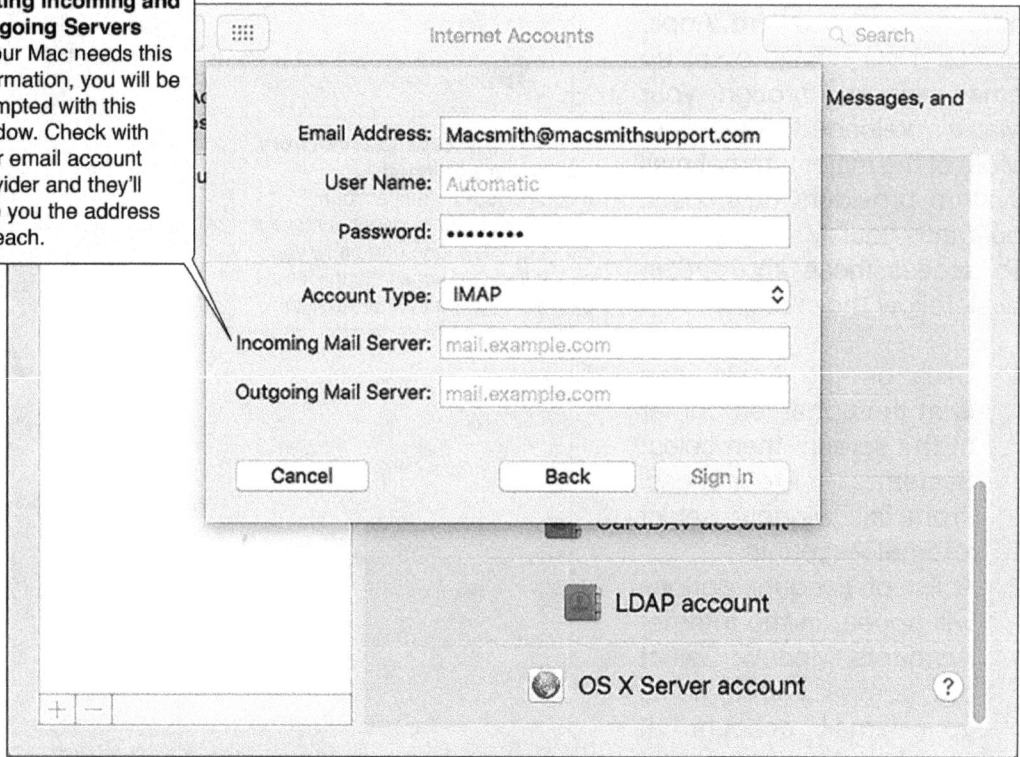

5. Fill in the information requested in the "Add a Mail Account" drop-down window as well as any subsequent information. If you don't know some of the answers (for example, your incoming or outgoing mail servers), contact your email account provider and they can help you with these items.

Enable or Disable an Account
To see the mail account in Mac Mail, it must be enabled. Click on the account name in the list so that it's highlighted, then check the "Enable this account" box.

If you want to keep the account information, but not receive or send mail, uncheck the "Enable this account" box. You can enable it again at any time.

Internet

Internet Accounts sets up your accounts to   other apps.

@ Macsmithsupport
    Mail

@ **Mail**

Email Address: macsmith11@macsmithsupport.com

Description: Macsmithsupport

Name: MacSmith 11

Password: ••••••••

☑ Enable this account

Add Another Account
You can access multiple email accounts through Mac Mail at the same time. To add another account, click the plus (+) button, and follow the steps shown again.

Remove an Account
If you no longer need access to an email account, select it in the list so that it highlights, then click the minus (-) button.

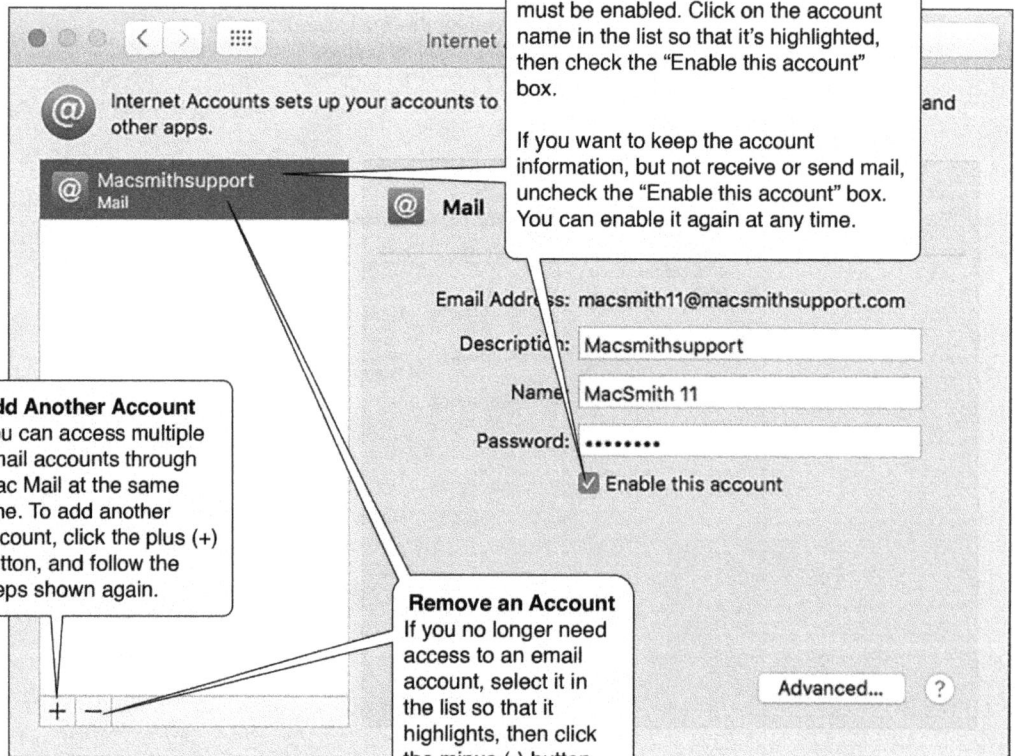

Advanced...   ?

58

6. Once the information for your accounts has been entered it will appear in the list area on the left side of the Internet Accounts window. Select it so that its background highlights, then check the box for "enable this account". The account will now appear when you open Mac Mail.

You can add multiple email accounts to Mac Mail so that all are accessible at the same time. To add another account, click the plus (+) button at the bottom of the accounts list, then follow the previous steps.

To access your email, simply click on the Mac Mail icon in the dock (the one that looks like a postage stamp). It will automatically open and show new mail associated with any email addresses that you have added.

Setting up Internet Access

To access the Internet wirelessly from your Mac you'll first need to have a network set up. Networks are available through phone and cable companies. Contact the company that you prefer and have them set up your network connection if you don't already have one.

The piece of equipment that brings the network into your house (usually from a phone line or the cable company) is called a modem. When your network is set up, you'll be provided with a modem along with a network name (or address) and password. Write down the name and password in the front of this book. You'll need to use them from time to time!

The equipment that lets you access this network wirelessly is called a router. Apple calls their router an "Airport." Some network providers now combine the modem and router into one unit, but make sure that you have both. If you don't, you'll need to connect your Mac directly to the network modem using an ethernet cable.

Once you have a network available to you wirelessly, you can access it with your Mac. Apple makes this quite easy by allowing your Mac to find available networks. To access a network, follow these steps:

1. Click on the Apple icon at the upper left corner of the screen, then select System Preferences. From this window, select NETWORKS.

2. You'll see some networking options available in the list on the left side of the Network window. Click on Wi-Fi to highlight it. If you don't see a Wi-Fi option in the list, add one by clicking the Plus (+) button beneath the list area, then selecting Wi-Fi from the drop-down menu.

Add Wi-Fi Connection
To add a new Wi-Fi connection, click the plus (+) button. A drop-down window will appear. Select the Wi-Fi option from the drop-down list beside the word "Interface."

3. Make sure that the drop-down menu for LOCATION is set to "Automatic."

4. The STATUS should indicated "Connected." If it doesn't, click the button that reads "Turn Wi-Fi On."

5. Click on the drop-down menu for NETWORK NAME and select your network.

6. Enter the network password in the drop-down window that appears. If you'll be using this network frequently, check the box beside "Remember this network." (Note that the "Show Password" option will simply show you what you are typing as you type. It will not show you an existing password.) Click the JOIN button when you are done.

7. Before you leave the NETWORK window, make sure that you have checked off the box beside "Show Wi-Fi status in menu bar." This will provide a useful shortcut in the future when you are accessing networks wirelessly.

8. Click on the APPLY button. You now can access the Internet wirelessly.

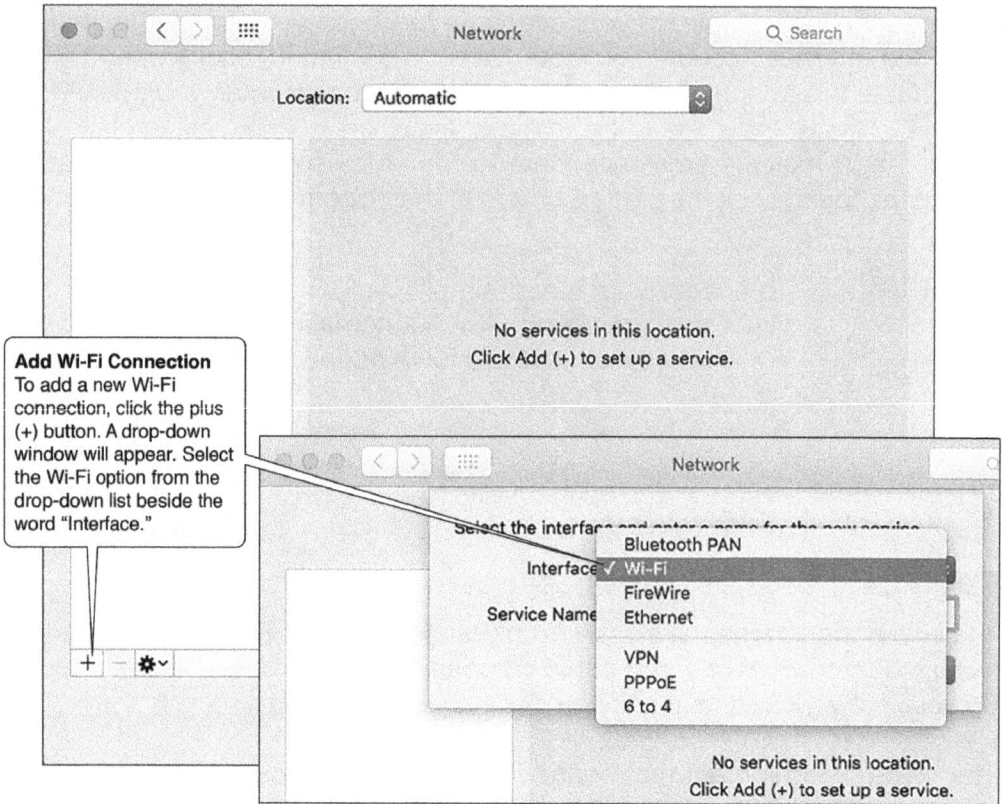

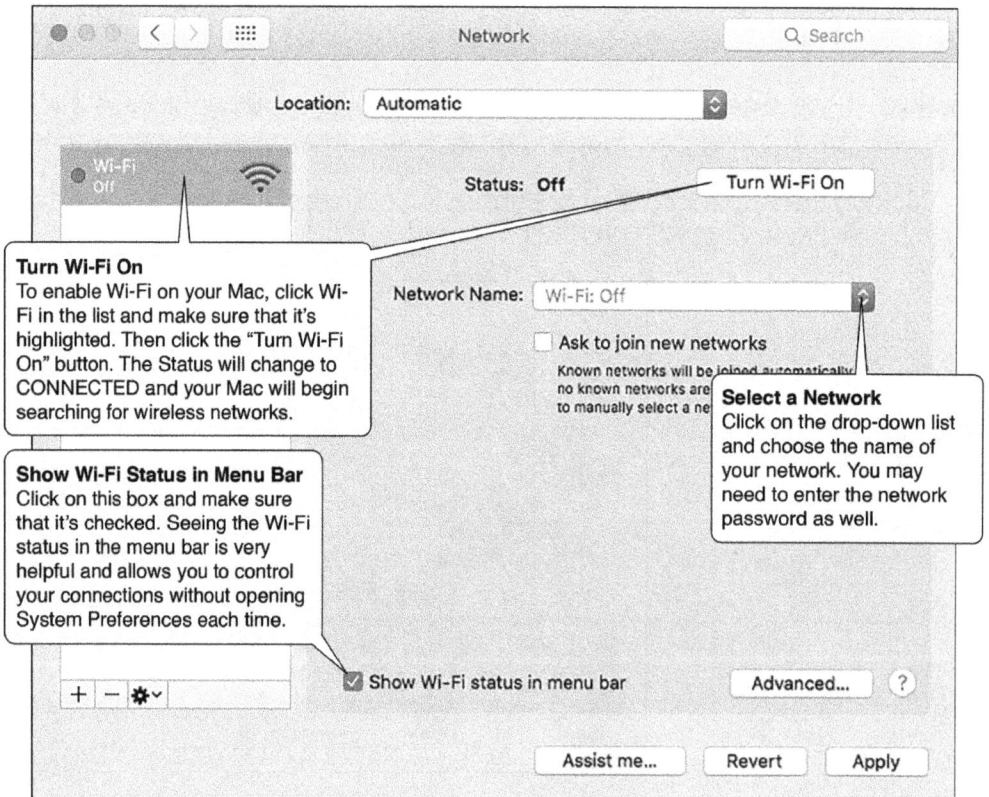

Turn Wi-Fi On
To enable Wi-Fi on your Mac, click Wi-Fi in the list and make sure that it's highlighted. Then click the "Turn Wi-Fi On" button. The Status will change to CONNECTED and your Mac will begin searching for wireless networks.

Show Wi-Fi Status in Menu Bar
Click on this box and make sure that it's checked. Seeing the Wi-Fi status in the menu bar is very helpful and allows you to control your connections without opening System Preferences each time.

Select a Network
Click on the drop-down list and choose the name of your network. You may need to enter the network password as well.

If you checked the box for "Show Wi-Fi status in menu bar" while in the NETWORK window (see step 7) you'll now have quick access to any networks that you've set up. The network icon is a series of curved bars that form a cone shape located on the right side of the Menu Bar. The number of bars indicates the strength of your network.

If you see only an empty cone outline, this means that your Wi-Fi has been turned off. Click on the cone, then select "Turn Wi-Fi On" from the drop-down menu.

To switch from one network to another, click on the cone (make sure that Wi-Fi is turned on), then select the network that you want from the drop-down menu. The network that is currently being used will have a check beside it. The strength of each network is shown by the number of bars in the cone corresponding to the network name on the list.

Sometimes a network is "hidden" which means that its name will not appear in the list of available

Wi-Fi Access in the Menu Bar
If the Wi-Fi icon is an empty cone shape, this means that the Wi-Fi is currently off and you will not be able to access your network wirelessly.

To turn the Wi-Fi back on, click on the Wi-Fi icon, then select Turn Wi-Fi on from the drop-down menu.

	Wed 5:33 PM MacSmith 11
	Wi-Fi: Off
	Turn Wi-Fi On

	Wed 5:33 PM MacSmith 11
	Wi-Fi: Looking for Networks...
	Turn Wi-Fi Off
✓	Our Network
	belkin54g
	linksys
	MPW Wireless Network
	Join Other Network...
	Create Network...
	...rk Preferences...

Select a Network
Click on the drop-down list and choose the name of your network. If the network has a lock icon on the right, this means it is secure and you'll need to enter a password.

Network Strength
The strength of each network is indicated by the icon on the far right. The more bars shown, the stronger the signal.

networks. To join a "hidden" network, select "Join Other Network..." from the list of network names, then follow the prompts to enter the network name and password (if needed).

It's important to note that some networks are secure while others are not. A secure network will have a lock icon to the right of its name and will require a password. Unsecure networks have no lock icon and do not need a password. Unsecure networks are fine to use for basic web browsing, but it is not advised that any personal information be sent on them, such as logging in to a banking web site or accessing personal email.

To use the Internet you'll need a web browser. Apple supplies one on your machine called Safari. Click on the Dock icon that looks like a compass to open Safari. There are quite a few browsers available now, including Chrome, Internet Explorer, Firefox, Opera, and many others. Use the one that works best for you.

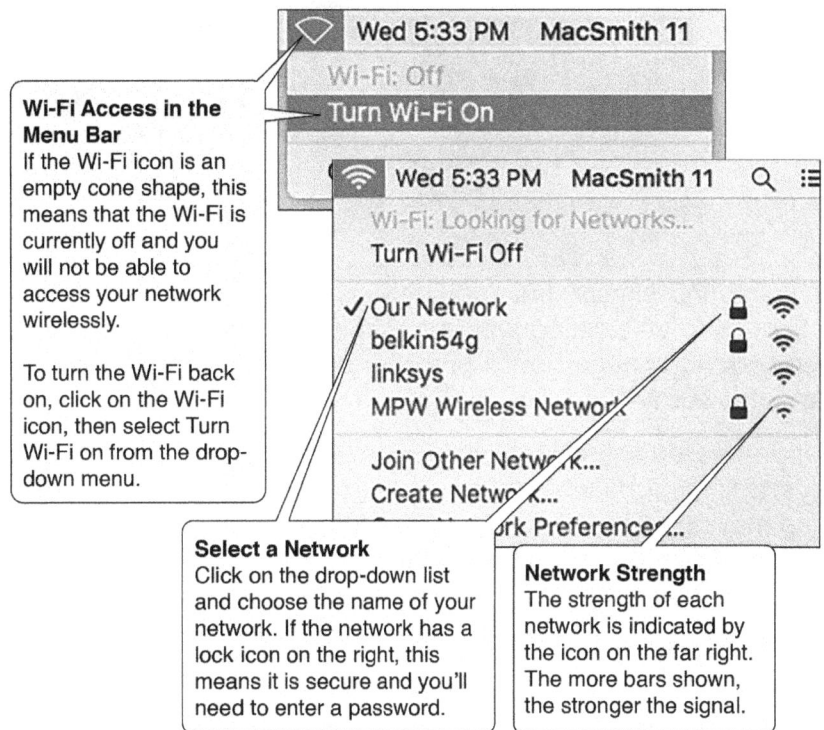

What is a Web Browser? What is a Search Engine?

If you want to find something on the Internet you'll need two things: a Web Browser and a Search Engine. The Web Browser is an application (software) on your computer that allows you to look at anything on the Internet. Examples of Web Browsers are Safari, Firefox, Google Chrome, or Internet Explorer.

A Search Engine is an online program that operates within a Web Browser, and finds items on the Internet using keywords. Examples of Search Engines are Google, Yahoo, Bing, or Ask. Sometimes the Search Engine that a Web Browser is using isn't obvious, especially if you're typing a search term into the URL field (the one that often starts with "http://..". The Search Engine that you're using will be shown when the search results appear.

You can use a Web Browser without needing a Search Engine if you know the specific web address ("URL" or "Uniform Resource Locator") of the site that you want to see. For example, you don't need a Search Engine to get to the Apple web site, you can just type in Apple.com in the address field of the browser. However, if you wanted to know where to find an apple orchard in your neighborhood, you would need to type "apple orchards" into a Search Engine, then view the results.

6 – APPS, UPDATES AND UPGRADES

What's Next in this chapter...

- **Understanding the App Store**
- **Running Updates**
- **Performing Upgrades**

They sound similar, but "updates" and "upgrades" are two very different things. Updates are smaller changes to an existing program that are usually fixes for minor problems or compatibilities. Overall, they really don't change how a program or app functions to any great extent. It's a good idea to keep your updates current.

Upgrades are entirely new versions of a program. They do change how the program (including an operating system) will function and may even make it incompatible with other programs. Upgrading your Mac is like moving to the next higher grade at school - it takes you to the next level where things can be quite different. You'll want to think carefully and do some research before performing an upgrade. Once you do upgrade, you typically cannot go back (without a great deal of time, trouble and expense!).

Before checking for updates or upgrades, however, let's look at Apple's App Store. This is the central location for downloading new apps, getting updates, or accessing upgrades.

Understanding the App Store

Most of the software as well as the operating system on your Mac is downloaded from the App Store. An "app" is simply a generic term for "application." Apple throws everything under this heading and makes it available in one centralized location: the App Store.

Open the App Store
Click on the Apple menu icon, the click on App Store.

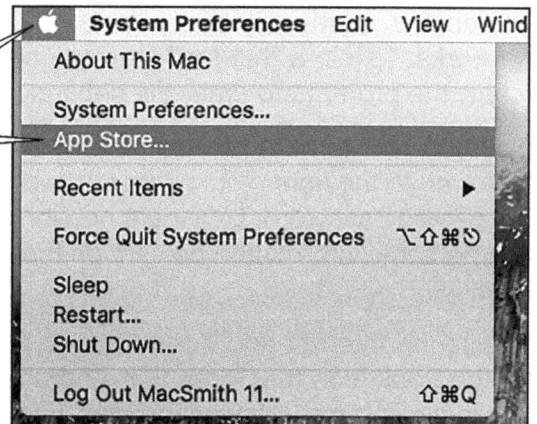

Accessing the App Store is very easy. Just click on the Apple menu in the upper left corner of the Menu Bar, then click on App Store.

System Preferences	Edit	View	Wind
About This Mac			
System Preferences...			
App Store...			
Recent Items			▶
Force Quit System Preferences			⌥⇧⌘⎋
Sleep			
Restart...			
Shut Down...			
Log Out MacSmith 11...			⇧⌘Q

A new window will appear with several options along the top. These allow you to navigate to other App Store windows. The five App Store windows are: Featured, Top Charts, Categories, Purchased, and Updates.

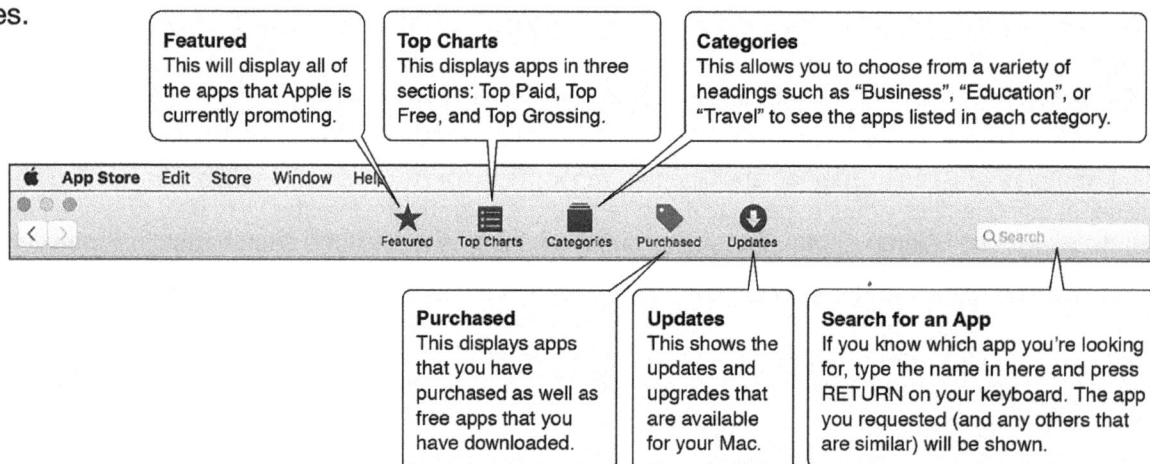

Featured
This will display all of the apps that Apple is currently promoting.

Top Charts
This displays apps in three sections: Top Paid, Top Free, and Top Grossing.

Categories
This allows you to choose from a variety of headings such as "Business", "Education", or "Travel" to see the apps listed in each category.

🍎 **App Store** Edit Store Window Help

★ Featured   ▤ Top Charts   ▦ Categories   🏷 Purchased   ⊙ Updates   🔍 Search

Purchased
This displays apps that you have purchased as well as free apps that you have downloaded.

Updates
This shows the updates and upgrades that are available for your Mac.

Search for an App
If you know which app you're looking for, type the name in here and press RETURN on your keyboard. The app you requested (and any others that are similar) will be shown.

Before you can access and download apps, however, you'll need one important thing: your Apple ID. Chances are, when you bought your Mac you created an Apple ID then. It's usually your email address, and also has a password that you set.

Every item that you download from the App Store is associated with the Apple ID used to download it. Apple does this for a reason: no matter what device you are on, you will always have access to your purchases on the App Store, as long as you are using the same Apple ID to download them each time.

Some people have multiple Apple IDs, or may have several within a family. This can create confusion if some apps were obtained with one Apple ID, and other apps with a different Apple ID. You will need to log in to the App Store under each ID to download or update any apps that you have purchased.

If you have forgotten your Apple ID, go to Apple's support web site (apple.com/support) and click on the link for "Apple ID."

Featured Apps

These apps are typically the latest that Apple is promoting. Access information by clicking on an app's name. Download an app by clicking on the price (or "Free") button.

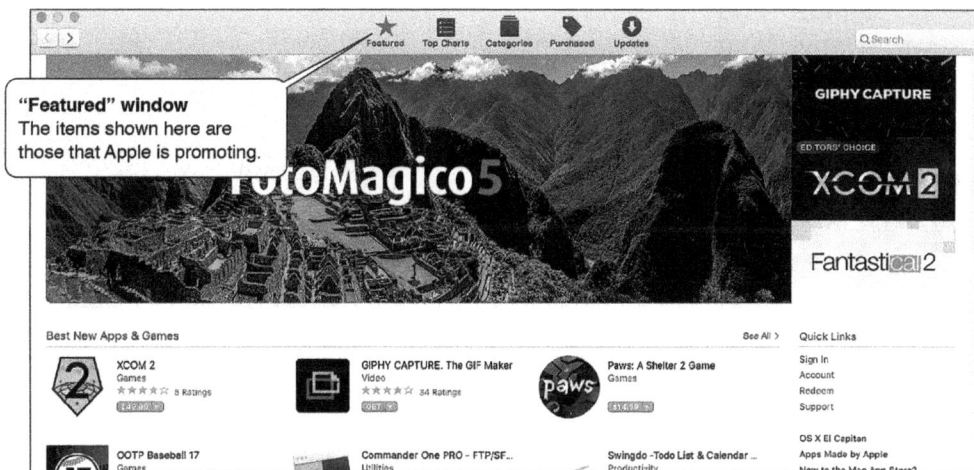

"Featured" window
The items shown here are those that Apple is promoting.

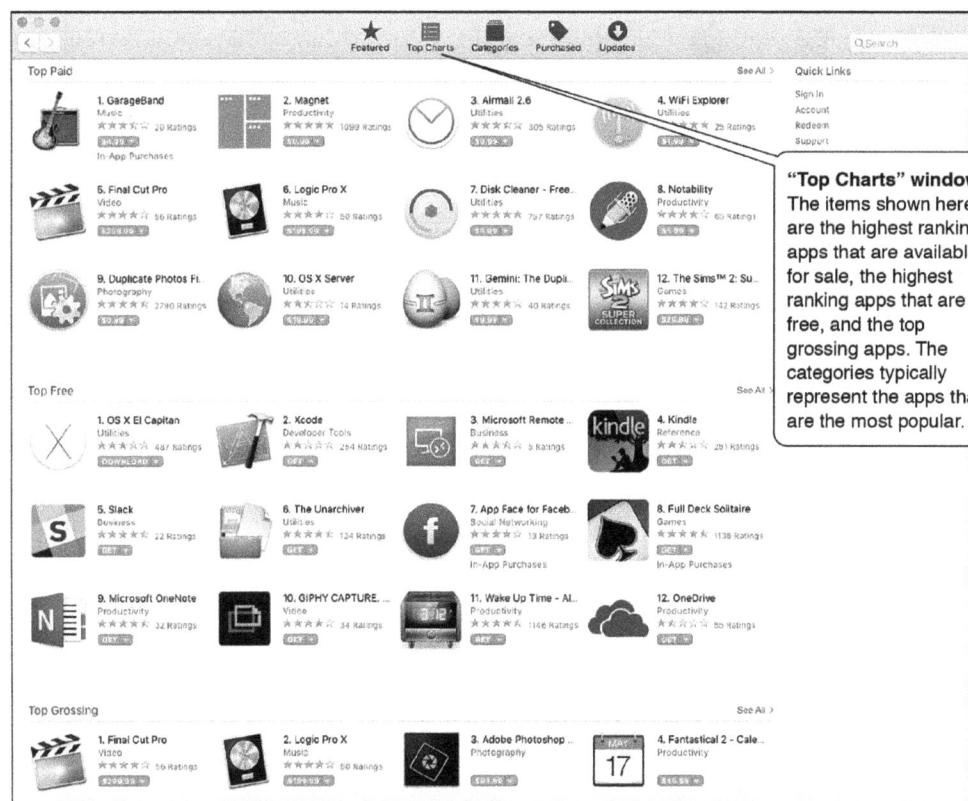

"Top Charts" window
The items shown here are the highest ranking apps that are available for sale, the highest ranking apps that are free, and the top grossing apps. The categories typically represent the apps that are the most popular.

Top Charts Apps

The apps listed here are in three classifications: Top Paid, Top Free, and Top Grossing. These give you a sense of which apps are the most popular. Top Paid apps are those that have been selling the best recently. Top Free apps are those that users have downloaded the most without having to pay for them. Top Grossing apps are those that have been making the most money overall (which can be skewed if an app is expensive).

Categories of Apps

This display window is very helpful if you need an app within a general interest area, but aren't sure what you're looking for. You can select a topic, then browse the apps available for that topic. Each app shows ratings and reviews (if any) from other users, which can provide you with helpful information before you download anything new.

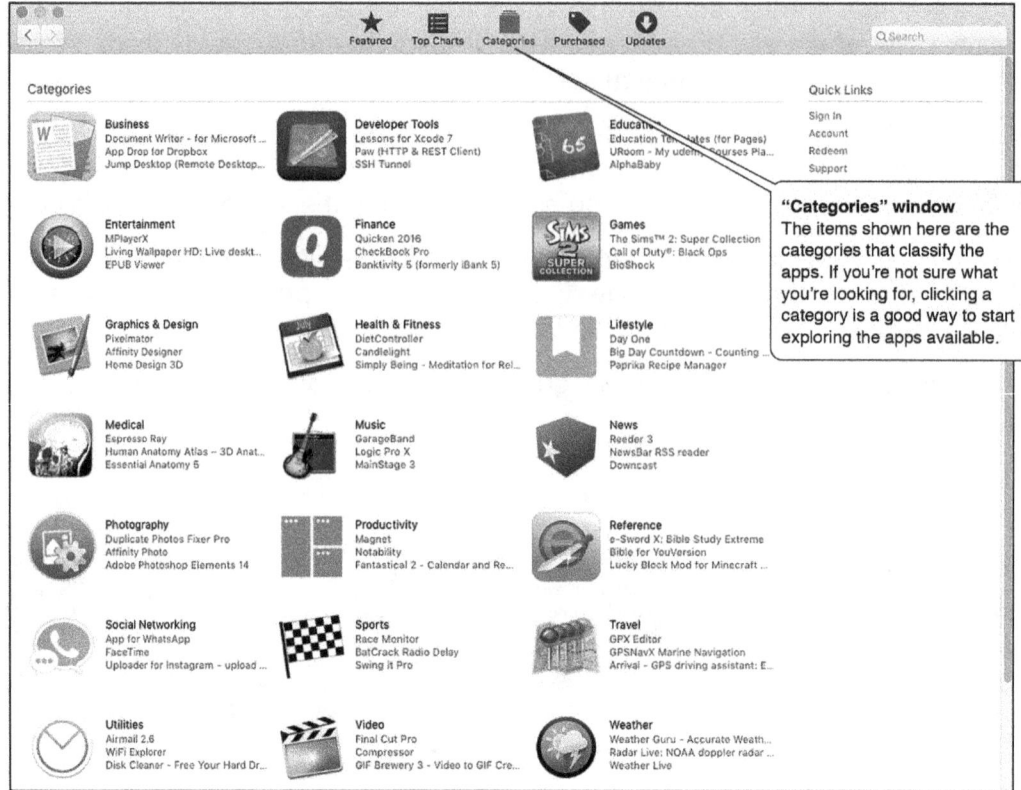

"Categories" window
The items shown here are the categories that classify the apps. If you're not sure what you're looking for, clicking a category is a good way to start exploring the apps available.

"Purchased" window
This window shows all of the apps that you have purchased from Apple's App Store as well as any free apps that you downloaded from the store. If you have put other software on your machine that you did not buy through the App Store, it will not be listed here.

Status Buttons
Each app will have an associated button on the right side of the window:

- DOWNLOAD - clicking this button downloads an app that is not yet on your machine.
- OPEN - Clicking this button simply opens the app in the same way as clicking on it in the Dock.
- PAUSE/RESUME - When an app is downloading, this button will allow you to stop or start the process.
- UPDATE - Apple periodically scans your Mac to see if any apps need updating. If updates are available, clicking this button will download them.

Purchased Apps

This window shows you a list of both purchased and free apps that you have already downloaded for the Apple ID that you're currently logged in as. It's very helpful because it also indicates the date of the app and the status of each on your Mac. You can check here to see if any apps need updating, to open an app, or to download a new app that you've purchased from the App Store but not yet installed on your Mac.

Note that this window will not contain any apps or software that you bought from vendors that are not available on the App Store. For example, Adobe software such as Photoshop or Acrobat is purchased and downloaded directly from Adobe's web site. You'll need to check back with these other vendors to see if these apps need updating.

Running Updates

Updates are smaller fixes or changes to your existing system that keep it current. It's a good idea to check periodically to see if any are available for your Mac. They can often affect the security of your Mac and allow it to function more smoothly.

Updates to Apple and App Store Software

Updates are available through Apple's App Store. To see if your system requires updates, click on the Apple menu in the upper left corner of the Menu Bar. The App Store line will indicate if your system needs updates right on the Apple menu, and will even tell you the number of updates that are available.

To run updates, follow these steps:

1. Click on the Apple icon at the upper left corner of the screen, then select APP STORE. The App Store window will appear.
2. Click on the UPDATES icon at the top of the App Store window. Your Mac will begin analyzing your computer to see which updates are needed, and will list them in the window.

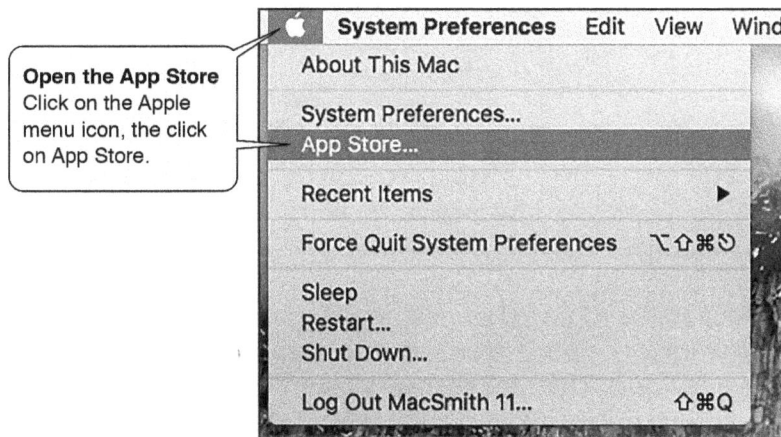

Open the App Store
Click on the Apple menu icon, the click on App Store.

App Store
Apple's App Store is where you can find updates for your Mac's software. New apps and software can also be purchased from the App Store. Select the UPDATES option to see the Updates that are recommended for your Mac.

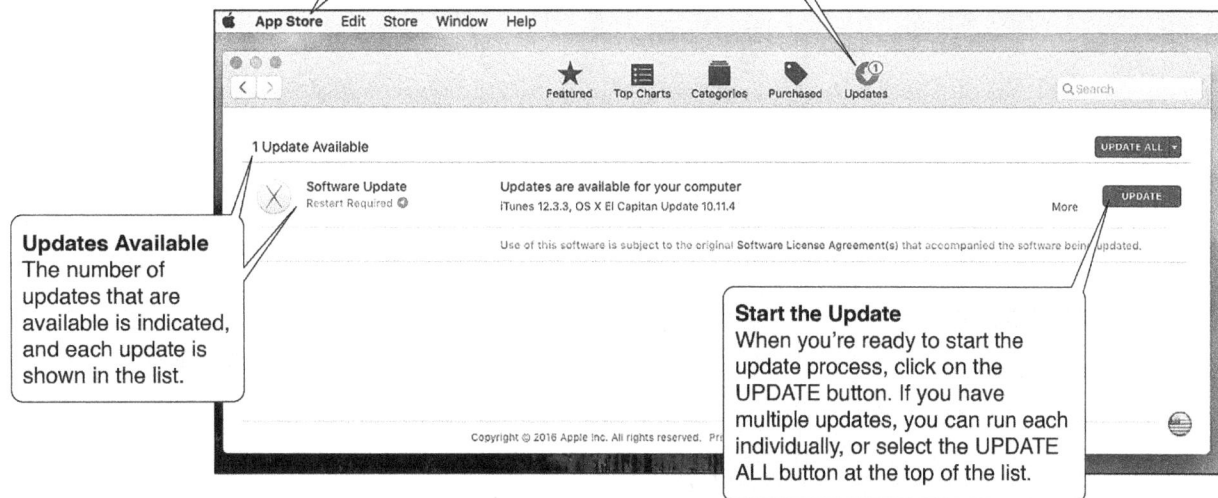

Updates Available
The number of updates that are available is indicated, and each update is shown in the list.

Start the Update
When you're ready to start the update process, click on the UPDATE button. If you have multiple updates, you can run each individually, or select the UPDATE ALL button at the top of the list.

3. Click the START UPDATE button to run an individual update, or to run all of them, click the UPDATE ALL button.
4. If an update requires that you restart your Mac, a drop-down window will appear to let you know. If this is the case, make sure that you have saved any work you've been doing, then quit out of all other programs that are open. This will help expedite the update process.

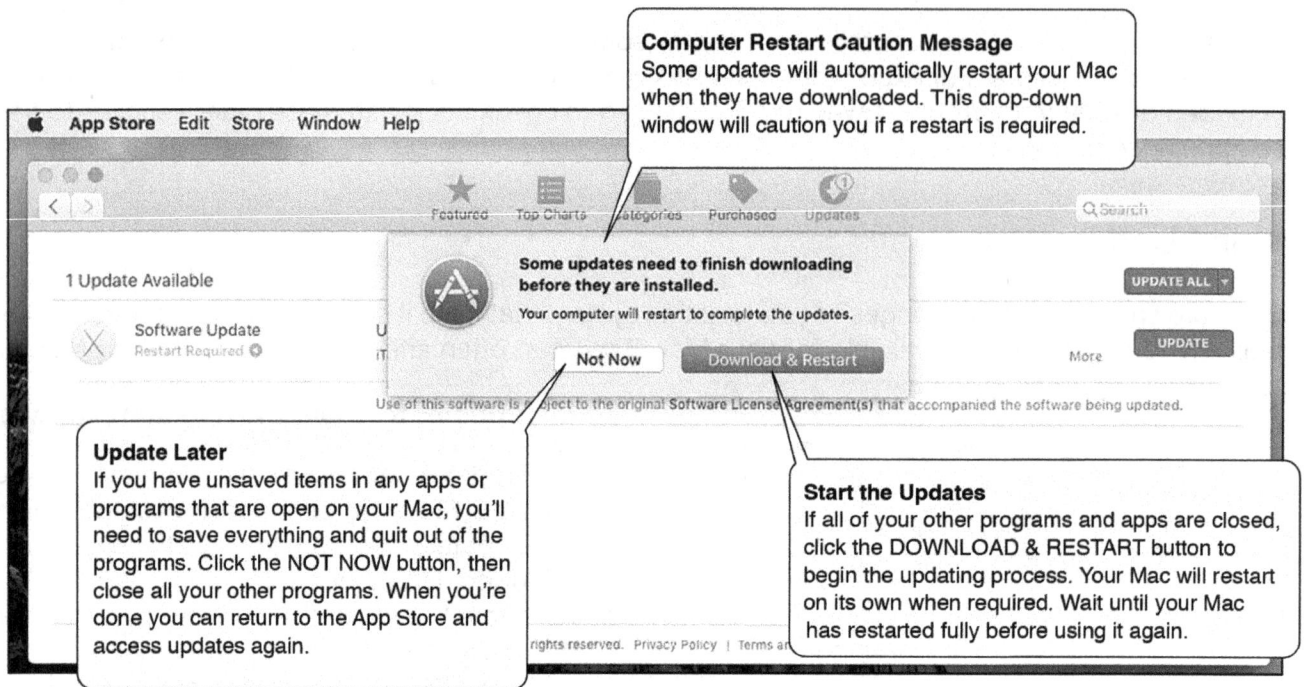

Computer Restart Caution Message
Some updates will automatically restart your Mac when they have downloaded. This drop-down window will caution you if a restart is required.

App Store   Edit   Store   Window   Help

Featured   Top Charts   Categories   Purchased   Updates   Q Search

1 Update Available

Some updates need to finish downloading before they are installed.
Your computer will restart to complete the updates.

Software Update
Restart Required

Not Now   Download & Restart   More

UPDATE ALL ▾

UPDATE

Use of this software is subject to the original Software License Agreement(s) that accompanied the software being updated.

Update Later
If you have unsaved items in any apps or programs that are open on your Mac, you'll need to save everything and quit out of the programs. Click the NOT NOW button, then close all your other programs. When you're done you can return to the App Store and access updates again.

Start the Updates
If all of your other programs and apps are closed, click the DOWNLOAD & RESTART button to begin the updating process. Your Mac will restart on its own when required. Wait until your Mac has restarted fully before using it again.

5. While an update is being downloaded and installed, a progress bar and accompanying information will be displayed. This will give you an idea of how long the update will take to complete. If you need to cancel an update, click on the CANCEL button beside it. The process will stop and you can continue to use your Mac. When you're ready to start the update again, just repeat these steps from the beginning.

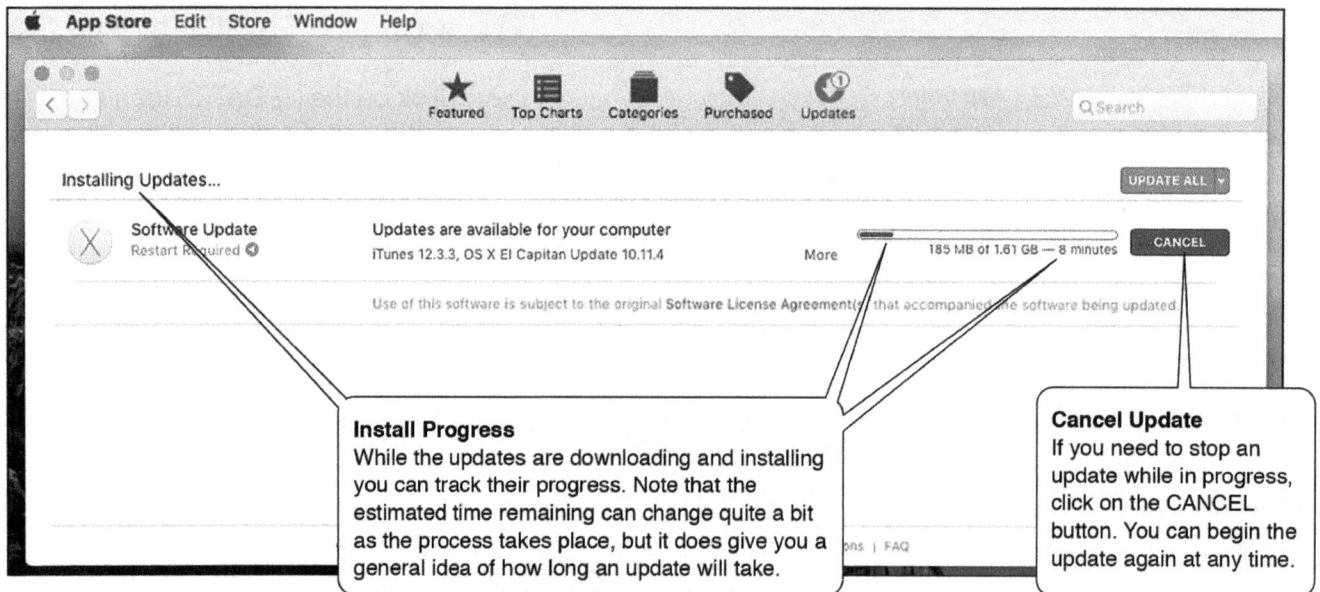

App Store   Edit   Store   Window   Help

Featured   Top Charts   Categories   Purchased   Updates   Q Search

Installing Updates...

Software Update
Restart Required

Updates are available for your computer
iTunes 12.3.3, OS X El Capitan Update 10.11.4   More

185 MB of 1.61 GB — 8 minutes   CANCEL

UPDATE ALL ▾

Use of this software is subject to the original Software License Agreement(s) that accompanied the software being updated.

Install Progress
While the updates are downloading and installing you can track their progress. Note that the estimated time remaining can change quite a bit as the process takes place, but it does give you a general idea of how long an update will take.

Cancel Update
If you need to stop an update while in progress, click on the CANCEL button. You can begin the update again at any time.

6. Wait for your Mac to restart automatically (if needed) then you can begin using it again.
7. When the updates are compete (and your Mac has restarted if necessary) open the Updates window in the App Store one more time (repeat steps 1-3). Review the list of updates that were installed and make sure that nothing else is required (your Mac will indicate if something else is needed).

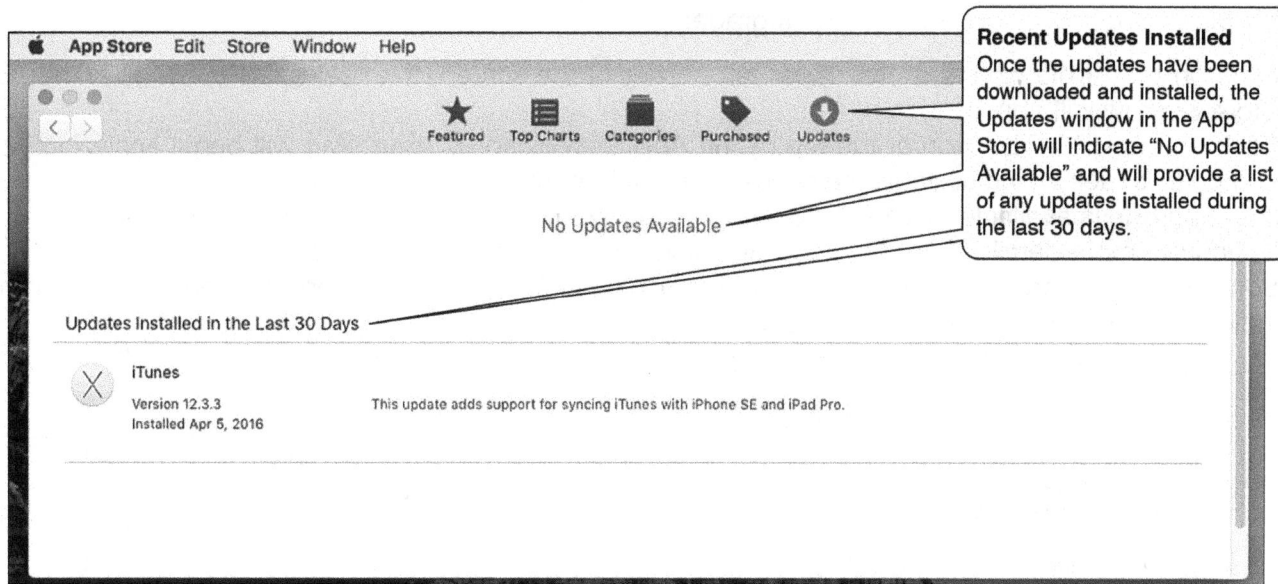

Recent Updates Installed
Once the updates have been downloaded and installed, the Updates window in the App Store will indicate "No Updates Available" and will provide a list of any updates installed during the last 30 days.

Some updates are reliant upon the ones that preceeded them. If you have not run updates for quite a while, you may need to repeat the process two or three times in a row before everything is current. The update process can be a bit time-consuming but it's important to keep your Mac running efficiently.

Updates to Non-App Store Software

Your Mac will indicate when updates are available for software purchased through the App Store. Some software is purchased from other sources, however (for example, Microsoft Office or Adobe Creative Suite products). Sometimes these companies will provide automated messages that you will receive when updates are available, but you may also need to visit the manufacturers' web sites to see if updates are available.

Performing Upgrades

As noted earlier in this chapter, an upgrade is completely different from an update. An upgrade is an entirely new version of software or an operating system. Deciding to upgrade requires some careful thought and usually a bit of research. Considering the following before deciding to upgrade:

*   Does your Mac have sufficient hard drive space or RAM for this upgrade to function effectively? Will the upgrade cause your Mac to run more slowly?
*   Will the new version require that you learn new methods for doing things? How long could this take?
*   Will the new version remove functionality that is important to you?
*   Will the new version still work with your existing software, or will you need to upgrade other things too? Is there an additional cost involved to do this?

Eventually you will need to upgrade your software and operating system simply because the companies that make them cannot continue to support older versions. Security issues are also often addressed with upgrades. Careful research and planning is all that's needed to make your upgrade go smoothly when you do decide that you're ready.

Upgrading the Mac Operating System (OS)

Just as with updates, upgrades to your Mac's operating system (OS) are done through Apple's App Store. And just as with updates, you'll need to use your Apple ID to login to the store and access the upgrade.

Follow these steps when you're ready to upgrade:

1. Click on the Apple icon at the upper left corner of the screen, then select APP STORE. The App Store window will appear.
2. Click on the UPDATES icon at the top of the App Store window. Your Mac will begin analyzing your computer to see which updates are needed, and will list them in the window.
3. If an upgrade is available, a large window announcing it will appear above any other updates.
4. To find out more details about the upgrade, click on the words "Learn More."
5. Some upgrades are free while others require a fee. To begin the upgrade click on the button that indicates either the price or FREE UPGRADE.

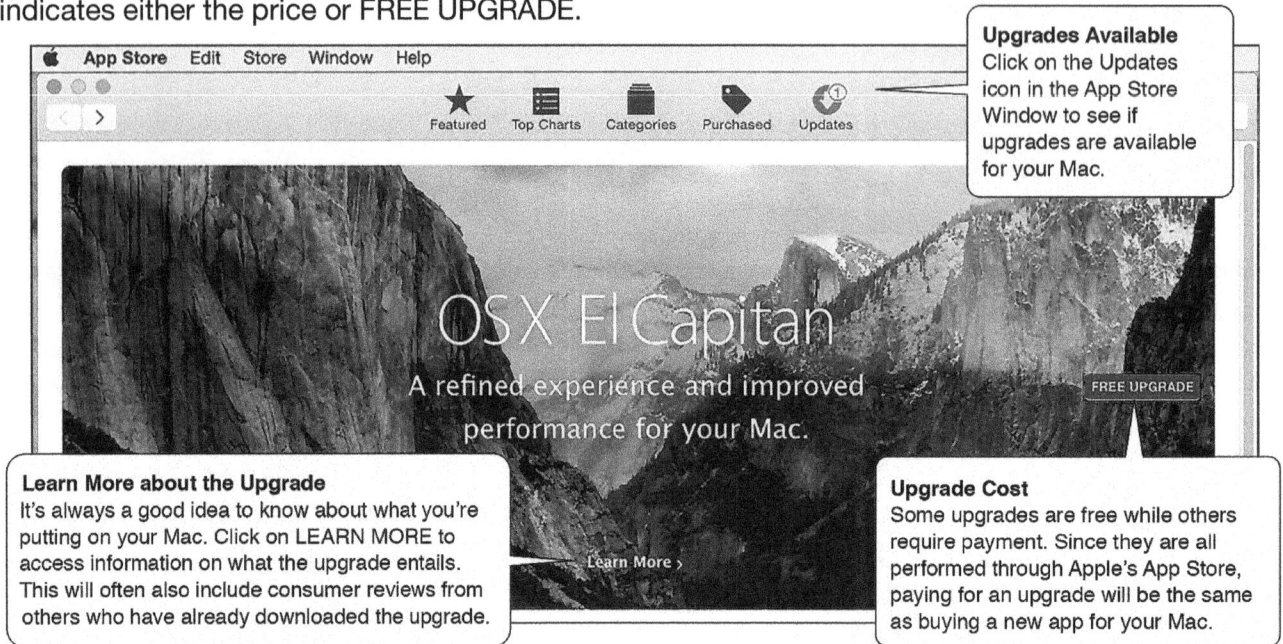

Upgrades Available
Click on the Updates icon in the App Store Window to see if upgrades are available for your Mac.

Learn More about the Upgrade
It's always a good idea to know about what you're putting on your Mac. Click on LEARN MORE to access information on what the upgrade entails. This will often also include consumer reviews from others who have already downloaded the upgrade.

Upgrade Cost
Some upgrades are free while others require payment. Since they are all performed through Apple's App Store, paying for an upgrade will be the same as buying a new app for your Mac.

6. If you have not already logged in with your Apple ID, a drop-down window will appear requesting your ID and password. Enter them in the specified fields and click on the SIGN IN button.
7. The upgrade will begin downloading. Let it finish this process, then follow the prompts to complete the upgrade.

Once the upgrade is complete, give yourself plenty of time to explore any new features and and get used to new functionalities.

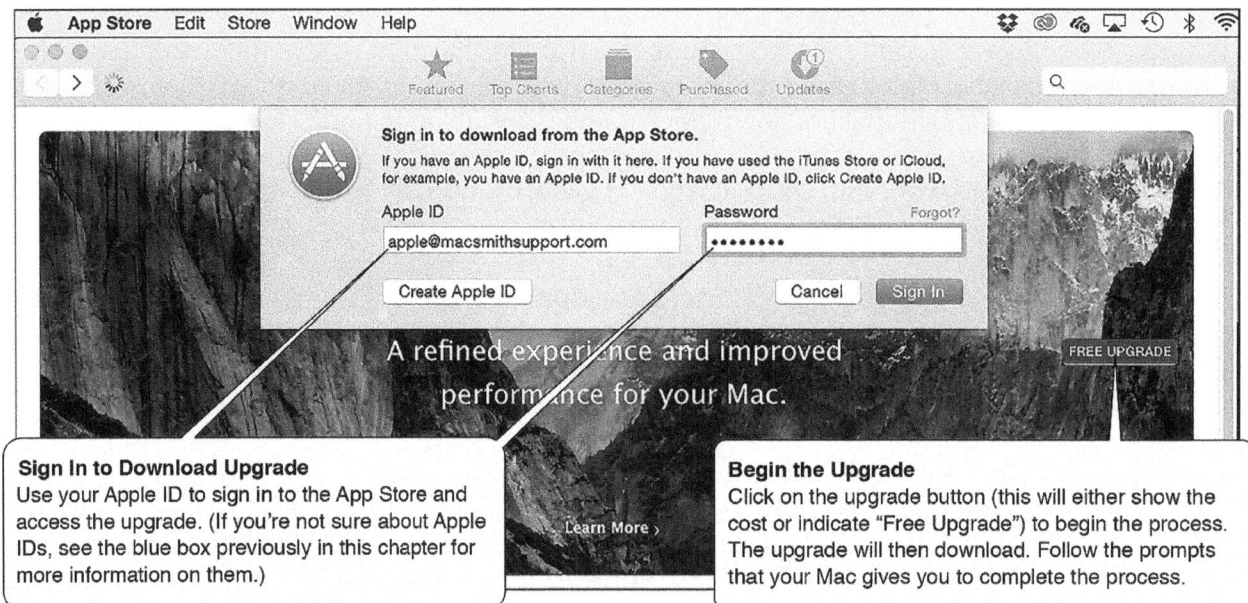

Sign In to Download Upgrade
Use your Apple ID to sign in to the App Store and access the upgrade. (If you're not sure about Apple IDs, see the blue box previously in this chapter for more information on them.)

Begin the Upgrade
Click on the upgrade button (this will either show the cost or indicate "Free Upgrade") to begin the process. The upgrade will then download. Follow the prompts that your Mac gives you to complete the process.

7 – KEEPING YOUR MAC SECURE AND PRIVATE

What's Next in this chapter...

- Understanding Users
- Understanding Keychain
- Security and Privacy

Security and privacy are always a concern, but fortunately Apple has quite a few measures built in that can help. Apple has established a very secure system on your Mac buy enforcing rigorous control over any software and apps that can be downloaded. Apple's operating system has also been developed in a closed environment that makes it more secure. These measures help, but there are other steps that you can take to safeguard your system.

Understanding Users

When you first received your Mac, you probably had a User identity created for you. This is what you use to log in to your Mac. Usually it's your name (or nickname) with a password that you created. Whenever you power up your Mac, you'll see it on a blank screen along with a picture within a circle. When you click on the picture, you are prompted to enter your password. Your Mac then displays the Desktop that you've become familiar with.

Login Screen
When you first power up your Mac, you'll see a login page with your name, a picture that you chose to accompany your name, and a field for entering your password.

MacSmith 11

Enter Password

Creating a New User

Each person who uses your Mac can have their own account. This means that they can log in separately and set up their desktop exactly the way that they want it without affecting the way you have yours set up. These separate accounts are called "Users" because usually each one belongs to its own different user.

Each individual "User" can be given different privileges based on the kind of account that they are given. The account options are:

- **Administrator** - This is the highest level of User available, and has complete control over your Mac. The User that was created for you (or that you created) when you first got your Mac was an Administrator account. An Administrator can add and manage other users, install apps, and change settings. Your Mac can have more than one Administrator level User.
- **Standard** - A Standard User can install apps and change settings for his or her own use, but cannot add other Users or change other Users' settings. Standard Users are set up by an Administrator.

- **Managed with Parental Controls** - Users who are Managed with parental controls can access only the apps and content defined by the Administrator who manages that user. The Administrator can restrict the Managed User's contacts and website access, and place time limits on computer use.
- **Sharing Only** - Sharing-only Users only have permission to access shared files remotely. They cannot log in to your Mac or change any of its settings.
- **Guest** - Guest Users can use your computer temporarily without you having to add new accounts for them as individual Users. Guest Users do not need a password, cannot change any settings, and cannot login remotely. Files created by a Guest User are stored in a temporary folder, but this folder and its contents are deleted when the Guest User logs out.

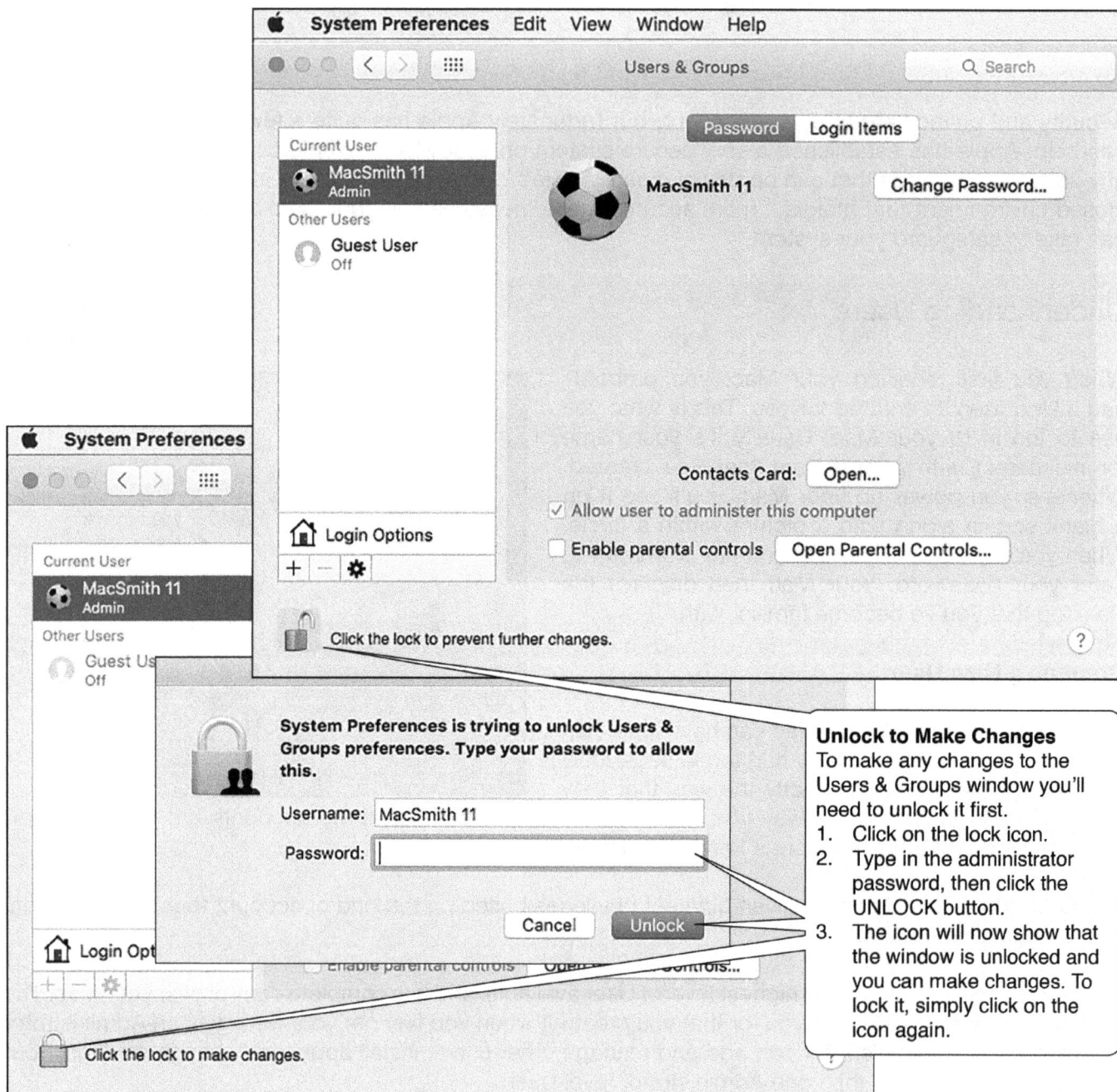

Unlock to Make Changes
To make any changes to the Users & Groups window you'll need to unlock it first.
1. Click on the lock icon.
2. Type in the administrator password, then click the UNLOCK button.
3. The icon will now show that the window is unlocked and you can make changes. To lock it, simply click on the icon again.

To create a new User on your Mac first make sure that you are logged in as an Administrator (usually your main User account that you first set up), then follow these steps:

1. Click on the Apple icon at the upper left corner of the screen, then select SYSTEM PREFERENCES. From this window, select USERS & GROUPS.
2. In the Users & Groups window, click on the lock icon in the lower left corner.
3. In the window that appears, enter the password for your username, then click the UNLOCK button. The icon will now show that your Users & Groups window is unlocked.
4. Click on the plus (+) button to add a new User.
5. In the drop-down window, click on the New Account menu button and select the kind of User that you would like to create.
6. Fill in the remaining information for the username and password. (Note: The password hint will appear after three failed login attempts. This can be helpful if you are not using this account often.)
7. Click the CREATE USER button. The new user will now appear in the "Other Users" section of the Users & Groups window.

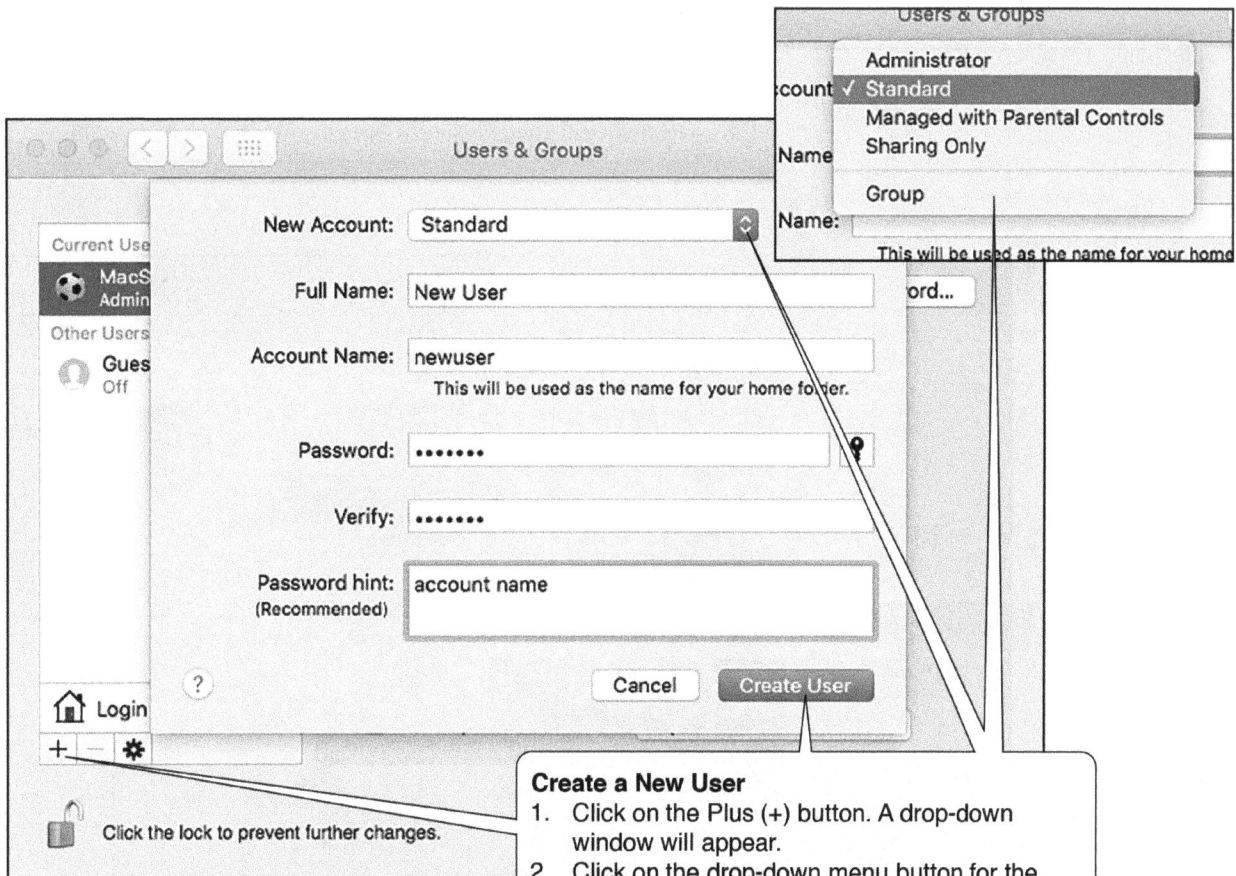

Create a New User
1. Click on the Plus (+) button. A drop-down window will appear.
2. Click on the drop-down menu button for the New Account field, then select the kind of User that you would like to create.
3. Fill in the name and password information on the New Account window, then click the CREATE USER button.
4. The new User will now appear in the "Other Users" list on the Users & Groups window.

Changing a User's Icon Image

Each User that you create on your Mac can have their own individual image that represents them quickly. When the User account is first created, an image is assigned automatically, but changing it is easy. First, make sure that you are logged in as an Administrator, then follow these steps:

1. Click on the Apple icon at the upper left corner of the screen, then select SYSTEM PREFERENCES. From this window, select USERS & GROUPS.
2. In the Users & Groups window, click on the lock icon in the lower left corner.
3. In the window that appears, enter the password for your username, then click the UNLOCK button. The icon will now show that your Users & Groups window is unlocked.
4. In the "Other Users" list on the left side of the Users & Groups window, locate the name of the User whose image you'll be changing and click on it.
5. Click on the image icon for that User that appears in the Users & Groups main window. A drop-down window will appear with a variety of images.
6. Select the image that you would like to use, then click on the DONE button. The new image will now appear for that User.

Change User Icon Image
Selecting different images for each User helps you to locate them easily. Make sure that you are logged in as an Administrator, then follow these steps:
1. Select the User from the "Other Users" list.
2. Select the icon image that appears in the main window area. A drop-down menu will appear with many new images.
3. Click on the image that you would like to use, then click the DONE button.
4. The selected image will now appear with that User's name.

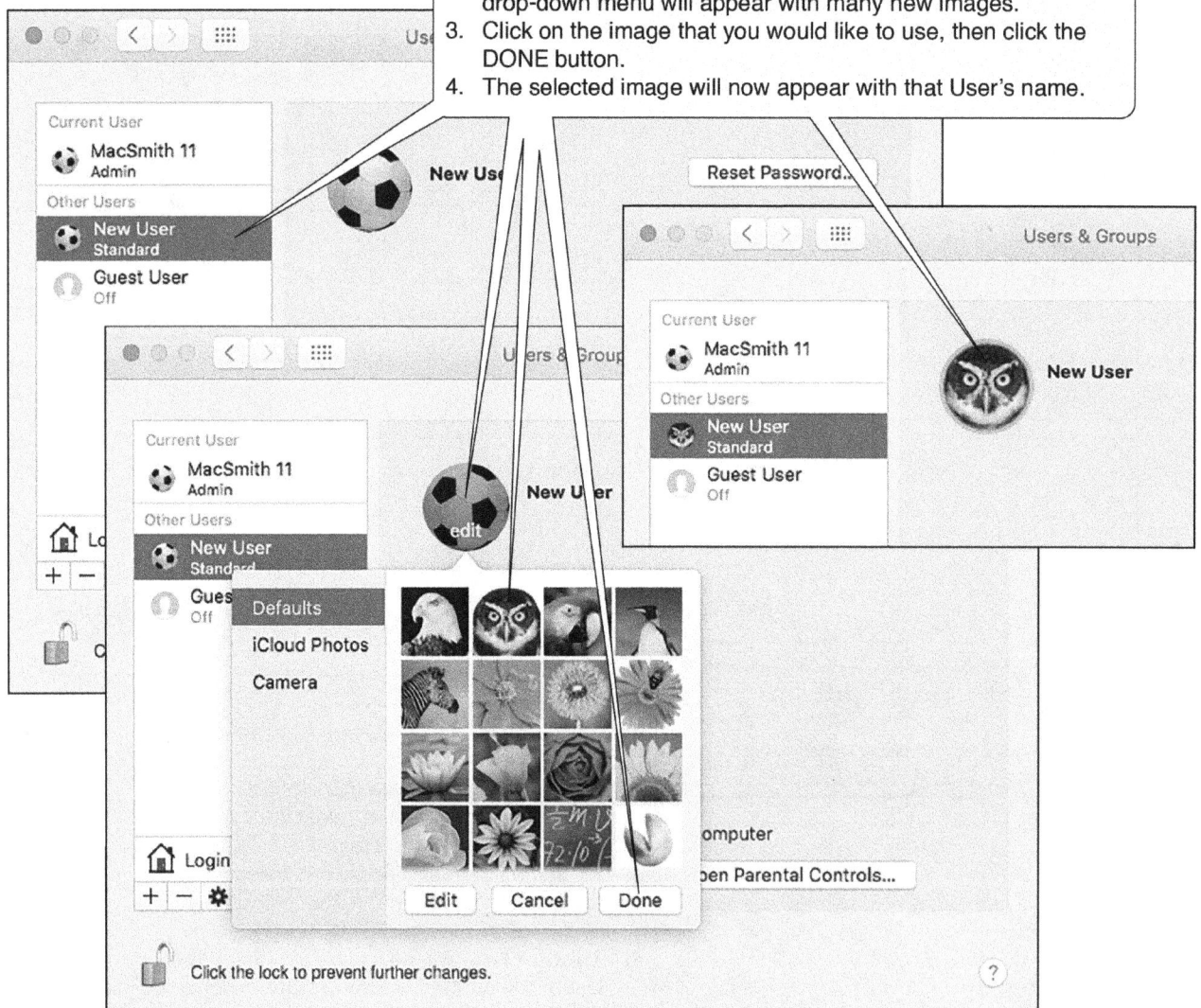

Changing a User Password

You will probably want to set a new password from time to time to ensure that your important data and information remain secure. You can change your password easily with these steps:

1. Click on the Apple icon at the upper left corner of the screen, then select SYSTEM PREFERENCES. From this window, select USERS & GROUPS.
2. In the Users & Groups window, click on the lock icon in the lower left corner.
3. In the window that appears, enter the current password for your username, then click the UNLOCK button. The icon will now show that your Users & Groups window is unlocked.
4. In the Users & Groups window, click on your username from the list on the left so that it is highlighted.
5. Click the CHANGE PASSWORD button.
6. Click in the OLD PASSWORD text field and type in your current password.
7. Click in the NEW PASSWORD text field and type in your new password, then type it in again in the VERIFY field.
8. If you want help remembering your password, type in a hint in the PASSWORD HINT field. The hint will appear after three failed login attempts.

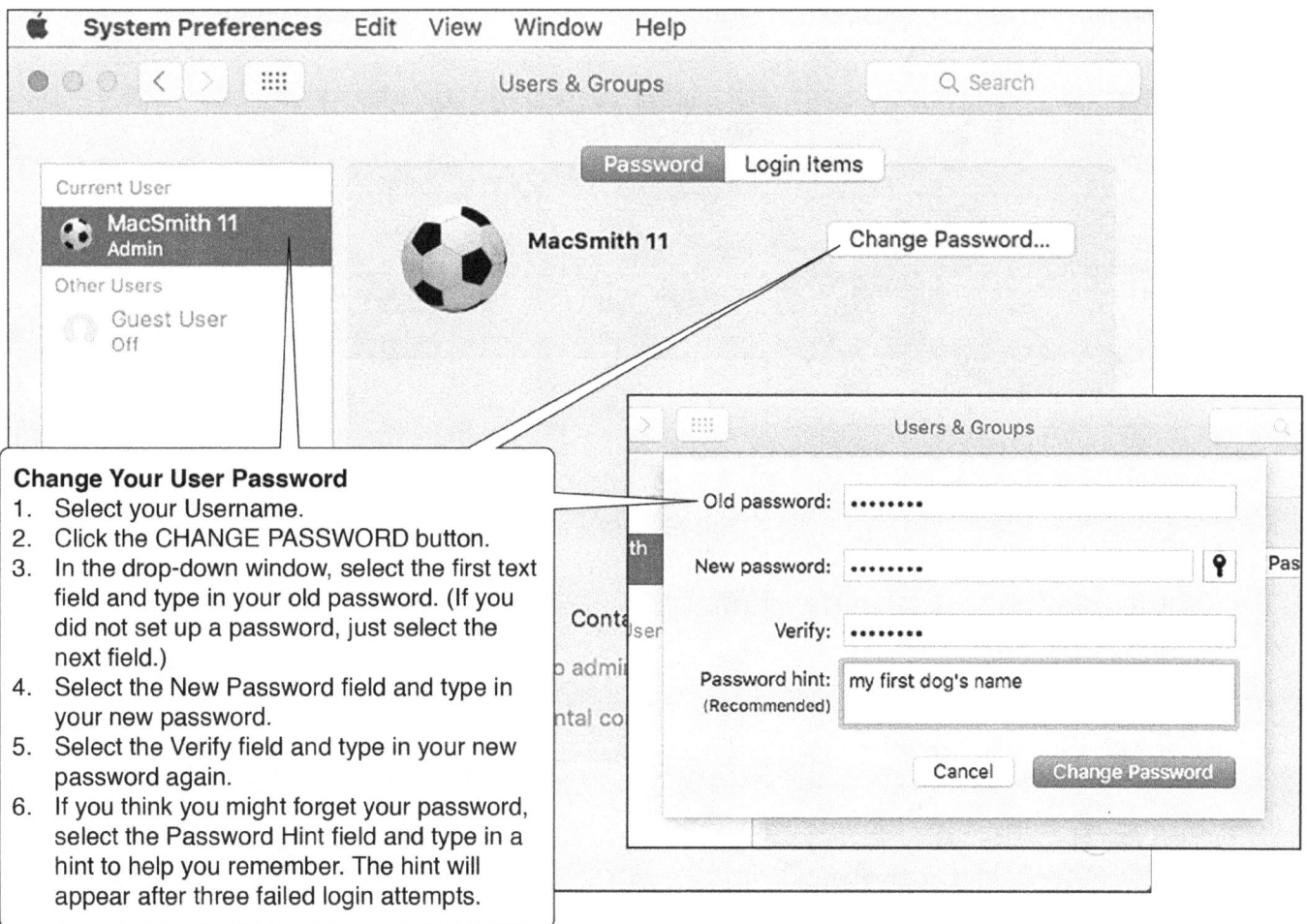

System Preferences Edit View Window Help

Users & Groups

Password Login Items

Current User
MacSmith 11
Admin

MacSmith 11   Change Password...

Other Users
Guest User
Off

Change Your User Password
1. Select your Username.
2. Click the CHANGE PASSWORD button.
3. In the drop-down window, select the first text field and type in your old password. (If you did not set up a password, just select the next field.)
4. Select the New Password field and type in your new password.
5. Select the Verify field and type in your new password again.
6. If you think you might forget your password, select the Password Hint field and type in a hint to help you remember. The hint will appear after three failed login attempts.

Users & Groups

Old password: ••••••••
New password: ••••••••
Verify: ••••••••
Password hint: my first dog's name
(Recommended)

Cancel Change Password

Allowing Another User to Become an Administrator

More than one User can be given Administrator status on your Mac. Think carefully before you implement this option, however. You are giving the other User full access to your Mac, including the ability to change settings, download new software and apps, or even delete items. Some people like to create a secondary Administrator to use simply as a backup in case they forget their password for the first one or in case it becomes corrupt in some way. If you choose to allow another User to become an Administrator, follow these steps:

1. Click on the Apple icon at the upper left corner of the screen, then select SYSTEM PREFERENCES. From this window, select USERS & GROUPS.
2. In the Users & Groups window, click on the lock icon in the lower left corner.
3. In the window that appears, enter the password for your username, then click the UNLOCK button. The icon will now show that your Users & Groups window is unlocked.
4. In the "Other Users" list on the left side of the Users & Groups window, locate the name of the User that you'd like to make an Administrator. Click on that User so that it is highlighted.
5. Click on the checkbox beside "Allow user to administer this computer" so that it is highlighted and a check mark appears.
6. A drop-down window will tell you that the change will not take place until you restart your Mac. You can restart whenever it is convenient for you.

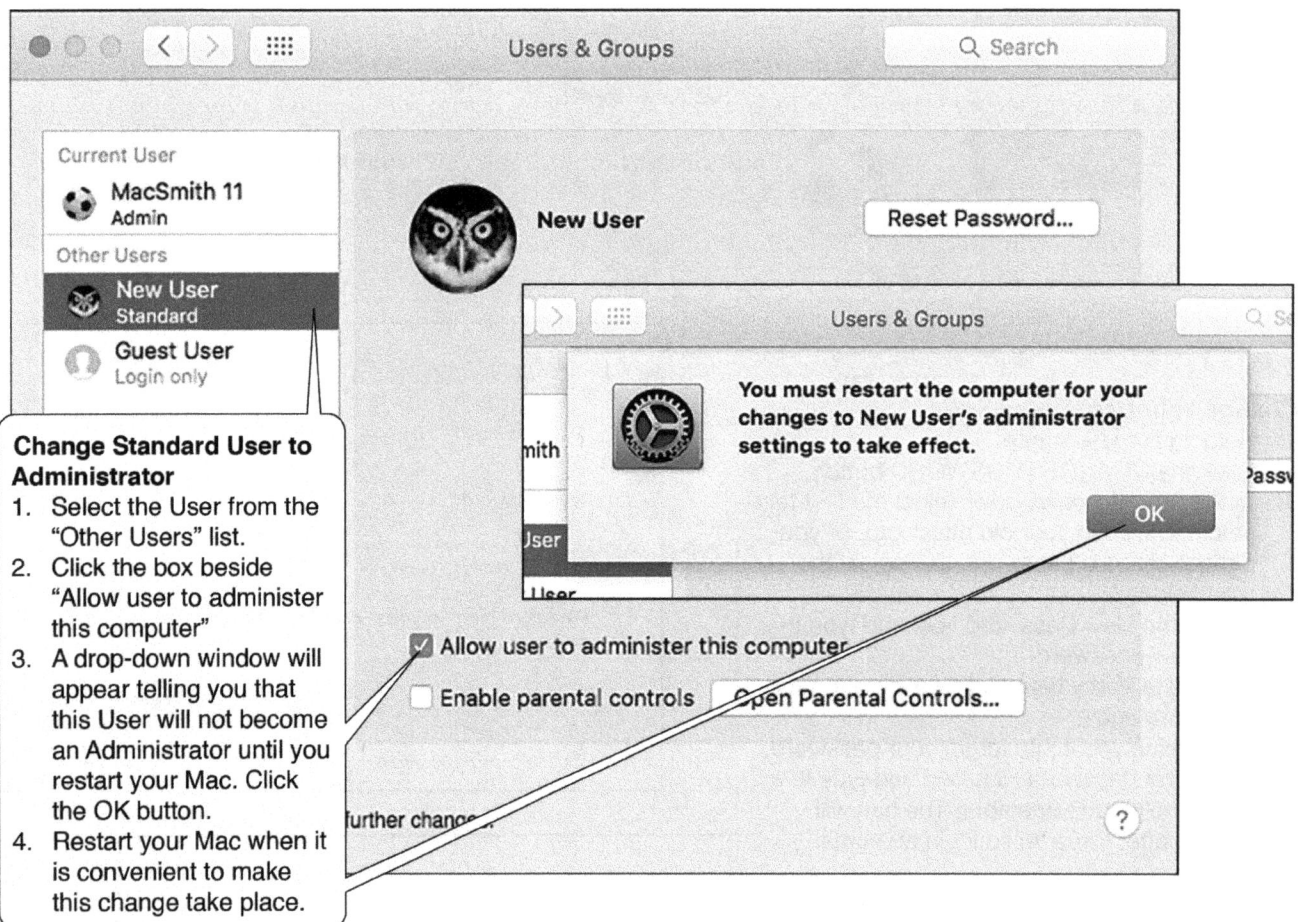

Change Standard User to Administrator
1. Select the User from the "Other Users" list.
2. Click the box beside "Allow user to administer this computer"
3. A drop-down window will appear telling you that this User will not become an Administrator until you restart your Mac. Click the OK button.
4. Restart your Mac when it is convenient to make this change take place.

Logging in a Second User

More than one User can be logged in to your Mac at one time. You may have multiple Users logged in, however only one User's account will be active (that is, only one User's screen will appear on the Desktop) at any one time. To login a second User from the first User's Desktop, follow these steps:

1. Login as you normally would when your computer starts up.
2. Click on the User name at the right side of the Menu Bar (the upper right corner of your screen).
3. From the drop-down menu, click on the name of the second User that you would like to login.
4. A new login screen will appear. Fill in the new User's password and click the arrow button.
5. If this is the first login for the user, you will be asked if you want to sign in with an Apple ID. If you do, check this box, fill in the Apple ID and password, then click the CONTINUE arrow button. If you don't want to sign in with an Apple ID, check the "Don't sign In" box. A pop-up window asking "are your sure?" will appear. Click the SKIP button, and the pop-up window will disappear. Now click the CONTINUE arrow button.
6. The second User's desktop will appear.

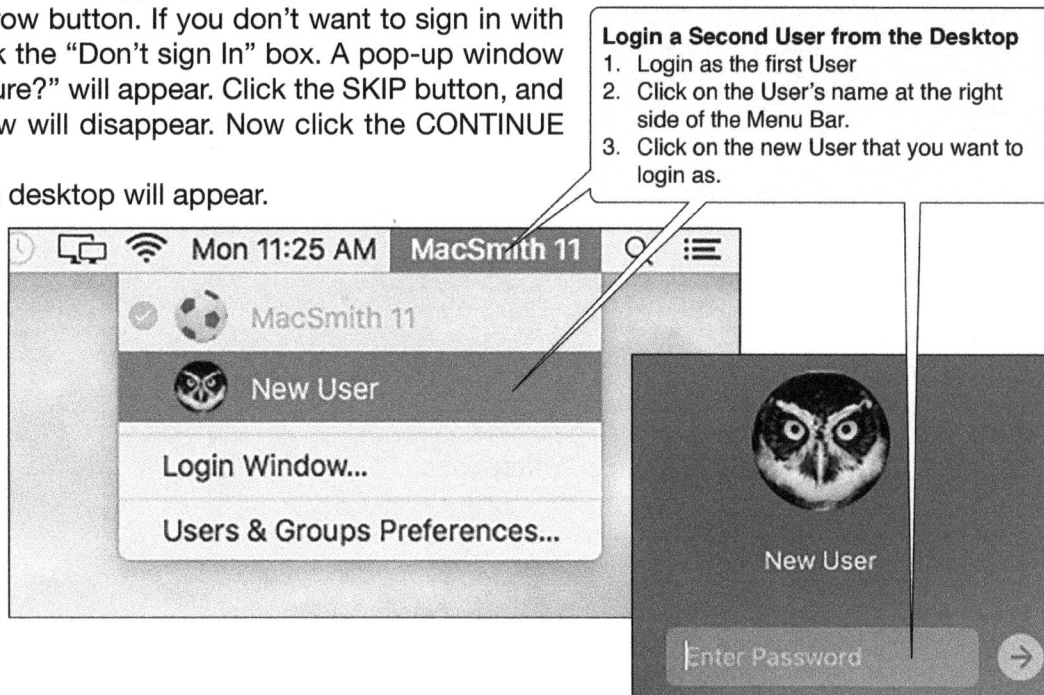

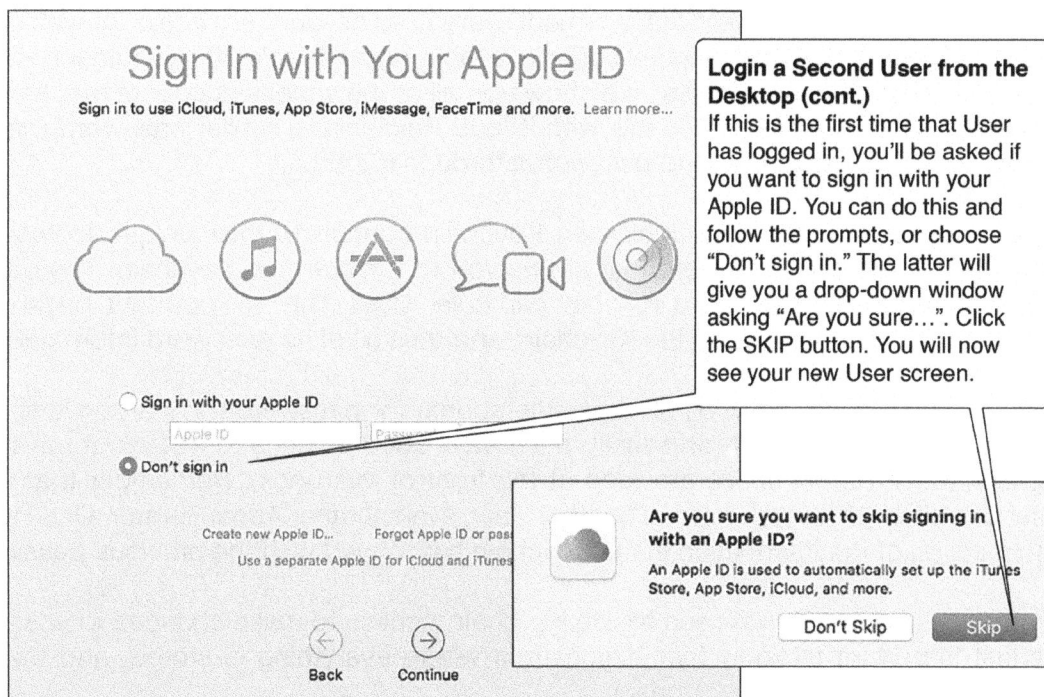

> **Login a Second User from the Desktop**
> 1. Login as the first User
> 2. Click on the User's name at the right side of the Menu Bar.
> 3. Click on the new User that you want to login as.

> **Login a Second User from the Desktop (cont.)**
> If this is the first time that User has logged in, you'll be asked if you want to sign in with your Apple ID. You can do this and follow the prompts, or choose "Don't sign in." The latter will give you a drop-down window asking "Are you sure...". Click the SKIP button. You will now see your new User screen.

Switch Between Users

When a machine has more than one user, you don't need to switch between them by logging out as one, then log in as another. Follow these steps to switch users from your desktop screen:

Switch Between Multiple User Logins
1. Click on the User name at the right side of the Menu Bar.
2. The drop-down menu will show the Users that are logged in. The current user will have a check inside a gold circle.
3. Click on the User that you would like to switch to.
4. If a password is required you will be prompted for it. Otherwise the screen will turn to show the second User's desktop.

1. On the right side of the menu bar, click on the user name.
2. The drop-down will display current users. All logged-in users are shown with a circle and a check mark inside. The user that is currently shown on the screen will be indicated by a gold circle with a check mark inside.
3. Click on the user that you would like to switch to. If the user is logged in, the screen will turn to display the new user's desktop. If the user is not logged in, or a password is required, you'll be prompted for this information.
4. To return to the previous user's desktop, simply repeat the steps above.

Understanding Keychain

Keychain is Apple's password management system. All of your passwords for web sites, networks, servers, etc. are stored in Keychain. An application available in your Mac's Utilities folder (located in the Applications folder) called "Keychain Access" will show you all of the various accounts that have information saved in Keychain. (Note: Don't confuse this with iCloud Keychain, a similar password management system that allows you to access logins and passwords through iCloud.)

Each User on your Mac has their own Keychain containing their unique logins and passwords. Each Keychain has its own password that allows you to "unlock" the Keychain. The password for a Keychain is the same as the password for that particular User. This is important because one User (even an Administrator) cannot access the Keychain, and thus all of its password information, of another User.

Keychain should not be used as your sole source for passwords. It's a convenience that allows you to access secure sites quickly and easily. It's always good practice to write your passwords down in another location (such as the space provided at the front of this book). Remember that any Administrator level User can change the password of another User, even another Administrator. Once this password has been changed, all of the information in the Keychain associated with the previous password is lost.

In most cases you will not need to use Keychain Access to make changes to your password information. It's just important to know that Keychain is where everything is stored, and that no User can access another User's Keychain information.

Opening Keychain Access
1. Click on the FINDER icon in the Dock
2. In the Finder window, click on the APPLICATIONS folder.
3. In the Applications folder, double-click on UTILITIES to open the folder.
4. In the Utilities folder, double-click on KEYCHAIN ACCESS to open the app.

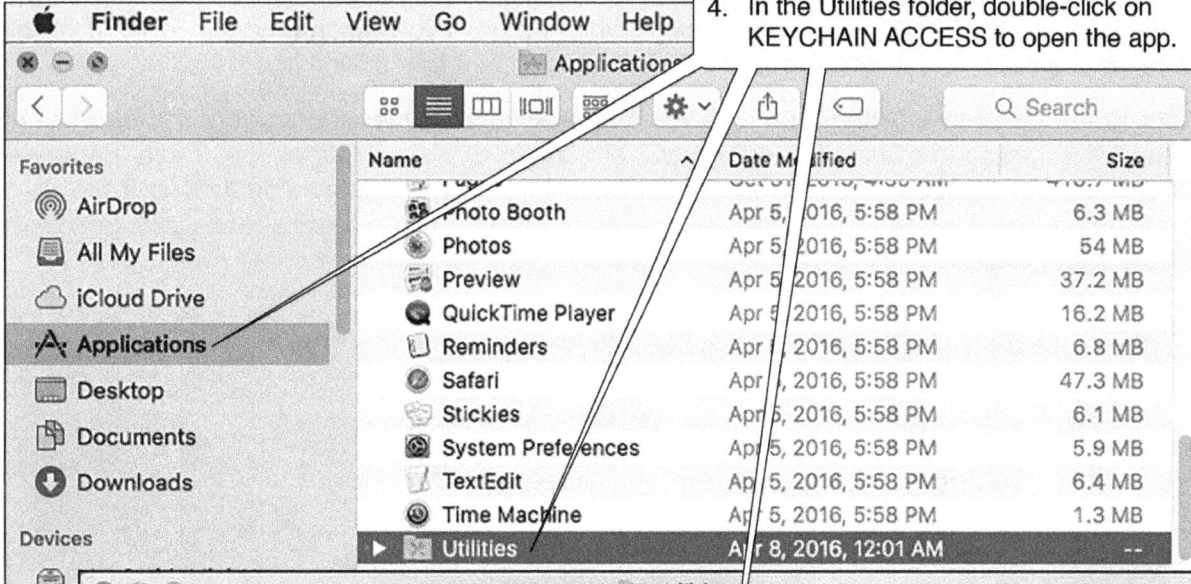

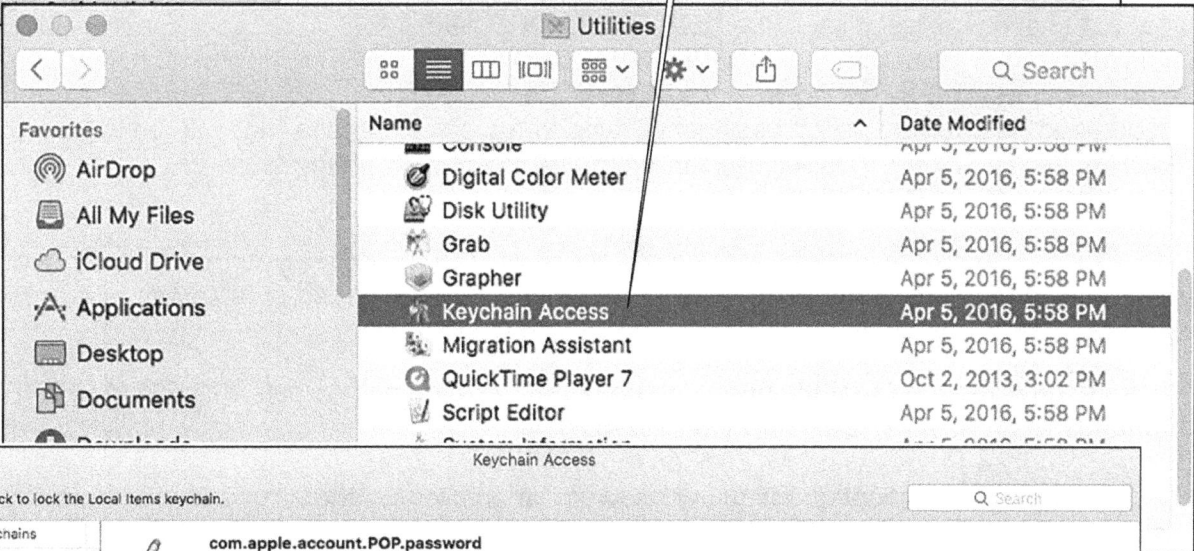

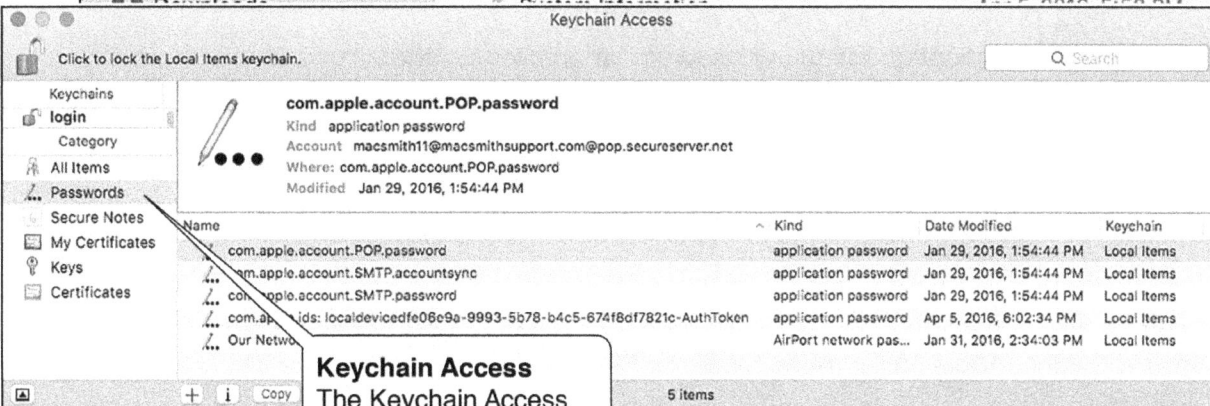

Keychain Access
The Keychain Access application shows information such as the logins that currently have passwords.

General

Passwords can be both helpful and annoying. They keep your system safe, yet they can be tiresome to type in every time you access your Mac. You may be tempted to leave your Mac's password option blank, so that you simply hit the RETURN key rather than typing in a password each time you login. If your Mac is in a secure location and you're comfortable with this option, feel free to use it.

It's important to note, however, that you MUST have an administrator level password in order to unlock and thus make changes to the Security and Privacy options in System Preferences. If you are logged in as an Administrator but do not use a password, your Mac will simply not allow you to unlock the Security and Privacy window. You will need to change your password from nothing to an actual word. Follow these steps to change your password while you are in the Security & Privacy window:

1. Click on the Apple icon at the upper left corner of the screen, then select SYSTEM PREFERENCES. From this window, select SECURITY & PRIVACY.
2. In the Security & Privacy window, click on the GENERAL button.
3. Click the CHANGE PASSWORD button. A drop-down window will appear.
4. Enter your current password in the OLD PASSWORD field. (If you don't have one, just click in the NEW PASSWORD field)
5. Type in your new password in the NEW PASSWORD field.
6. Type in your new password again in the VERIFY field.
7. If you need help remembering passwords, type in a word or phrase that will remind you of it in the PASSWORD HINT field. This will appear after three failed login attempts.
8. Click the CHANGE PASSWORD button.

Your Mac gives you several options for use of your password to access your machine. To require that a password be entered after a set period of time when your Mac is asleep or in screen saver mode, follow these steps:

1. Click on the Apple icon at the upper left corner of the screen, then select SYSTEM PREFERENCES. From this window, select SECURITY & PRIVACY.
2. In the Security & Privacy window, click on the GENERAL button.
3. Check the box that indicates "Require Password" then click on the arrows for the drop-down menu. Select the time period that your Mac will wait before it requires a password to be entered.
4. If you would like a message to appear when someone attempts to access your Mac, check the box beside "Show message when the screen is locked" then click on the SET LOCK MESSAGE button and type in your message.
5. If you want your Mac to require a password each time it is accessed, check the "Disable automatic login" box.

An additional option provided in the General window of Security and Privacy affects the apps that you download to your Mac. Apple has screened and approved all apps that it provides through the App Store, so the "Mac App Store" option is the most secure. Other major developers (such as companies like Adobe or Microsoft) have secure and reliable apps that are safe for you to download, so the "Mac App Store and identified developers" option is generally quite secure but not fully approved by Apple. Many other apps have been developed and are available, but their security could be questionable so click the "Anywhere" option only if you know about the developer who created the app and are comfortable with this downloading option.

Change User Password
1. Click the CHANGE PASSWORD button to access the drop-down window.
2. Type in your current password. (If none, select the New Password field.)
3. Type your new password in both the New Password and Verify fields
4. Type in a password hint to help you remember your password. This will appear after three failed login attempts.
5. Click the CHANGE PASSWORD button on the drop-down window. It will disappear and your new password will now be in effect.

Require Password
1. Click to place a check in the box for "Require password"
2. Click on the arrow button to access the drop-down menu.
3. Click on the time period after which your Mac will require a password for access.

Security & Privacy

Old password: ••••••••

New password: ••••••••

Verify: ••••••••

Password hint: my first dog's name
(Recommended)

Cancel   Change Password

Security & Privacy

General   FileVault   Firewall   Privacy

immediately
5 seconds
1 minute
5 minutes
✓ 15 minutes
1 hour
4 hours
8 hours

A login password has been set for this user   Change Password...

☑ Require password 15 minutes after sleep or screen saver begins

☑ Show a message when the screen is locked   Set Lock Message...

☐ Disable automatic login

Set Lock Message
This option will display a message on your Mac's screen when it is locked.
1. Click the SET LOCK MESSAGE button.
2. Enter the message that you would like your Mac to display when it is locked, then click the OK button.

Security & Privacy

Set a message to appear on the lock screen:

This Mac is currently locked. Please contact the owner for access.

Cancel   OK

Allow apps downloaded from:
○ Mac App Store
◉ Mac App Store and identified developers
○ Anywhere

Automatic Login
Check this box if you do not want your Mac to log you in automatically. Your Mac will require you to enter a password each time it is accessed.

Click the lock to prevent further changes.

Unlock the Window
Make sure that you have unlocked the page to change settings. If the page is locked, click the lock icon, then enter your Administrator level password. You cannot unlock the Security & Privacy window if you are using a blank password.

Downloading Apps
- "Mac App Store" - This option only allows downloads from the App Store
- "... and identified developers" - This option allows downloads from the App Store as well as other major software developers that Apple deems safe.
- "Anywhere" - This option allows downloads from any developer and is the least secure.

FileVault

FileVault is an application that encrypts the information on your Mac. It provides an extra level of security beyond your username and password, and is useful if you store sensitive information on your Mac. When FileVault is set up on your Mac it will ask you to create a master password and recovery key for the computer. If you forget your User password, the master password can be used to access the files instead.

This may sound like a great idea, but there are two important things to consider. First, if you forget the master password along with the User login information you have lost all access to any of your files, applications, and software currently residing on your computer. Breaking through File Vault to regain this information can be done, but it is extremely difficult and will most likely be expensive. Second, FileVault may slow down the overall performance of your Mac. For these reasons, think carefully as to whether or not you really need to use FileVault.

The main FileVault page comes with a warning:

> **WARNING: You will need your login password or a recovery key to access your data. A recovery key is automatically generated as part of this setup. If you forget both your password and recovery key, the data will be lost.**

They are not kidding. If you choose to turn on FileVault, DO NOT lose your login password or recovery key. Write them down at the front of this book.

FileVault is now automatically turned on when you first set up your Mac although you are given the option to turn it off. You can do so during the initial setup process, or follow the steps below. It's also recommended to turn off FileVault if you are upgrading to the next operating system on your Mac.

To turn on FileVault, follow these steps:

1. Click on the Apple icon at the upper left corner of the screen, then select SYSTEM PREFERENCES. From this window, select SECURITY & PRIVACY.
2. In the Security & Privacy window, click on the lock icon in the lower left corner.
3. In the window that appears, enter the password for your username, then click the UNLOCK button. The icon will now show that your Security & Privacy window is unlocked.
4. Click on the FILEVAULT button to access FileVault options.
5. Click the TURN ON FILEVAULT button.

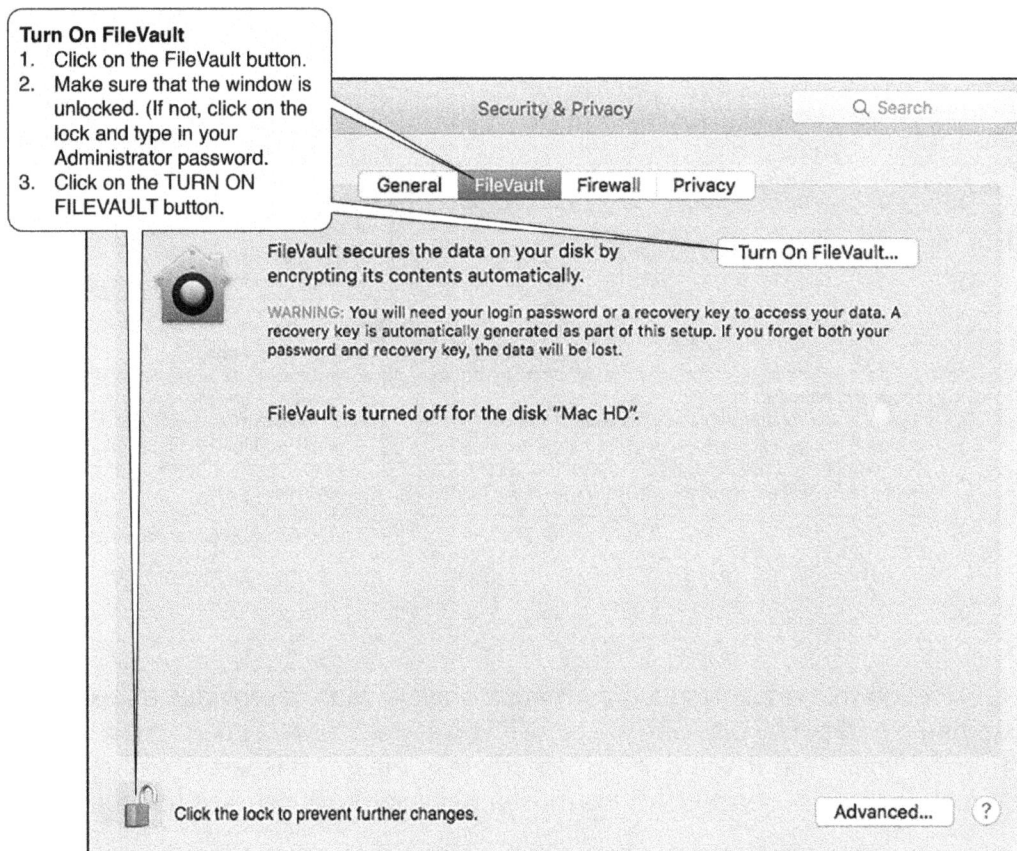

Turn On FileVault
1. Click on the FileVault button.
2. Make sure that the window is unlocked. (If not, click on the lock and type in your Administrator password.
3. Click on the TURN ON FILEVAULT button.

Security & Privacy

General | FileVault | Firewall | Privacy

FileVault secures the data on your disk by encrypting its contents automatically.

Turn On FileVault...

WARNING: You will need your login password or a recovery key to access your data. A recovery key is automatically generated as part of this setup. If you forget both your password and recovery key, the data will be lost.

FileVault is turned off for the disk "Mac HD".

Click the lock to prevent further changes.

Advanced...

6. A message may appear asking if you want to set up your iCloud account to reset your password. If you do, select this option and follow the prompts. Otherwise, select the option to create a recovery key.
7. A new window will appear containing the automatically generated recovery key. It is critical that you write this down (do not write it in a file on your computer!) and keep it in a place that you will remember and can easily access later. When you have done this, click the CONTINUE button.

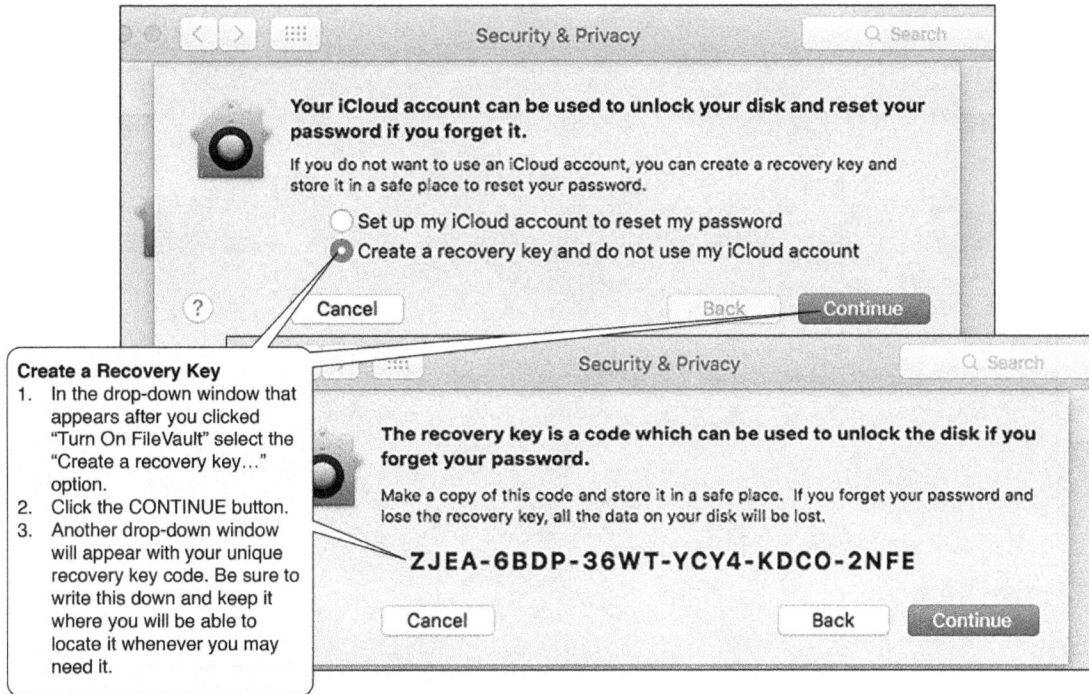

Create a Recovery Key
1. In the drop-down window that appears after you clicked "Turn On FileVault" select the "Create a recovery key…" option.
2. Click the CONTINUE button.
3. Another drop-down window will appear with your unique recovery key code. Be sure to write this down and keep it where you will be able to locate it whenever you may need it.

ZJEA-6BDP-36WT-YCY4-KDCO-2NFE

8. If your Mac has more than one User, a window will appear requesting the password for each user. Click the "Enable User" button beside each User's name. A drop-down window will appear requesting the User's password. Enter it and click the OK button.

9. When all Users have been enabled, click the CONTINUE button.

10. A new drop-down window will appear requesting that you restart your Mac. Click the RESTART button.

11. When your Mac restarts, the FileVault window will now show an Encrypting status bar which will indicate when the encryption process is complete. This Process will most likely take quite a while and will slow down your Mac.

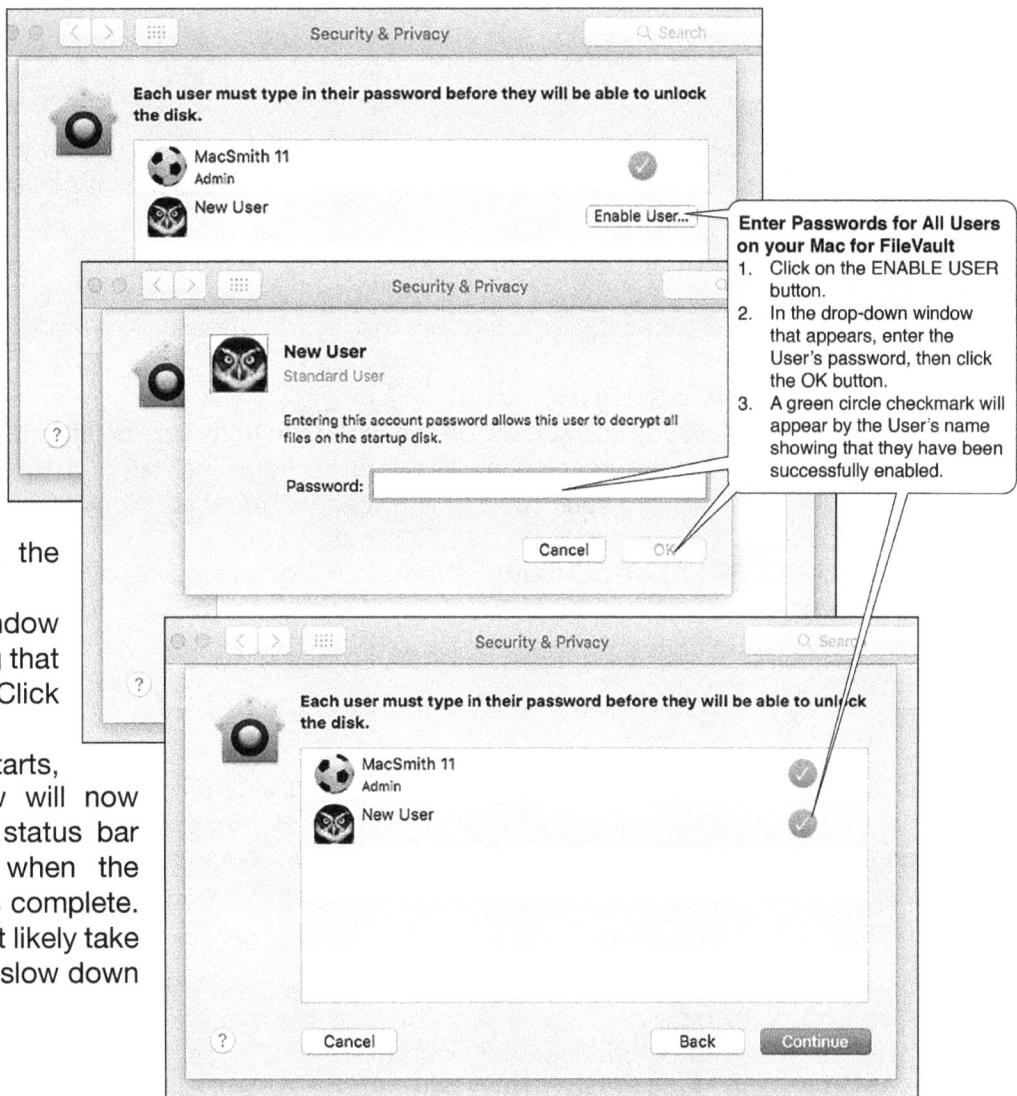

Enter Passwords for All Users on your Mac for FileVault
1. Click on the ENABLE USER button.
2. In the drop-down window that appears, enter the User's password, then click the OK button.
3. A green circle checkmark will appear by the User's name showing that they have been successfully enabled.

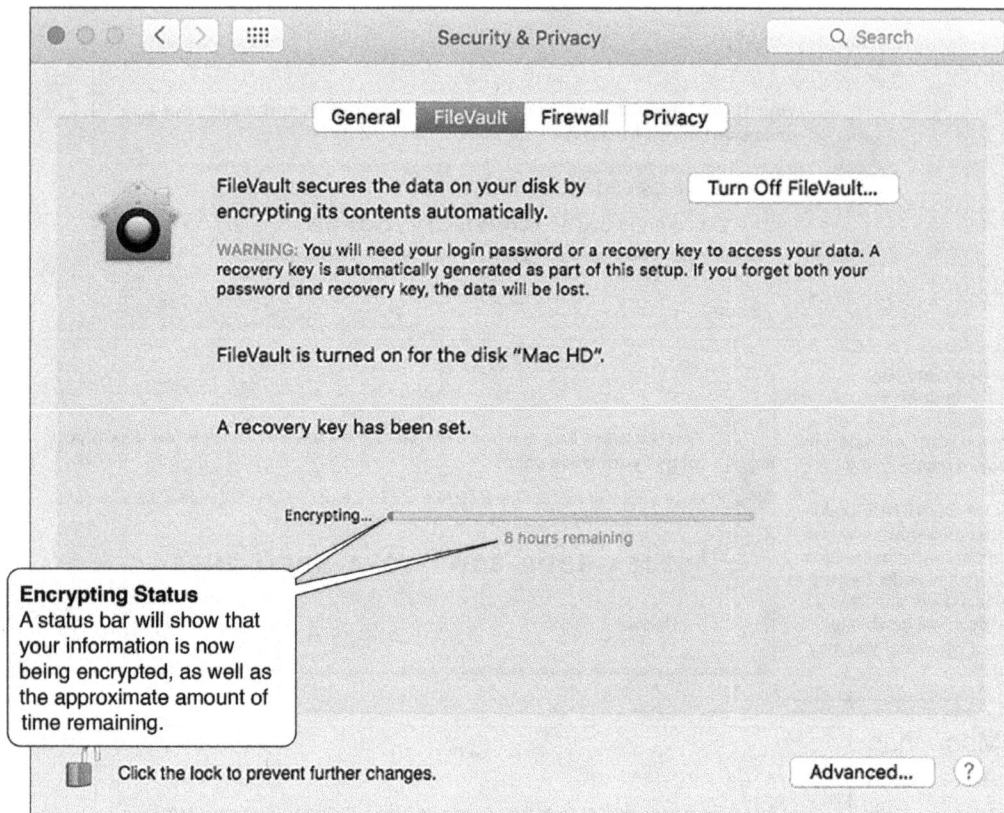

Encrypting Status
A status bar will show that your information is now being encrypted, as well as the approximate amount of time remaining.

If FileVault seems to become stuck during the encryption process, you may need to get assistance in resetting your system. Since any problems may be specific to your Mac it's best to contact Apple Support directly at support.apple.com.

To turn off FileVault follow these steps:

1. Open System Preferences by clicking on the Apple drop-down menu, then selecting SYSTEM PREFERENCES.
2. Click on the SECURITY & PRIVACY icon.
3. In the Security & Privacy window, click on the lock icon in the lower left corner.
4. In the window that appears, enter the password for your username, then click the UNLOCK button. The icon will now show that your Security & Privacy window is unlocked.
5. Click on the FILEVAULT button to access FileVault options.
6. Click the TURN OFF FILEVAULT button (Note: this process may take some time since all of your data is being unencrypted).
7. Restart your Mac.

Firewall

A Firewall is a security system on your Mac that blocks unauthorized access. It allows you to access the outside world, but prevents any to you from the outside unless you've given prior approval. The firewall system on your Mac allows you to enable the firewall and have it apply to everything, or you can apply different firewall settings to individual apps and specific software so that you can block some while leaving others open.

By default, your Mac's firewall is turned off. Many security experts say that for the average computer user, a firewall doesn't really offer much protection beyond the systems that are already in place. It can also interfere with some of the operations of your software and apps. However, if you feel more comfortable having it turned on, the steps are explained here.

To turn on the full system firewall, follow these steps:

1. Click on the Apple icon at the upper left corner of the screen, then select SYSTEM PREFERENCES. From this window, select SECURITY & PRIVACY.
2. In the Security & Privacy window, click on the lock icon in the lower left corner.
3. In the window that appears, enter the password for your username (the one that you use to login to your Mac), then click the UNLOCK button. The icon will now show that your Security & Privacy window is unlocked.
4. Click on the FIREWALL button at the top of the window.
5. Click the TURN ON FIREWALL button.
6. The window will now indicate "Firewall: On" along with a green dot.

Turn On Firewall
1. Make sure that your window is unlocked. (If not, click the lock and type in your password at the prompt.)
2. Click the FIREWALL button.
3. Click the TURN ON FIREWALL button.
4. The window will now indicate "Firewall: On" with a green dot.

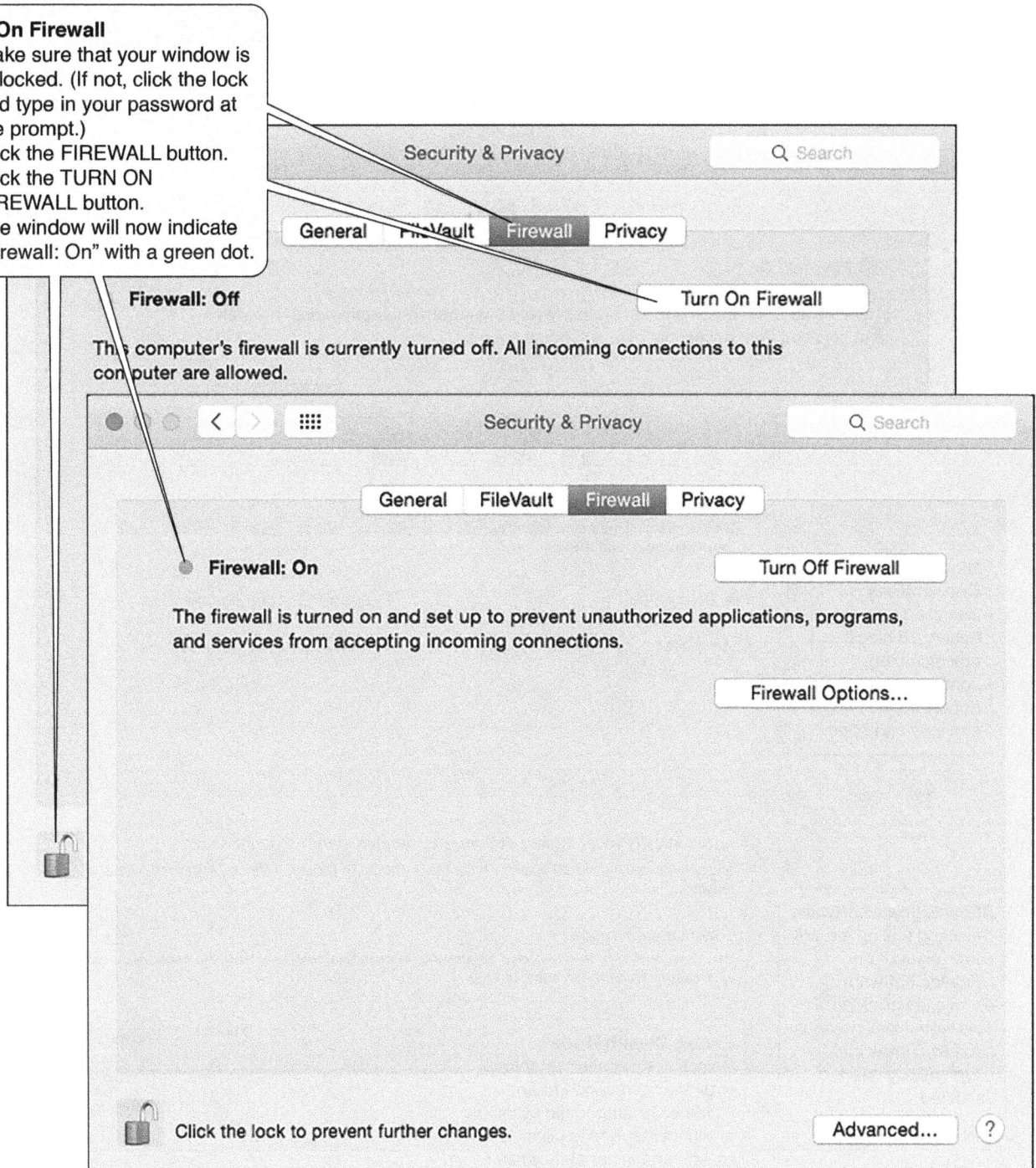

Security & Privacy   Q Search

General   FileVault   Firewall   Privacy

Firewall: Off   Turn On Firewall

This computer's firewall is currently turned off. All incoming connections to this computer are allowed.

Security & Privacy   Q Search

General   FileVault   Firewall   Privacy

Firewall: On   Turn Off Firewall

The firewall is turned on and set up to prevent unauthorized applications, programs, and services from accepting incoming connections.

Firewall Options...

Click the lock to prevent further changes.   Advanced...   ?

To access more specific settings, Click the FIREWALL OPTIONS button. A drop-down window will provide the following options:

- BLOCK ALL INCOMING CONNECTIONS - Checking this option prevents all sharing services, such as File Sharing and Screen Sharing from receiving incoming connections. If you use sharing services, don't select this option.
- AUTOMATICALLY ALLOW SIGNED SOFTWARE TO RECEIVE INCOMING CONNECTIONS - Some software and apps have been previously validated or "signed" (a good example is iTunes). By checking this option you are allowing these items to connect to your Mac automatically. If an app is unsigned, your Mac will prompt you with a window asking if you want to allow or deny the connection. If you choose allow, your Mac will add it to the signed list so that you won't be prompted with the question again.
- ENABLE STEALTH MODE - Some unauthorized apps can send queries to your Mac in order to detect it. Stealth Mode makes your Mac invisible to these. Authorized apps will still have access to your machine.

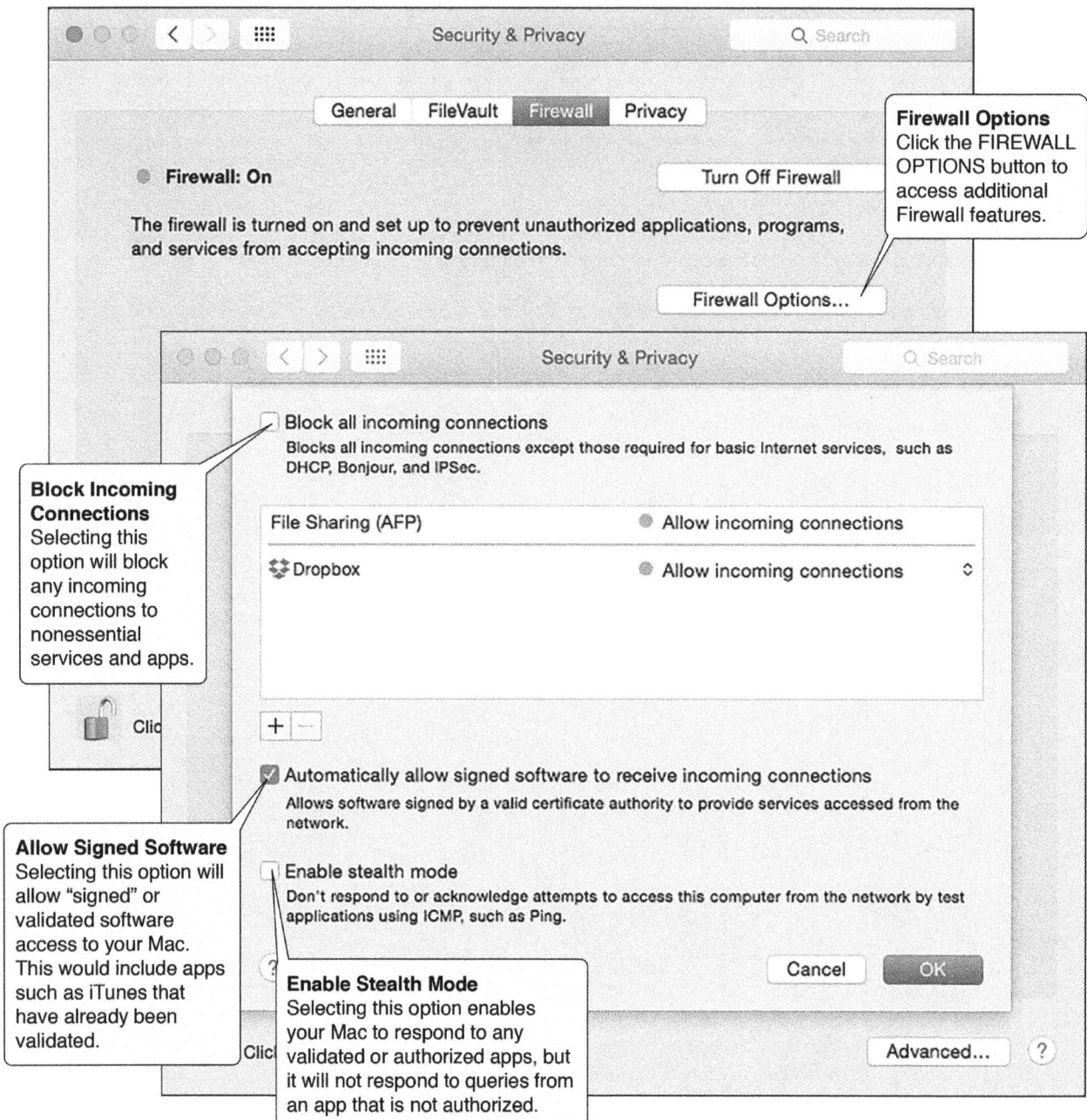

Firewall Options
Click the FIREWALL OPTIONS button to access additional Firewall features.

Block Incoming Connections
Selecting this option will block any incoming connections to nonessential services and apps.

Allow Signed Software
Selecting this option will allow "signed" or validated software access to your Mac. This would include apps such as iTunes that have already been validated.

Enable Stealth Mode
Selecting this option enables your Mac to respond to any validated or authorized apps, but it will not respond to queries from an app that is not authorized.

84

In Firewall Options you can also control access to specific apps on your Mac. Select the app on the list, then click on the drop-down list arrow to either allow or block incoming connections.

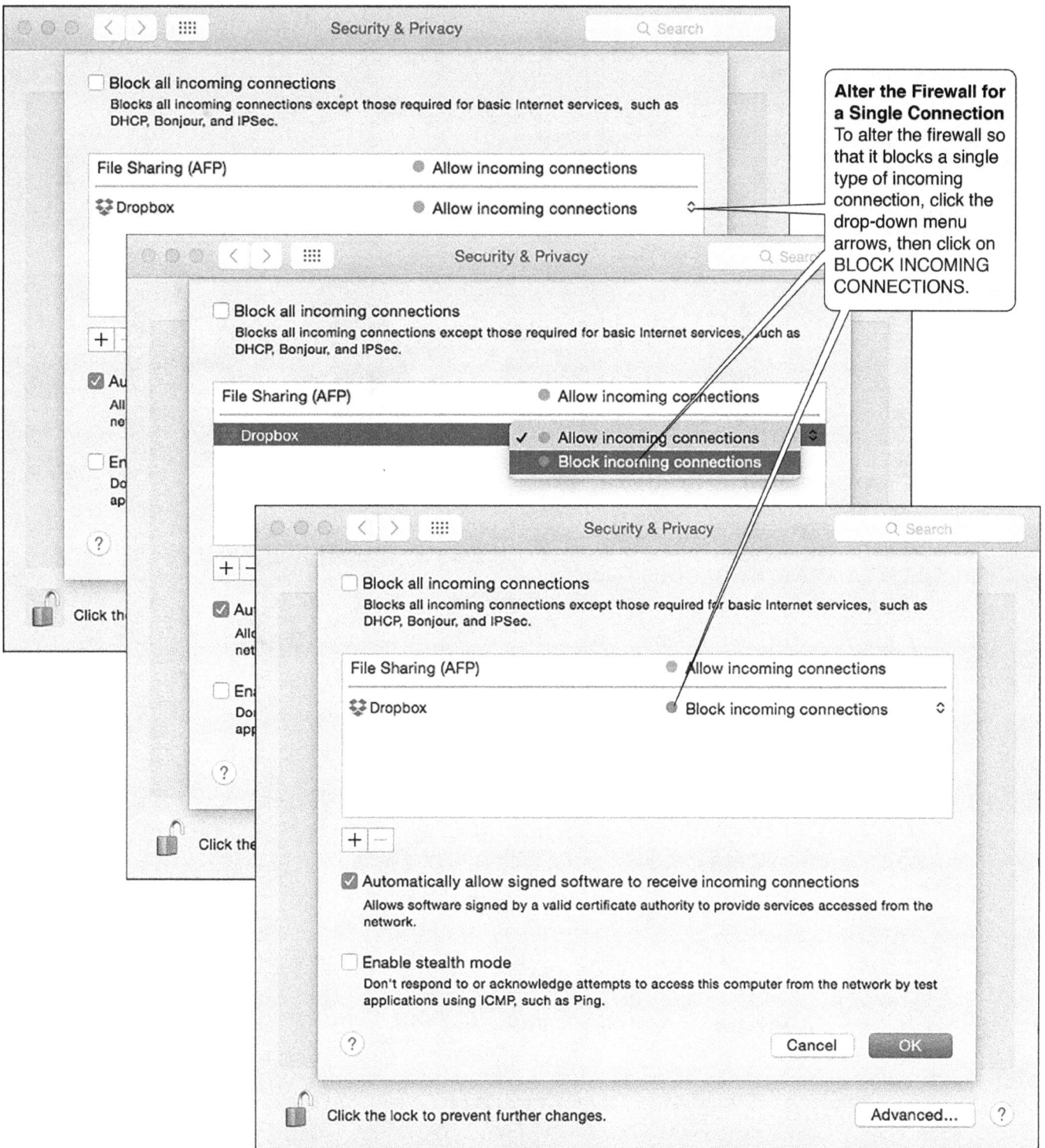

Alter the Firewall for a Single Connection
To alter the firewall so that it blocks a single type of incoming connection, click the drop-down menu arrows, then click on BLOCK INCOMING CONNECTIONS.

To add more apps to the list, click on the plus (+) sign, navigate through the drop-down Finder window to locate the app that you want, then click the ADD button. To delete items from the list, select the app, then click on the minus (-) button.

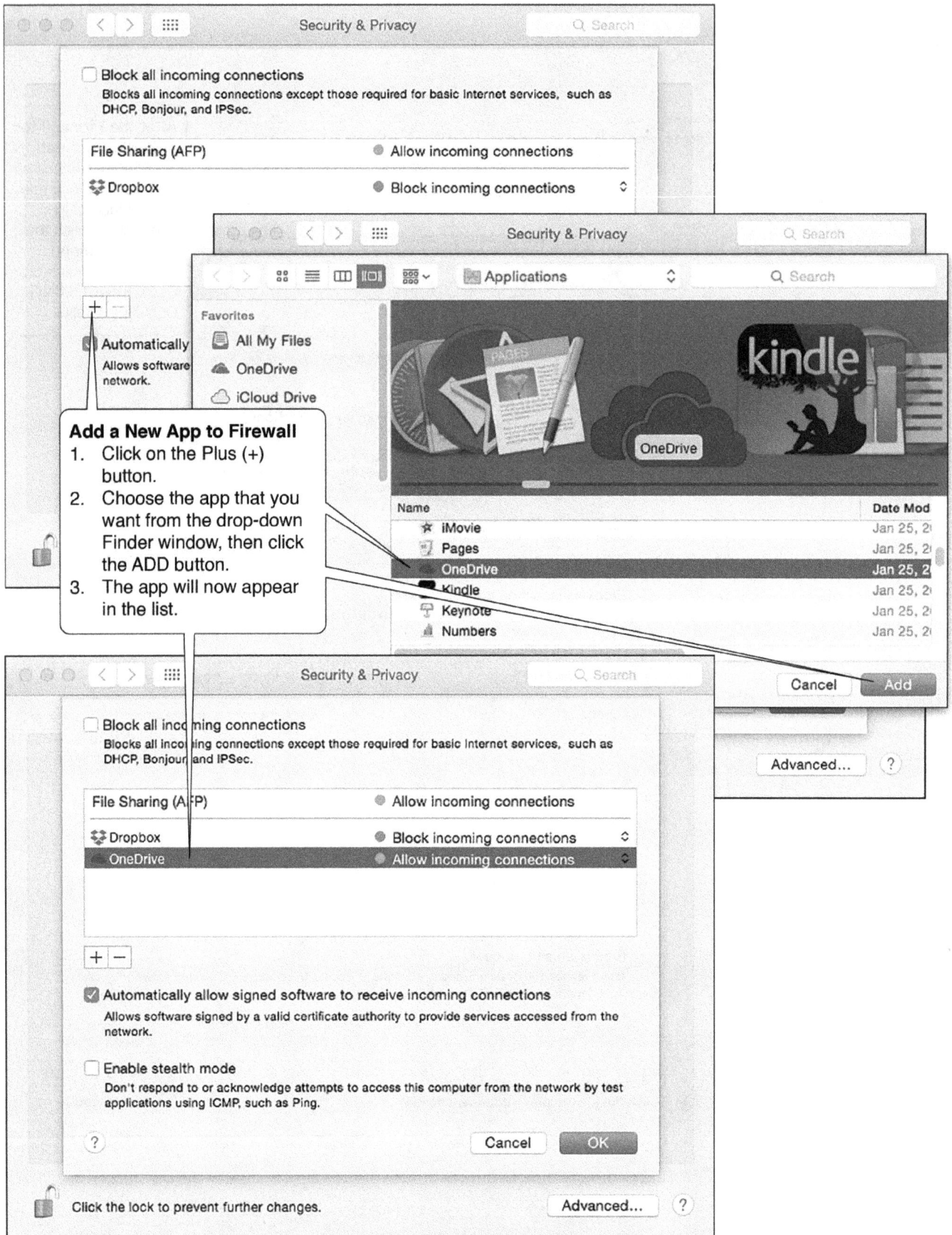

Add a New App to Firewall
1. Click on the Plus (+) button.
2. Choose the app that you want from the drop-down Finder window, then click the ADD button.
3. The app will now appear in the list.

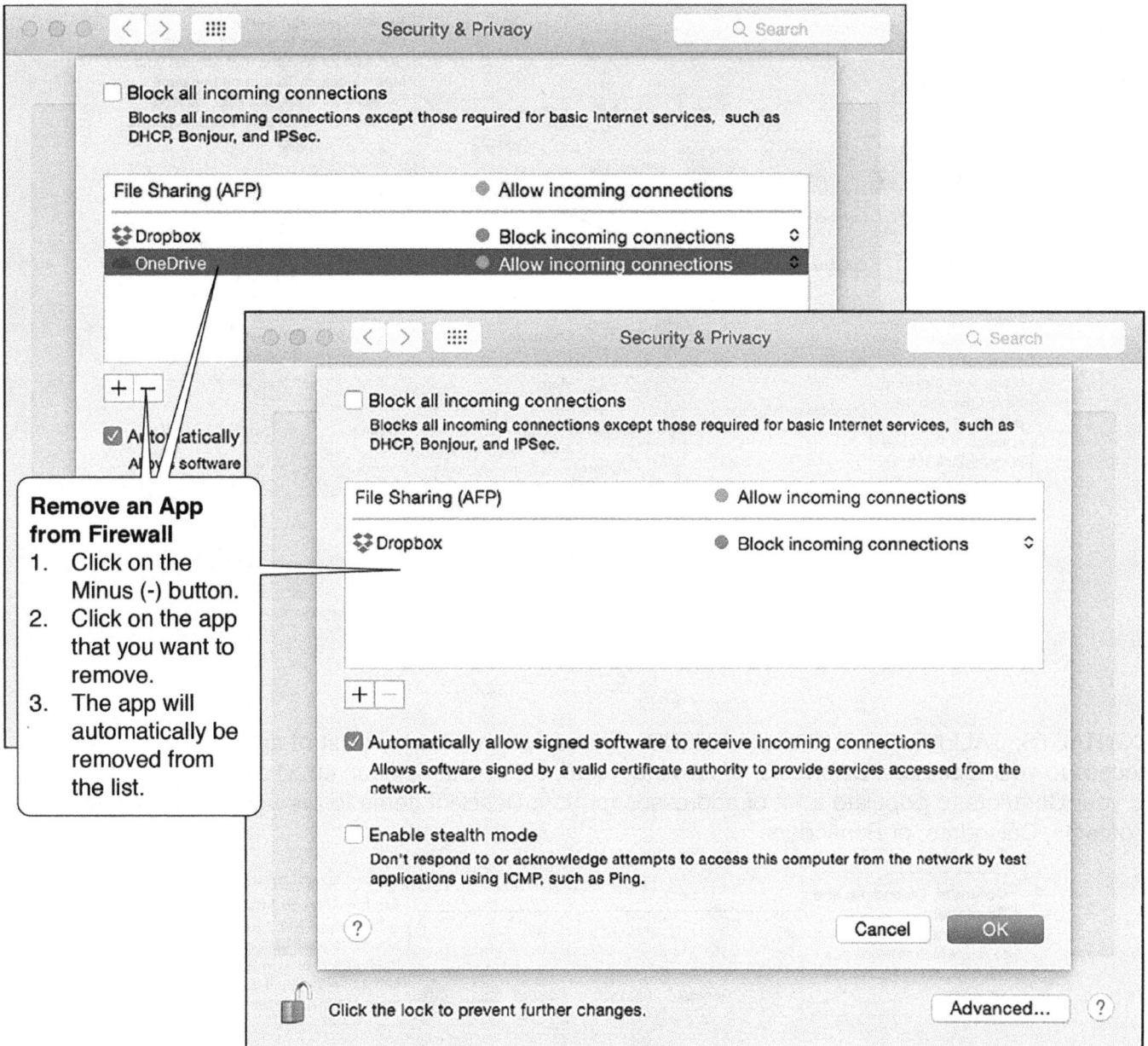

Remove an App from Firewall
1. Click on the Minus (-) button.
2. Click on the app that you want to remove.
3. The app will automatically be removed from the list.

Privacy

Your Mac may be interacting with the outside world quite a lot to determine your location, make sure you have updated software, or to remind you of that important dentist appointment coming up. Privacy settings allows you to control how your Mac is accessed by various apps and services.

LOCATION SERVICES - When you turn on Location Services, you allow apps and websites to use your Mac's current location to provide information, services, and features appropriate to where you are. For example, if you search for "take-out pizza" with Location Services enabled, your Mac will provide a list of pizza restaurants that are located near you, rather than a random list of restaurants across the nation that may have the word "pizza" in their name. SYSTEM SERVICES allows the location of your Mac to be used by your Mac's search app Spotlight or Spotlight Suggestions in Safari.

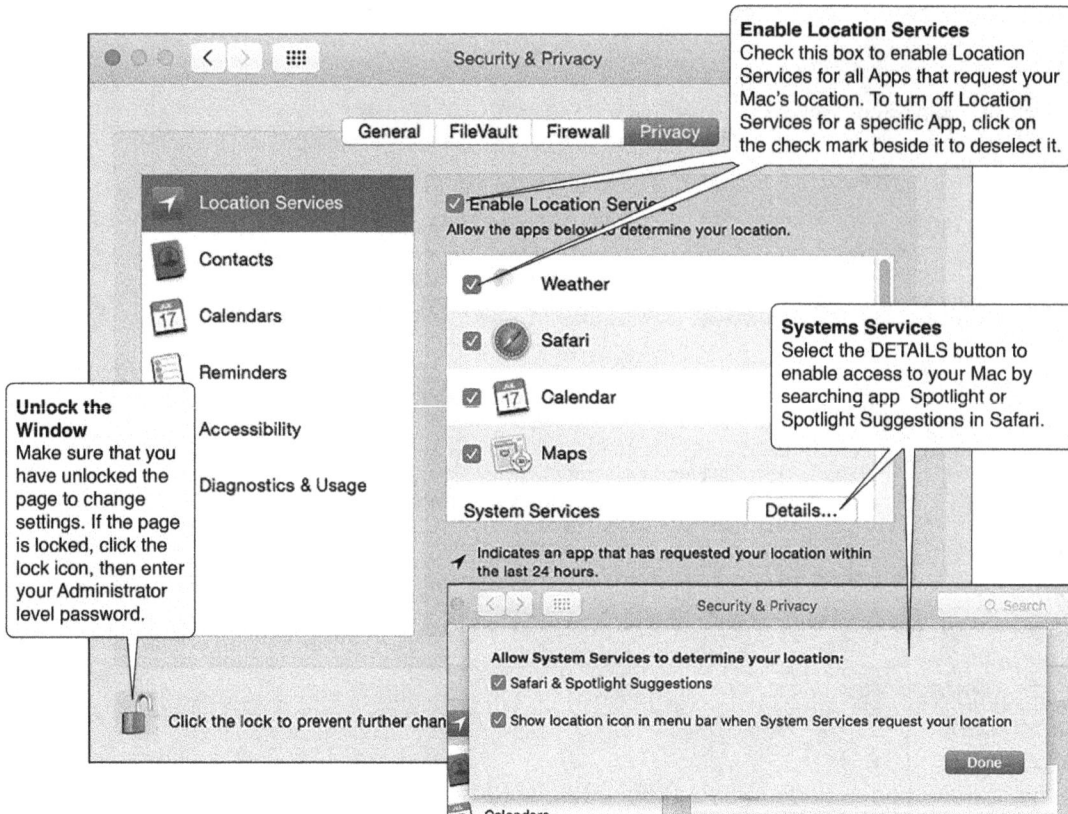

Enable Location Services
Check this box to enable Location Services for all Apps that request your Mac's location. To turn off Location Services for a specific App, click on the check mark beside it to deselect it.

Systems Services
Select the DETAILS button to enable access to your Mac by searching app Spotlight or Spotlight Suggestions in Safari.

Unlock the Window
Make sure that you have unlocked the page to change settings. If the page is locked, click the lock icon, then enter your Administrator level password.

CONTACTS, CALENDARS, AND REMINDERS - These options display a list of apps that have requested access to your Contacts, Calendars, or Reminders apps. For example, an email app may request access to your Contacts to populate a list of addresses for you. Deselect items to prevent them from accessing Contacts, Calendars, or Reminders.

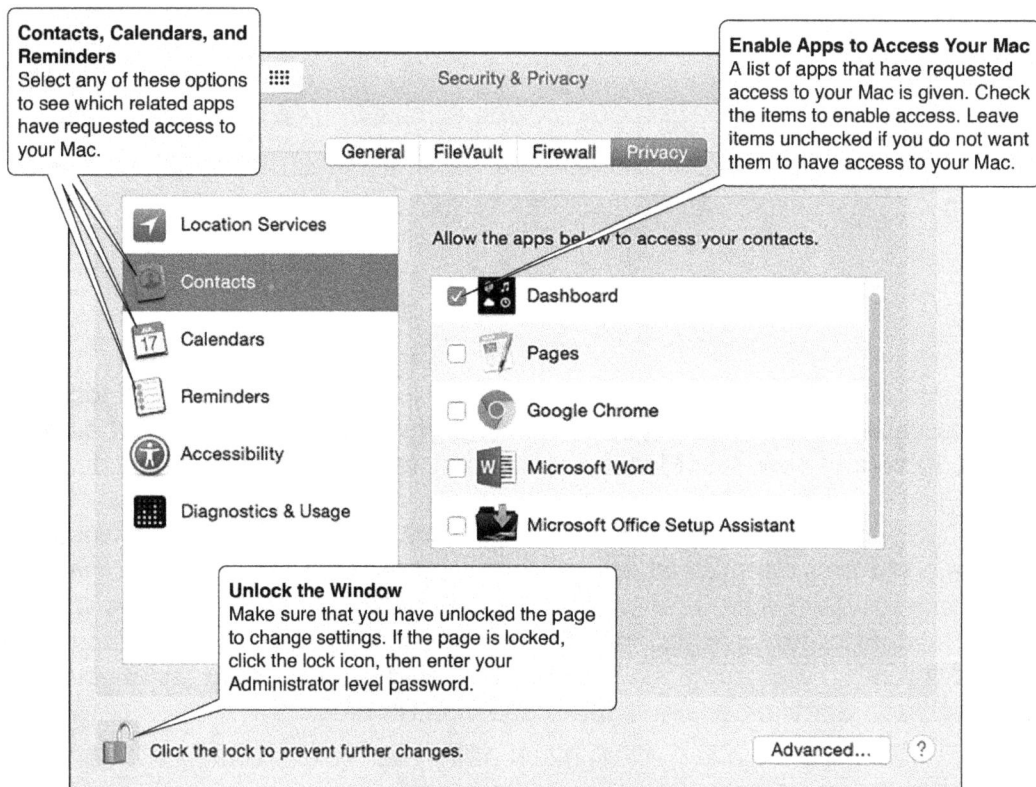

Contacts, Calendars, and Reminders
Select any of these options to see which related apps have requested access to your Mac.

Enable Apps to Access Your Mac
A list of apps that have requested access to your Mac is given. Check the items to enable access. Leave items unchecked if you do not want them to have access to your Mac.

Unlock the Window
Make sure that you have unlocked the page to change settings. If the page is locked, click the lock icon, then enter your Administrator level password.

Accessibility
Select this option to see which scripts and apps have requested access to your Mac.

ACCESSIBILITY

This option displays the apps that run scripts and system commands that control your Mac. You will receive an alert for any outside app requesting access, and the app will be placed in the Accessibility list whether it has been approved or denied. If you deny access to an app but want to enable it later, open the Accessibility list and check the box beside the app to approve it.

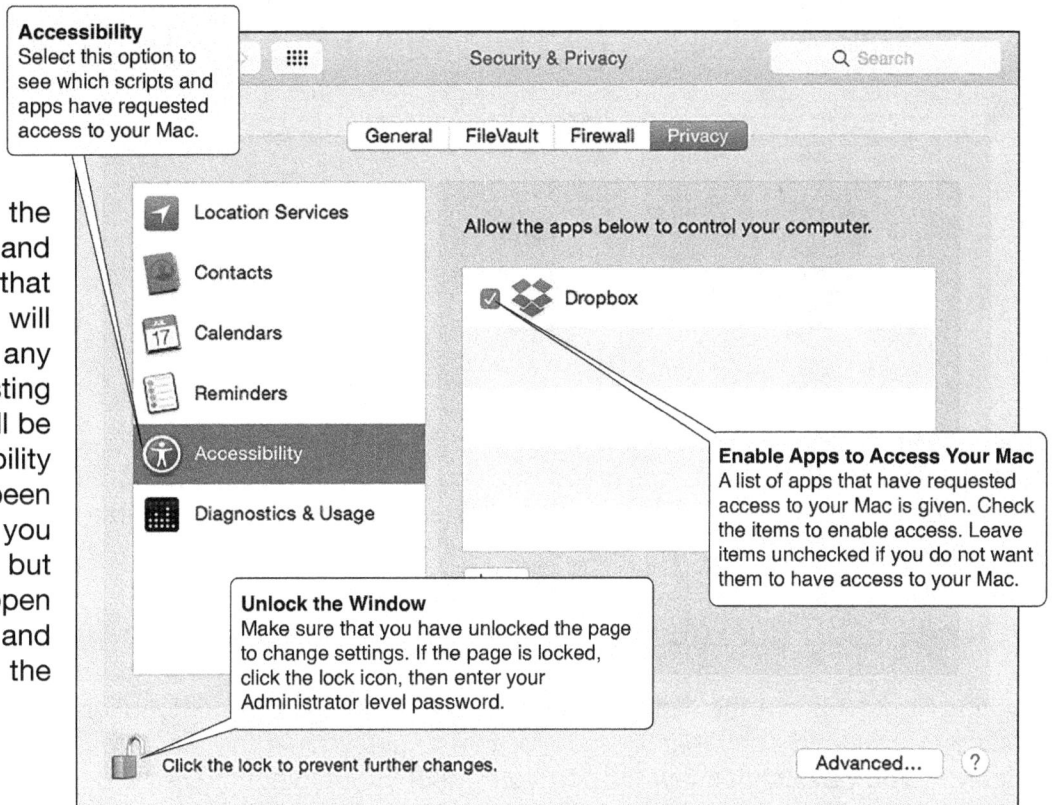

Security & Privacy

Q Search

General   FileVault   Firewall   Privacy

Location Services

Contacts

Calendars

Reminders

Accessibility

Diagnostics & Usage

Allow the apps below to control your computer.

☑ Dropbox

Enable Apps to Access Your Mac
A list of apps that have requested access to your Mac is given. Check the items to enable access. Leave items unchecked if you do not want them to have access to your Mac.

Unlock the Window
Make sure that you have unlocked the page to change settings. If the page is locked, click the lock icon, then enter your Administrator level password.

Click the lock to prevent further changes.

Advanced...   ?

Share Data with Apple
Check either of these options if you want to share data about your Mac's usage and performance with Apple.

Diagnostics & Usage
Select this option to allow your Mac to share data with Apple.

DIAGNOSTICS & USAGE

This option enables your Mac to automatically send information to Apple about your Mac's performance and usage. Apple uses the information to improve the products that they create. Select this option if you agree to participate.

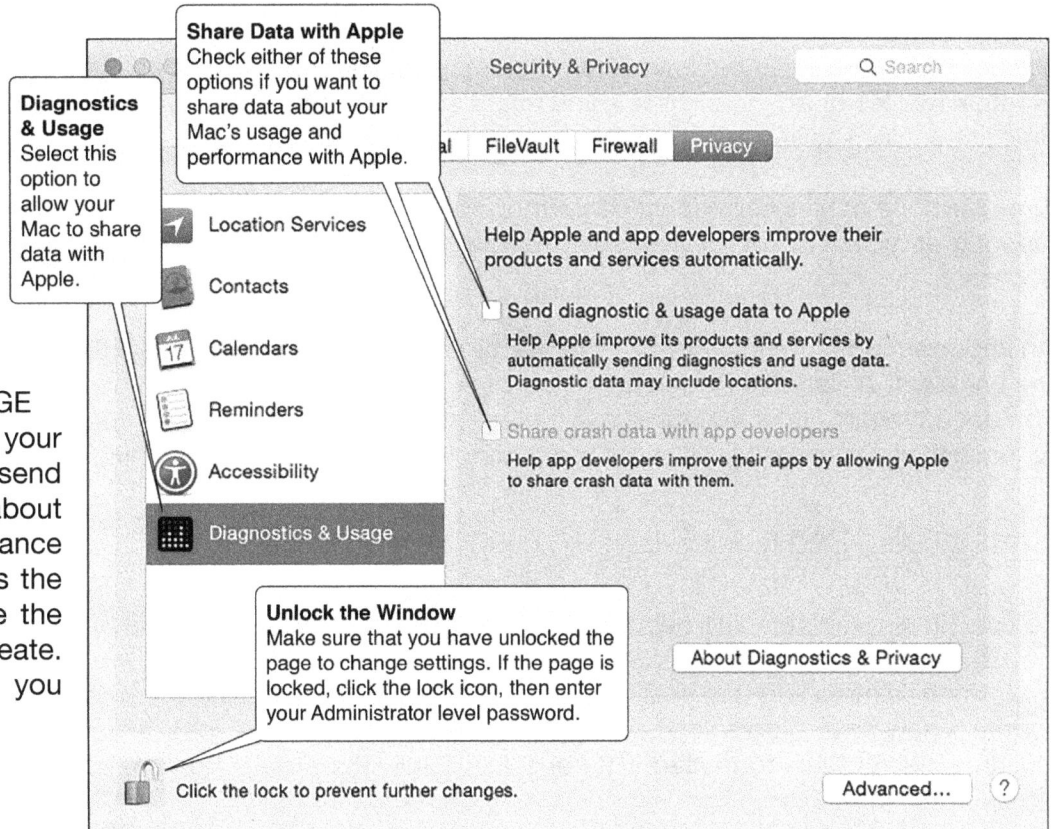

Security & Privacy

Q Search

al   FileVault   Firewall   Privacy

Location Services

Contacts

Calendars

Reminders

Accessibility

Diagnostics & Usage

Help Apple and app developers improve their products and services automatically.

☐ Send diagnostic & usage data to Apple

Help Apple improve its products and services by automatically sending diagnostics and usage data. Diagnostic data may include locations.

☐ Share crash data with app developers

Help app developers improve their apps by allowing Apple to share crash data with them.

Unlock the Window
Make sure that you have unlocked the page to change settings. If the page is locked, click the lock icon, then enter your Administrator level password.

About Diagnostics & Privacy

Click the lock to prevent further changes.

Advanced...   ?

8 – BACKING UP WITH TIME MACHINE

What's Next in this chapter…

- Understanding Backups
- Setting Up Time Machine
- Running Time Machine Backups
- Restoring Files from a Time Machine Backup

Everyone knows how important it is to back up your information on your computer. Yet few people actually take the time to do it. Apple has made backing up fast and easy through the app Time Machine. All you need is an external device (typically a hard drive that you can buy at your local office supply store) that your data will be backup up on, and you're ready to go!

Understanding Backups

Backing up files is not the same thing as copying them to another location, then erasing the originals. A backup is a second copy that is ready for you to use should the first copy become corrupt or disappear entirely. If you have only a few files on your Mac, you could just create duplicates and copy them to an external drive. That system works well until you have lots of files. Then it becomes cumbersome and potentially confusing.

Backing up also should be done on a regular basis. Depending on how often you use your computer and create new files or add to old ones, you might schedule backups to happen daily, weekly, or on any other time schedule. The key is to have a schedule and stick with it.

Time Machine makes backing up very simple. Once you've set it up, backups will take place automatically (as long as your backup device, such as the external hard drive, is connected), and they'll be easy to access.

An important point to note is that Time Machine backs up using a special file format. You'll be able to see the backup files listed in Finder, but if you click on them, you will not be able to access your data. Also, if you open them in finder you run the risk of corrupting them so that Time Machine cannot read them. Best to leave them alone. You'll always need to use the Time Machine application to retrieve any backup files.

Setting Up Time Machine

To use Time Machine, you'll need an external drive that your data will be backed up onto. Typically these drives are about the size of a deck of cards and connect to your Mac with a USB port. Usually they're preformatted (meaning that your Mac can automatically start using them) but occasionally you'll need to format a new drive before you use it. When you plug in the drive for the first time, your Mac will tell you if the drive needs to be formatted. If it does, just follow the prompts on the screen.

Some newer model Mac laptops have only one port. This is called a USB-C port. Unfortunately, it does not accept a standard USB device. If you have this kind of Mac you will probably need to buy a USB-C to USB Adapter in order to connect your USB external hard drive to your Mac.

After plugging in your external drive, follow these steps to set up Time Machine:

1. Click on the Apple icon at the upper left corner of the screen, then select SYSTEM PREFERENCES. From this window, select TIME MACHINE.
2. Click SELECT BACKUP DISK.
3. Click on the external hard drive icon for the drive that you have plugged in to your Mac, then click USE DISK.
4. It's handy to have access to Time Machine in the Menu Bar. To do this, click on the checkbox at the bottom of the window that says, "Show Time Machine in menu bar."

Time Machine is Switched On
With Time Machine on, backups will take place automatically (if the backup drive is connected to your Mac).

Show Time Machine Icon in Menu Bar
Check this box to put the Time Machine icon on the right side of the Menu Bar. This will allow you to easily access Time Machine to run and pause backups.

Select the Backup Drive
1. Click SELECT DISK to choose the backup drive that you would like to use.
2. A dropdown menu will appear that displays all of the drives currently connected to your Mac.
3. Select the drive that you want to use for the backup, then click on USE DISK. As long as this drive remains connected to your Mac, all of your backups will automatically go here.
4. You can switch to a different drive just by using the SELECT DISK option again.

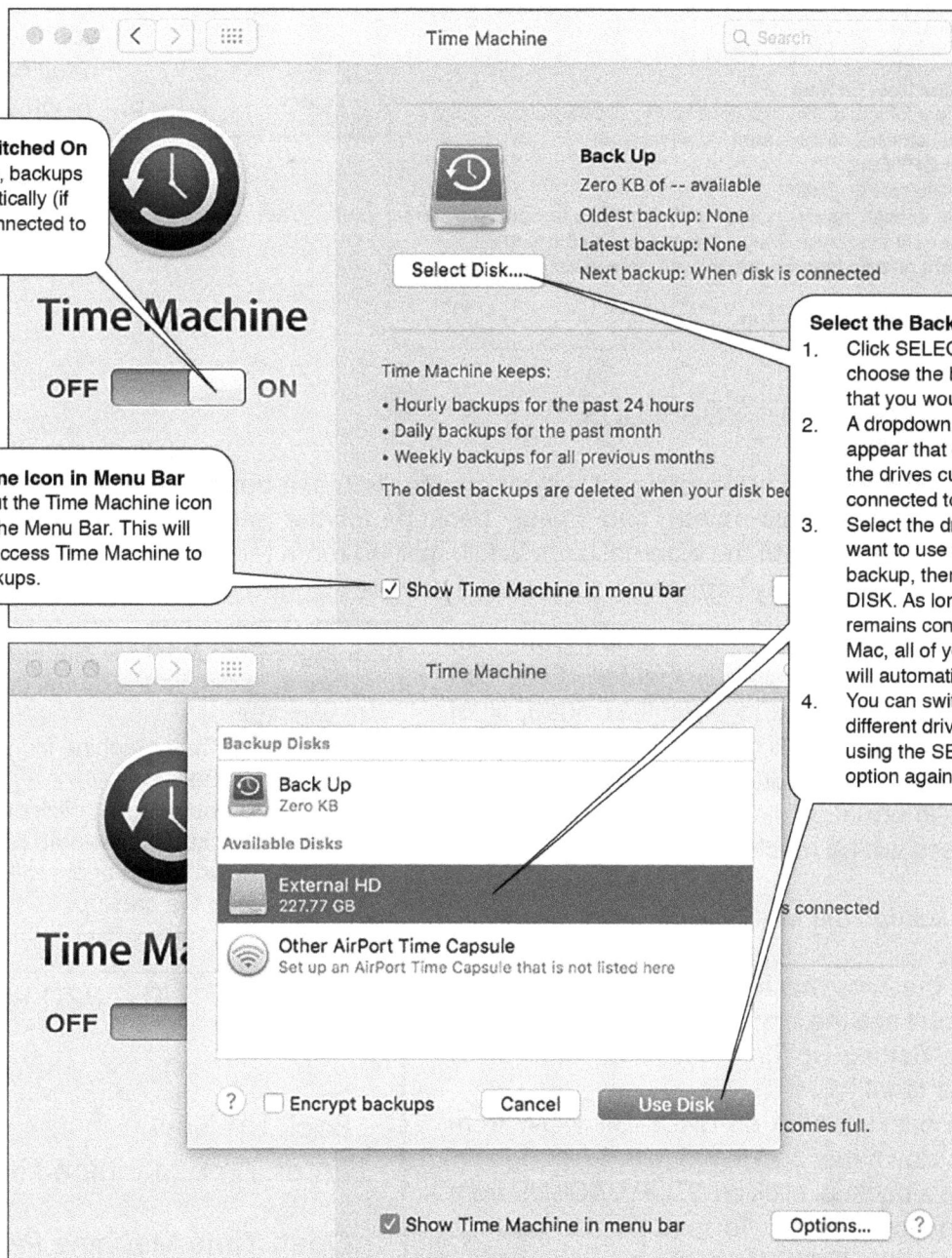

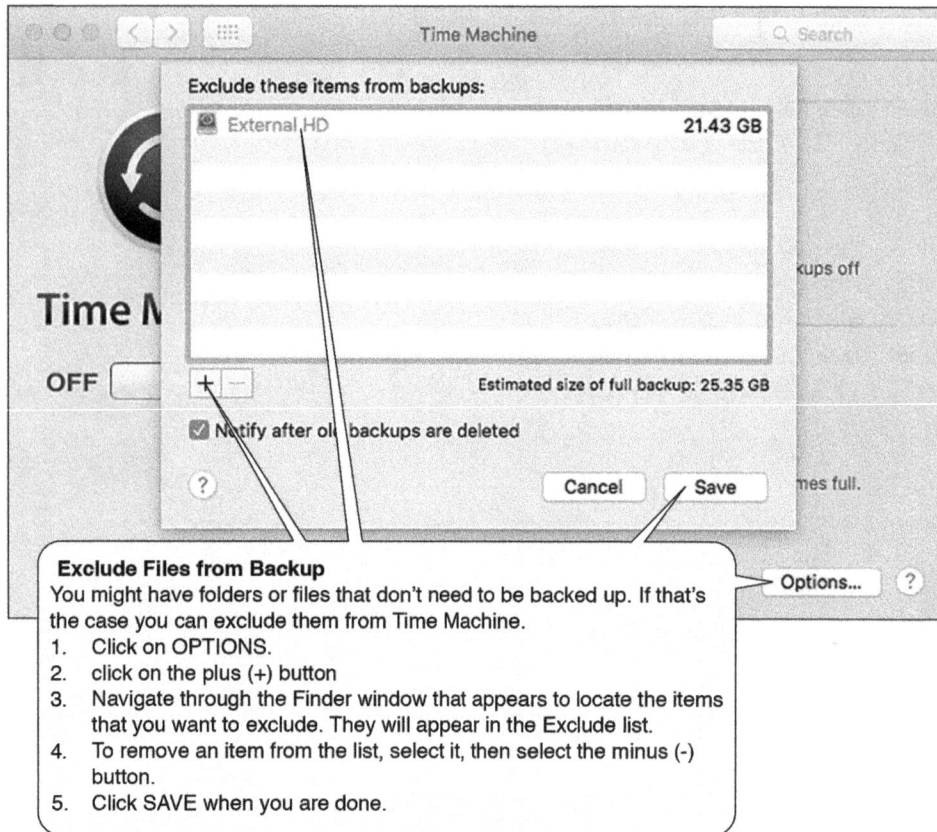

Exclude Files from Backup
You might have folders or files that don't need to be backed up. If that's the case you can exclude them from Time Machine.
1. Click on OPTIONS.
2. click on the plus (+) button
3. Navigate through the Finder window that appears to locate the items that you want to exclude. They will appear in the Exclude list.
4. To remove an item from the list, select it, then select the minus (-) button.
5. Click SAVE when you are done.

5. Click on the OPTIONS button. A new window will drop down. This window allows you to add files or folders that you do not need backed up. For now, you can keep this empty. Click on the checkbox at the bottom that says "Notify after old backups are deleted" if you want to know when this happens. This window also tells you the estimated size of a full backup.

6. When you are done, click on the red button at the top left of the window to remove the window from your display.

Running Time Machine Backups

Once you have set up Time Machine, it will automatically make hourly backups for the past 24 hours, daily backups for the past month, and weekly backups for the past year. The oldest backups will be automatically deleted when the external drive is full, making room for new backups. Remember, however, automatic backups will only happen if your external drive is plugged in!

Your first backup may take a long time if you have lots of files that you've already created. Files can include anything from text to photos to video, all of which take up a great deal of space. Once the initial backup has been made, each new backup includes just the new information since the previous backup, so the process will be much faster.

To control backups manually, follow these steps:

1. Click on the Time Machine icon in the Menu Bar. (If you don't see the icon, go back to the previous section, "Setting Up Time Machine," and follow the steps to #4.)
2. To run a backup, click on BACK UP NOW from the drop down menu.
3. To pause a backup, click on STOP BACKUP from the drop down menu. To resume the backup, click on BACK UP NOW again.

Running a Time Machine Backup
1. Make sure that your external drive is plugged in to your Mac.
2. Click on the Time Machine icon on the right side of the Menu Bar.
3. In the drop-down menu, click on BACK UP NOW.
4. Once the backup has started running, selecting this drop-down menu again will give you the option to stop the backup.

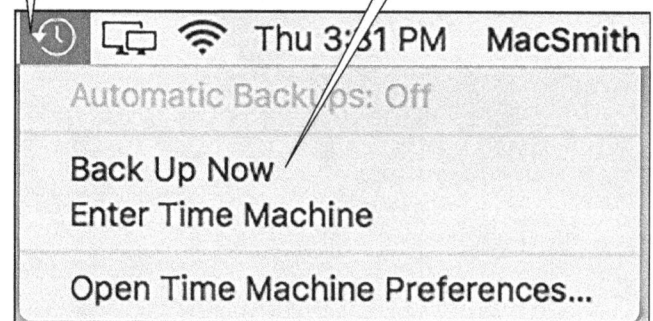

Stopping Time Machine From Running Automatic Backups
1. Click on the Time Machine icon in the Dock, or go to the Apple menu, select SYSTEM PREFERENCES, then click on Time Machine.
2. Click on the ON/OFF switch. It will slide to the OFF position.
3. Time Machine will no longer back up your Mac automatically, but you can still run backups manually.

Use these steps to stop automatic backups:

1. Click on Time Machine from the dock, or open it through System Preferences (Click on the Apple icon at the top left, then SYSTEM PREFERENCES, then click on the Time Machine icon).
2. Click the OFF/ON switch icon at the left side of the Time Machine window so that it slides to the OFF position. (Note: you will still be able to do manual backups, even if Time Machine is switched off.)

While TIme Machine is backing up, you can still use your Mac as you would normally.

Restoring Files from a Time Machine Backup

When you first enter the Time Machine backup interface, it will look very strange. You'll see what appears to be a stack of windows stretching back into space. These are, in fact, Finder windows that stretch back in Time. Each one represents a different backup that Time Machine carried out. A timeline on the right edge of your screen helps you to locate the Finder window with the correct date.

Use these steps to enter Time Machine and restore a file:

1. Make sure that your external drive used for backing up is plugged in to your Mac.
2. Click on the Time Machine icon in the Menu Bar. (If you don't see the icon, go back to the section, "Setting Up Time Machine," and follow the steps to #4.)
3. Click on ENTER TIME MACHINE in the drop down menu.
4. Your Mac will first open Finder, then the desktop will shift to show a stack of Finder windows stretching back into time.
5. Move your cursor to the right side of the screen, move it up or down to locate the backup date and time that you need, then click on it.
6. The Finder window representing that date and time will move to the front. Simply navigate through as you would normally in Finder to locate the file that you need.

7. Click RESTORE and the file will be restored to it's original location. You will now be able to access it once you exit Time Machine.
8. Click on CANCEL to leave Time Machine and return to Finder. You can now access the file that you restored.

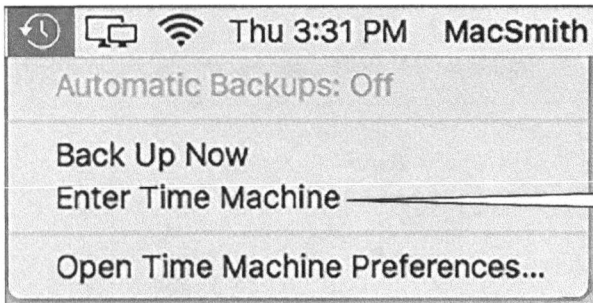

Restoring Files from Time Machine
1. Make sure that your external drive is plugged in to your Mac.
2. Click on the Time Machine icon on the right side of the Menu Bar.
3. In the drop-down menu, click on ENTER TIME MACHINE.
4. The desktop will change to show a series of Finder windows stacked on top of each other, and a timeline at the right of the screen.
5. Find the Date and Time in the timeline, then navigate through that finder window to locate the file that you need.
6. Select the file, then click the RESTORE button.

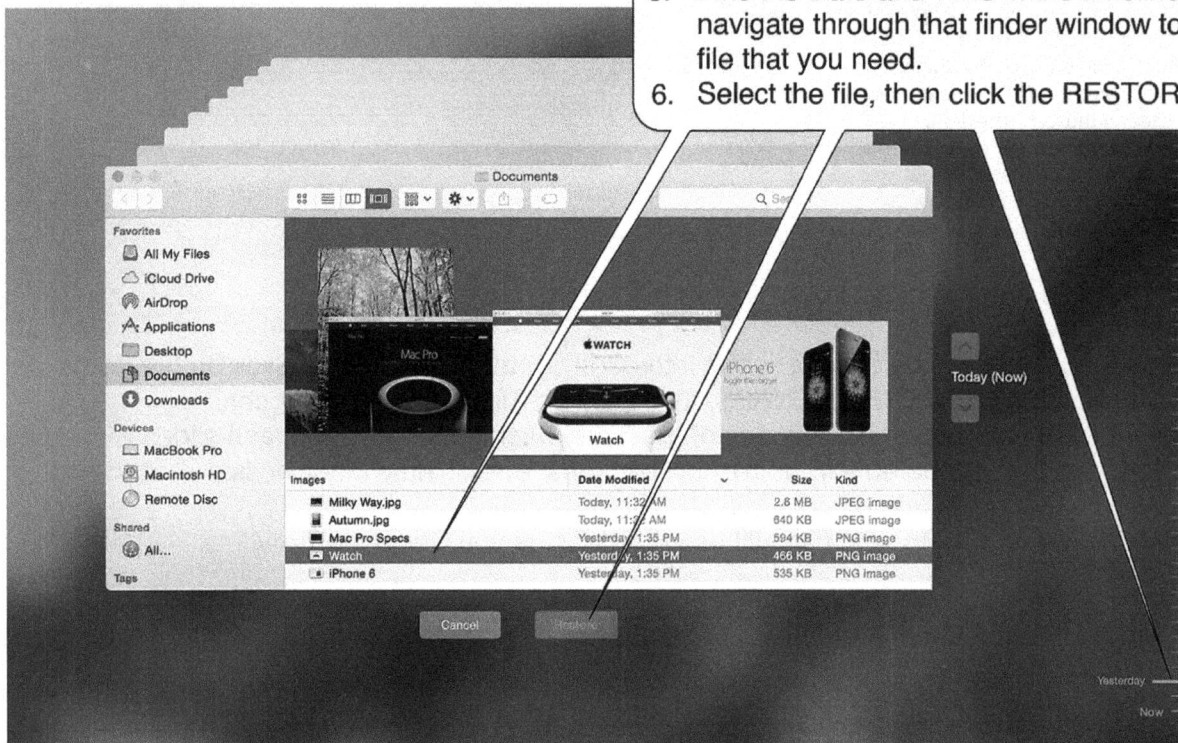

GLOSSARY

- **Administrator** – The highest level of control for a User enabling the ability to load, delete, update and upgrade apps and the operating system on a Mac. (p. 69)
- **Alert** – The sound a computer makes in order to gain the users attention. (p.41)
- **Application** – Smaller software programs that focus on a particular need although the term is now more broadly applied. (p.1)
- **App** – A shortened version of the term Application.
- **Apple ID** – a unique login and password for a user account that allows access to Apple's online products and services. (p.63)
- **Browser** – a software application that enables access to the Internet. Examples include Safari, FireFox and Chrome. (p.61)
- **Contacts** – A storage app populated by the Mac user that contains names, addresses, telephone numbers, and email addresses. (p.88)
- **Desktop** – The major portion of a Mac's screen consisting of the space between the Menu Bar at the top and the Dock on the bottom (or side). (p.2)
- **Disk** – see Hard Drive.
- **Dock** – a band located at the bottom (or side, depending on user preference) of a Mac's Desktop that contains icons for software and apps, enabling quick access to commonly used items. (p.2)
- **Drive** – see Hard Drive.
- **Encrypt** – The process of converting data so that it cannot be read or accessed without a specific key or code to prevent unauthorized access. (p.79)
- **Ethernet** – A method of networking between two or more computers as well as with the Internet, typically using a specific set of cords and connectors. (p.59)
- **External Hard Drive** - A self-contained drive that is separate from a computer but can be connected to it for use as additional storage. (p.90)
- **File** – The generic term for a self-contained unit of storage on the computer that can hold a such things as photos, documents, or even an app. Many file types can be used by multiple applications and programs. (p.9)
- **FileVault** - An app that encrypts data on a Mac and requires a specific key to access the data. If the key is not provided, the data is irretrievable and lost. (p.79)
- **Firewall** – the part of a computer system that blocks incoming communication while allowing outgoing communication. (p. 82)
- **Folder** – A container that can hold files and other folders. (p.9)
- **Hard Drive** – a data storage device containing the computer's operating system, software and apps, as well as all user files and data. (p. 6)
- **Highlight** – The change in background color behind a piece of text or an icon that indicates it has been selected. (p. 34)
- **iCloud** – Apple's cloud storage system that allows a user to keep personal files as well as apps for multiple devices in a way that is synced and accessible to each one. (p. 76)
- **Icon** – A small graphic that represents a computer program or file. Often the user can click on an icon to open the program. (p. 2)
- **Keychain** – a password management system that contains account names, passwords, and other information for quick access so that users do not need to type in these items each time they are used. (p. 76)
- **LCD** – Liquid Crystal Display. The technology used in displays for smaller computer screens such as laptops. (p. 35)
- **Menu Bar** – the horizontal band at the top of the screen. On the left side it contains commands for the program currently active, while on the right side it contains icons to access different apps and utilities. (p. 1)

95

- **Modem** – A device that allows a computer to transmit and receive data through telephone lines, cable television lines, and other analog systems. (p. 59)
- **Mouse** – A handheld input device that controls the cursor on the screen allowing the user to easily select and move items. (p. 36)
- **Network** – a group of computers connected together so that files, folders, Internet access and some software and apps can be shared between them. (p. 31)
- **Operating System** – The software that controls all of the Mac's basic functions and supports the workings of all the apps that are loaded on the system. (p. 6)
- **Power Adapter** – The device, usually consisting of a cord that plugs into a wall outlet, another cord that connects to the computer, and a small block between them that converts power for use. Power adapters are used to recharge a mobile device or laptop. (p. 33)
- **Processor** – the chip within a computer that performs the basic functions of the machine. Also referred to as the CPU or Central Processing Unit. (p. 6)
- **RAM** – Random Access Memory. A type of computer memory used for short-term storage when processing tasks where data can be stored randomly and overwritten. (p. 6)
- **Router** – A device (or software) that enables data to be transmitted from one computer or server to another until reaching its final destination. (p. 59)
- **Screen saver** – An app that fills the screen with moving, user-defined content such as images or text. (p. 22)
- **Scroll** – The process of moving information in a window up and down or from side to side typically using bars along the side or bottom of the window. (p. 34)
- **Scroll Bar** – The graphical device along the side or bottom of a window that a user selects to move window contents up and down or from side to side. (p. 34)
- **Search Engine** – a program, commonly used when accessing the Internet, that searches for items based on keywords and other reference information. (p. 61)
- **Serial Number** – A unique number assigned to every Mac that identifies it. (p. 6)
- **Sidebar** – the portion of a window (usually on the left) that allows for quick access to frequently used items. (p. 9)
- **Sleep** – a power saving option that allows the computer to shut down all but the basic functions that enable operation. (p. 7)
- **Spaces** – The separate desktops created within the Mission Control app that allow the user to organize windows and tasks. (p. 46)
- **Toolbar** – the portion of a window (usually at the top) where buttons, icons, and menus are located. (p. 8)
- **Trackpad** – a pressure-sensitive touchpad that allows the user to control the cursor on the screen to easily select and move items. (p. 36)
- **Update** – A release of an augmentation for an app or software program that fixes existing problems or adds minor features. (p. 65)
- **Upgrade** – A new version of an operating system, software, or an app that replaces the previous version. (p. 67)
- **URL** – Uniform Resource Locator. The address of an Internet web site, for example http://apple.com. (p. 61)
- **User** – A separate login created on a Mac so that multiple people can access the same machine. Each user has access to the Mac's software and apps, but not another user's files (unless specifically defined). (p. 69)
- **Wi-Fi** – A wireless system that enables networking with the Internet. (p. 60)
- **Widget** – A small application or part of an interface that performs a specific function or task. (p. 45)
- **Window** – A viewing area of the computer screen that contains an open app, folder, Internet information, etc. Windows can be moved on the screen and resized independently. (p. 4)